Fight for fieldsports and bollocks to Blair

Johnny Scott

a greener life clarissa dickson wright and johnny scott

enjoy your greener life

Clarissa Dick Wrig

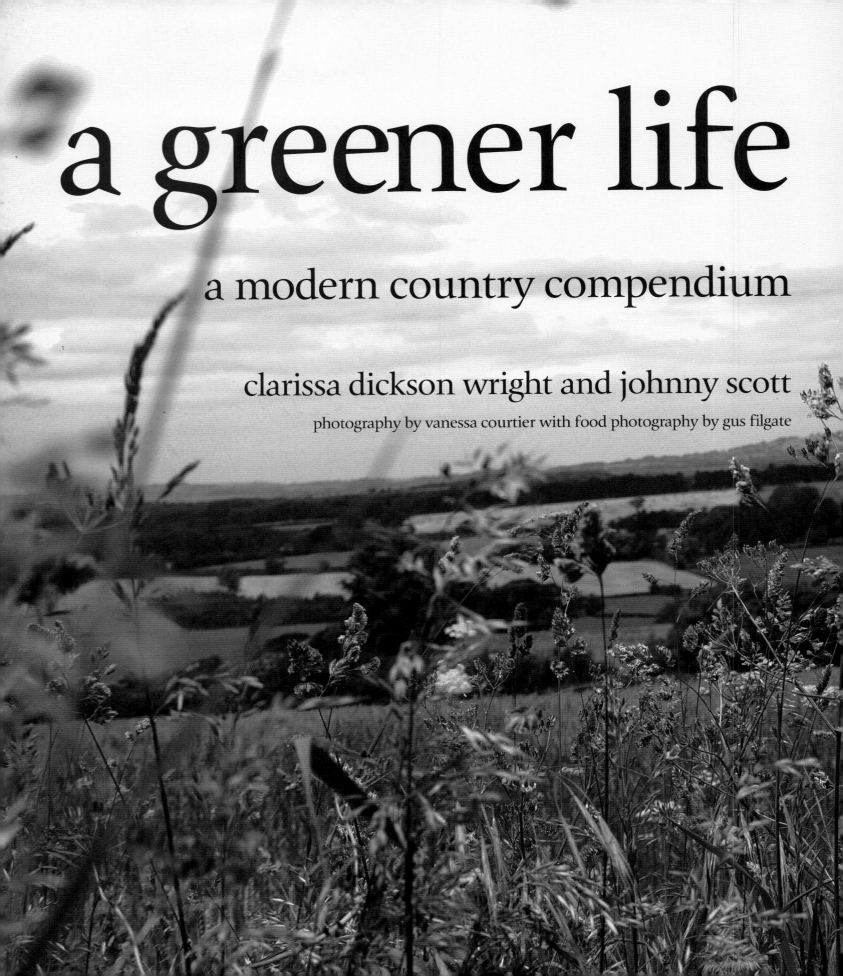

a greener life

a modern country compendium

clarissa dickson wright and johnny scott

photography by vanessa courtier with food photography by gus filgate

enjoy your greener life

Clarissa Dickson

kyle cathie limited

Dedication

Clarissa Dickson Wright:
To Tom Tibbitts, the energy spokesman for the Green Party,
for showing us all the way.

Johnny Scott:
To Rosie Scott and a dog named Jack.

First published in Great Britain in 2005 by
Kyle Cathie Limited
122 Arlington Road
London NW1 7HP
general.enquiries@kyle-cathie.com
www.kylecathie.com

ISBN 1 85626 534 X
ISBN (13-digit) 978 1 85626 534 8

© 2005 by Clarissa Dickson Wright
and Johnny Scott
Special photography © 2005 by Vanessa Courtier
and Gus Filgate
[See also other photography credits on page 250]

Project editor and copy editor Hilary
Mandleberg
Design Geoff Hayes
Picture research Sophie Allen
Home economy Jane Suthering
Styling Wei Tang
Index Alex Corrin
Production Sha Huxtable and Alice Holloway

Clarissa Dickson Wright and Johnny Scott are
hereby identified as the authors of this work in
accordance with Section 77 of the Copyright,
Designs and Patents Act 1988.

A Cataloguing in Publication record for this title is
available from the British Library.

Printed in Italy by Stige

Authors' acknowledgements

Clarissa Dickson Wright: Thanks to
Douglas Wain-Heapy for his advice on
vegetable growing and other gardening
matters; to April O'Leary for help with
spinning; to Marianne More-Gordon for
advice on mending, weaving, knitting,
and to Jane Burnett for advice on
composting.

Johnny Scott: Thanks to all the country
men and women who have shared their
priceless knowldege with me.

contents

introduction

When I was a child in the 1950s, my family, like the majority of other rural families, was self-sufficient. They had to be. The working week was Monday to Saturday lunchtime and shops were shut on Sunday. Few people had cars and a visit to the nearest town was an occasional outing.

Most people kept chickens, ducks, geese or bees. Many agricultural workers fattened a pig on their household waste. Bacon and the produce from the all-important cottage garden was the staple diet. The countryside was full of rabbits, and farmers were only too happy to allow ferreting over their land. Exchanging produce was commonplace. Those who had a surplus of one thing would exchange with someone who had a surplus of another. As farmers, we ate all our own produce and drank our own milk. When we killed for the house, there was always enough to share with the people who worked for us and, during the season, there was never any shortage of game.

the war years

To supplement their food, country people harvested wild foods from hedgerows and woods for centuries. Nor was nature's bounty just for those who lived with it on their doorstep. A desperate shortage of food during the war years led the Ministry of Food to actively encourage the civilian population to make the most of the countryside through their publication *Hedgerow Harvest*. Rationing was with us until 1954 and urban dwellers were as self-sufficient as their rural cousins, bottling, salting and preserving produce through the growing seasons to bolster their diet through the winter.

In the 1960s and 1970s, advances in agricultural technology and intensified farming led to the destruction of much of the old rural landscape and an exodus of people from the countryside as machinery replaced manpower. Communications improved and with it a dependence on out-of-season produce. This became available through the new and readily accessible supermarkets that started to crop up in every town – a result of Socialist policies to feed the nation on cheap foreign imports. All this led to a change in eating habits and standards. Myxomatosis destroyed the wild rabbit population and battery-reared chickens replaced rabbits as the nation's cheap food. Lifestyles changed and, to meet people's economic needs, both adults in a family were required to work. Even country people found there was less leisure time to spend picking wild produce and much country food lore became forgotten.

return to the countryside

Since the 1980s, an increasing number of people have moved into the countryside. Computers have removed the necessity of commuting and distance from work is now no longer necessarily a consideration when choosing where to live. Many of the cottages once occupied by shepherds in this part of the world are now homes to people who earn their living connected by a computer to a London office.

With this new lifestyle, a growing interest has arisen in what country living has to offer. This has coincided with a complete turn-around in agricultural policy. Where the ministries of agriculture in Europe and America in the 1960s and 1970s spent millions destroying huge tracts of permanent pasture, moorland, marsh and thousands of kilometres of hedgerow through reclamation schemes, the modern equivalent, DEFRA, is spending equivalent sums putting it back as it was. The countryside has fewer farmers, but is beginning to look more as it did just after the Second World War.

Our book offers practical advice on how to be self-sufficient, giving this new generation of country dwellers the opportunity to live as their ancestors did, in harmony with the seasons and enjoying our rural heritage and the delicious wild food that nature has always provided.

the green
outdoors

growing your own food

If you want a garden you will find a way so let us start on this exercise assuming that the desire is there and the spirit is willing. What I am dealing with here is a garden that will supply all or some of your needs. It is not about growing flowers but about feeding yourself, healing yourself, having a garden that smells nice and squirreling away food for the hungry months. Just because you don't have a 2-hectare garden it doesn't mean you can't grow some food. Allotments can be rented in most areas (see page 221) and you can grow anything there from only potatoes, as some people do, to a year's supply of vegetables. Even in a small urban garden (see page 16) you can grow vegetables among the flowers in your borders and have a dwarf fruit tree or two.

basic principles

The word on everyone's lips at the moment is 'organic'. It is the new buzzword but as such should be viewed with caution. At one end of the scale there is pure organic gardening such as Prince Charles practises on his Highgrove Estate in Gloucestershire.

On announcing, at the age of 21, that his favourite ancestor was George III, everyone banged on about lunacy, America and talking to trees. What I think Charles was referring to was the triumph of the Agrarian Revolution with its search for excellence in both plant and animal husbandry. George III himself had a keen interest in agriculture and was known as 'Farmer George'. At Highgrove, all the bits fit; it is organic production at its best. Even the air vibrates with health and life.

At the other end of the scale is the use of systemic pesticides, polythene and hydroponic cultivation, all of which dominate the production of what most people eat when they shop in supermarkets. In this world the vibrations are those of rape, ill-health and misery.

Somewhere in the middle lies what is known as best practice, where you aim for the high altar of organic production but incorporate a layer of pragmatism. This tells you that you don't have the time or energy for true organic but you will do the best you can. If you adopt this path you will find the way easier and the progression to the pinnacle structured. You choose how you want to proceed. We are not offering you the lowest rung of the ladder – the totally non-organic approach – but you can pick any rung on the rest of the ladder.

what is meant by organic gardening?

This is the growing of plants and trees using only organic compost or manure, in other words, compost made using only organic matter and manure from animals that have been raised organically. These will both be in short supply until you provide your own.

You also don't use any artificial or chemical fertilizers and are limited as to what pesticides you can use, although there are plenty of alternatives available. Nicotine and pyrethrum are effective plant derivatives that are used in botanical insecticides.

If you live in the UK and decide that you want to register for organic status in order to sell your produce as organic, it will take you three years and you will have to go through a lot of hoops. You should contact the Soil Association who will tell you all you need to know. If you live elsewhere contact the relevant Organic Association of your country.

To tell you where I stand, my compost heap takes what it gets and my manure comes from people who use best practice. The meat and poultry I eat at home comes from beasts raised by best practice from known suppliers, but is not necessarily organic.

permaculture

The term permaculture was first used by the Australian ecologist Bill Mollison in 1978 and, like Topsy, the word grew. Now it is a great buzzword and woe betide the gardening course that doesn't include a section on permaculture.

We live in an age where we have developed a passion for renaming something and imagining we invented it. Permaculture has been around for a very long time; it is simply holistic gardening, which every good vegetable gardener has tried to achieve since time immemorial. Mollison describes permaculture as integrating human habitation with plant life, creating microclimates by the use of annual and perennial plants, and mimicking the patterns found in nature. I would have said that was simply a description of pre-twentieth-century gardening.

The growth in the use of chemicals and the shortage and increased cost of labour have led us away from these principles but ever since Lady Eve Balfour laid down the principles of organic gardening in *The Living Soil* published in 1943, it is what we have been striving for.

The use of plants, shrubs and trees as windbreaks for more delicate plants isn't new and permaculture garden designers, with their layered growth, are echoing all the great vegetable gardeners of history. The Frenchman who plants a rose at the end of his row of vines, to attract pests and diseases and to make them easily identifiable before they attack the vines, is practising permaculture.

Dr Mollison is an Australian and the use of plants to cast shade and protect tender plants from wind dehydration, as well as the use of sheet mulching to preserve moisture, are all techniques my grandmother used in that self same climate. However all credit to him. Anything that inspires people to more organic and better gardening practices is to the good. The one drawback I can see to layered permaculture however is in small gardens, where the yield will be reduced. But on balance I am glad that Bill Mollison has got us all buzzing about permaculture because it is the right way to garden.

lunar planting

Felicity, who ran the vegetable garden at Lennoxlove House in East Lothian where I used to work, was very keen on lunar planting, aka bio-dynamic planting. If you consider that the moon governs the tides, women's bodies and many other things, why should it not also govern planting rhythms?

If you use lunar planting you will most certainly see your seeds germinating better and growing more strongly. To take advantage of the moon's power for promoting the growth of your crops, you must plant, and indeed transplant, your seeds and seedlings as the moon begins to wax, which is three days after you see a new, or crescent, moon.

There is no doubt that it works; I've even planted some seeds on a waxing and a waning moon and seen the difference with my own eyes.

tools

Don't stint on the quality of your tools or, as is always the case in life, it will prove more expensive in the end. Stainless-steel tools, though somewhat heavy, require the least maintenance and will last the longest, but they cost dear. If money is short, you can always start off with just a spade and a fork.

Secondhand tools are another option. I often go to county shows and there is

always a stall selling old tools. I have found some of my dearest friends on such stands. They are especially good places to find inexpensive trowels, hand forks, rakes and garden lines. They made things better in the past, so take a look. And remember, you can always replace handles if necessary. My marvel weedcutter, similar to a narrow cleaver, is perfect for splitting lobsters. My gardening friends gaze at it enviously.

the basic kit

1 a spade with a strong thin blade and a good step on top for digging

2 a round-pronged fork for digging and breaking up the soil

3 a flat-pronged fork for lifting root crops

4 a Dutch hoe with a 10cm blade

5 a trowel

6 a hand fork

7 a hand cultivator or a rake

8 a dibber with a steel point

9 secateurs

10 a wheelbarrow – don't stint on this. You will use it a lot. Buy a wooden wheelbarrow or one of galvanized steel with a hard rubber tyre

11 a watering can, preferably of galvanized steel with a screw-on brass rose (avoid push-on roses as they wear loose and can drown your row of precious seedlings. A dribble bar is a useful addition if you are watering on fertilizer or weedkiller. If you are buying a plastic watering can, choose the stiffest and best balanced you can find. Car boot sales are often a good source of watering cans.

You may wish to add, at a later date, a draw hoe, a 7cm onion hoe, a spring-tine rake, and a garden line.

If you can use a hosepipe in your area, buy one with a reel to store it on and an adjustable spray head.

Look after your tools well. Always clean and oil them before putting them away and dress the handles with linseed oil from time to time to stop them from drying out.

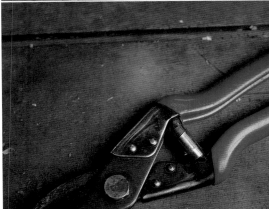

small-space gardening

The excitement I just heard in our publicist's voice because at last she was to have a garden of her own said it all. Many of you will have or will be starting with a small urban garden. The main thing to remember is that you should not attempt to grow large crops or keep large animals in a small garden. Apart from that, the same principles apply as to a larger plot.

As if to prove the point, my nephew, who has a garden in south London, even keeps chickens in his. They come indoors and roost on the rack for drying clothes. His main problem is the urban foxes. He has rescued one of his chickens from the mouth of a fox. Urban foxes are a menace that the councils will not touch. Buy *Countryman's Weekly* and find yourself a pest-controller with a silenced rifle is my advice. And before you scream at me, think of the danger fox mange poses to pets and children alike. Foxes are vermin; they are not, despite what anyone tells you, protected, except, impossibly, from fox-hounds!

organic or not?

You may be asking yourself if it is really possible to produce food organically in your small urban garden. Lynda Brown, in her brilliant and sadly out-of-print book *Gardeners' World Vegetables for Small Gardens* makes the point that whilst organic gardening is easier in a small garden, where everything interacts, it is in just such a garden that you want every lettuce and broad bean to count, so you should not feel guilty if now and again you use a few slug pellets or some inorganic pesticides.

raised beds

Your best way to grow vegetables is in raised beds, which are prettier than tyre planters. I must say I don't really fancy tyre planters myself; the smell of hot rubber on a sunny day doesn't appeal and I think the garden ends up looking rather like a junk yard. It's not that hard to build a small raised bed. The Chinese have used them for centuries where space is limited.

They need to be narrow, double-dug (see page 26) – hopefully your subsoil is not too full of rubble – and infilled with lots of compost and manure before the soil is replaced. This raises the soil above the level of the sub-soil so they look like tumulus mounds without the grass. In a garden I once had I took down the old air-raid shelter and filled the foundations with composted soil. It was fantastic. I grew Jerusalem artichokes, tomatoes, wild strawberries and herbs. It kept me very happy.

You will need to edge the beds with bricks, log rolls or old coping stones; use your imagination. Once the beds are finished you will never walk on them again so design them for easy access. You can make them any shape you like but you must be able to walk round them or at least reach across them. A bed about 1.2 metres long and 4–4.5 metres wide is probably the optimum.

Divide the beds with paths, not with grass as that would harbour slugs and snails and be impossible to cut. Wood shavings, gravel, bark or bricks are all good. Make sure to leave room for yourself and of course for a wheelbarrow. Because the beds aren't walked on, drainage is better, yields are improved, the soil warms up quicker, rotation is simpler, there are less weeds and the beds look wholesome and attractive.

Another attractive idea is to find an old cartwheel, treat it, paint it with non-toxic paint, build a raised bed to its measurements, lay the cartwheel on top and grow herbs through the divisions.

If you don't want to restrict your garden to vegetables then grow the vegetables among other plants. Remember roses love alliums.

And remember that a garden with slugs does have some benefits. It is probably a sheltered garden with a microclimate of its own.

the disadvantages of an urban plot

The main disadvantages of an urban plot are too much shade, problems of access and pollution. If trees overhang you may cut them back but do remember to tell your neighbours first or war might ensue. If they are merely casting shade you have no right of light but talk to your neighbours or your local council and see if you can have them trimmed. If the tree is very tall you could have some legal remedy as it may pose a threat to your house or to people. If all else fails, you can console yourself that you will have the ingredients for really wonderful leaf mould. If the shade really is too bad, you will simply have to grow what you can in tubs in the sunny bits, or perhaps in just one raised bed and a few containers.

Consider access carefully while you are planning your urban garden, especially if you have to bring everything through the house. You don't want to go off and buy a wheelbarrow which won't fit through the hall or an established fruit tree that could scrape your wallpaper.

As to pollution, lead is the main worry. If there is too much in the soil plants may still grow but will have a toxic content that is harmful to children. Modern fuels are a lot less toxic but if you are worried get your local council to test your soil.

If your soil is polluted, always wash vegetables carefully, especially soft-leafed ones, and peel all root vegetables. If the soil is badly contaminated the only solution is patience – grow green compost for several years and dig it in. Have the soil re-checked before growing any fruit or vegetables.

fruit and vegetable growing on a terrace

All the gardening shows on television, which I avoid like the plague, seem to advocate decking and slab terraces. Well, you can grow all sorts of things up the pillars of your decking – beans, squashes and raspberries spring to mind – and you can easily grow fruit and vegetables in containers on your paved terrace. The advantage of a paved terrace is that it gets a lot of reflected light and heat, but remember to keep watering and feeding.

Good-looking terracotta pots are now readily and inexpensively available. You can get them in a variety of shapes and sizes, so choose what is best for your terrace and for the crop you plan to grow. Make sure you put a layer of small stones or crocks at the bottom to help with drainage before you plant.

If you are growing in containers you will need soil that drains well but is not too fine. It would be nice to think that you have your own compost or leaf mould, or maybe you have an allotment where you are composting or you have a kind and generous friend with lots to spare. If not, you will have to use potting compost. Alternatively, if you can, get your hands on some organic compost. A national composting association should be able to put you in touch with someone who can supply this.

I like to mix a little garden soil in with my compost for containers as I feel it helps drainage and root development. It's not the end of the world if you don't have any. Use a bit of fine gravel instead.

Don't feel confined to growing herbs in your containers, but read the fruit and vegetable sections carefully (pages 48–67) and select accordingly.

(pages 48–67)

vegetables for your containers

Chillies of different varieties are good to grow in your containers as they look attractive and unusual and do well. I have a friend who grows Scots Bonnets, the hottest of all the chillies. He deep fries them in batter and eats them like potato chips!

Pot marigolds are another good plant. They give off a scent which deters garden pests and are good for eating in salads and stews. **Nasturtiums** are another idea. They will hang down prettily over the sides of the container and are excellent in salads or eaten on bread and butter, as we did as children.

Dwarf beans thrive in containers and so do **tomatoes**. I have even seen some in growbags on the roof of Westminster Cathedral. For window boxes plant the dwarf variety. **Aubergines** and **peppers** make unusual plants for containers but look a bit stark in window boxes.

Horseradish is another option. As it needs to be grown in a bucket to keep it under control, it does well in a container on a terrace. Its lush leaves look very rustic and it will grow well in shade. **Tree onions** and **chives** also do well and give an unusual look.

fruit and vegetable growing on a balcony

You will have seen how much use people make of their balconies in foreign towns, albeit that they probably have more sun. Herbs, geraniums, squashes, beans, tomatoes and even melons spring to mind as possible balcony crops. Your main drawback other than space is insect predation, especially the dreaded whitefly (see pages 44–47).

As well as pots, growbags do well on balconies but they aren't very glamorous and dry out quickly, so always remember to water. If you construct a wooden container for your growbag it will keep it structured and will look better.

fruit and vegetable growing in hanging baskets

I am not fond of hanging baskets but recently saw some at a friend's in Dorset. She had strawberries growing very well and happily there. There was no danger of slugs or damp rot and no back-breaking picking. I am told that you need to feed strawberries grown this way once a week with tomato food and add a meagre teaspoon of sugar for bigger, juicier fruit. No doubt you may think of other fruit or vegetables which are suitable. As I have never owned a hanging basket, perhaps you would let me know!

window boxes and windowsills

It is amazing what you can grow in a window box – I have even grown dwarf leeks. Make sure your box is secure, that you can get to it easily and remember to feed and water regularly.

Sometimes all you have is a windowsill, but do not despair. Herbs such as chives and garlic grow well while a pot of basil will keep away the flies.

large gardens

Large gardens really fall into three categories – open, walled and partially walled gardens.

clearing an open garden

If you are starting to make a paradise from a common field then you will need to clear it. When I worked at Lennoxlove House in East Lothian, the vegetable garden had not been touched in fifteen years, so I borrowed two Tamworth sows that had been clearing bracken on a nearby hill and we penned them in with an electric fence. They cleared the whole lot in about ten days, rootling out and eating all the couch-grass roots and nodes, and turning everything over better than any rotovator – and manuring as they went. So using pigs to clear and break up the ground is one option. Another is to use a crop such as potatoes which will help break up the soil, but in this case it will take you a year before you begin to see any results at all.

Possibly you will have inherited a garden rather than a field. Though it may be overgrown and weed-ridden, there may be a fruit tree or two in it. However gnarled they seem, don't grub out a fruit tree until you see what it can do. Pruning works wonders.

starting to plan the garden

The first thing to do with your open garden is identify the prevailing wind and see whether it poses any major problems. If it does then you must create windbreaks. Whether these are walls, wattle fencing, quick-growing trees such a poplars (remember never plant a poplar close to a house – I can't tell you how many law cases there are about this) or a nice crop of densely sown Jerusalem artichokes, depends on you. Wind is not in itself a bad thing, as it disperses the spores of rust, mould and blackspot, but it can be drying and in extreme cases destructive.

You will also need to note where the sun strikes your plot and plan your planting accordingly. On a large sheet of graph paper, mark out where you will put your greenhouse, cold frames, hot beds and compost and manure heaps. Also mark out the paths – gravel, brick or slab for preference – to give access to these and to the beds, and remember that box hedges will keep out rabbits and deer.

beds for fruit and vegetables

Decide where you are going to plant your fruit trees and canes and other permanent or semi-permanent plants such as rhubarb. Once all these are in place on the graph paper, divide the remaining areas into beds and decide what you want to grow. This is important as you don't want gluts and you may dislike some vegetables and fruit, in which case don't grow them. Work out how many people you are feeding and remember that freezers are all very well but green people search for seasonality. Now read the sections on crop rotation (see page 40), companion planting (see page 46) and What to Grow (see pages 48–75), and off you go.

partially walled gardens

These are gardens with one south-facing wall up which you can grow your tender fruit trees, and with box hedges to divide the garden from the rest of the surrounding land. They were common in poorer areas where there was less manpower available to build expensive, labour-intensive brick walls. The vegetable garden at Lennoxlove House was an example. Here, in good old Scottish tradition, rows of 2.5 metre high beech hedges were grown perpendicular to the wall and at some distance from it. They protected the fruit trees growing against the wall from frost, allowed air to circulate, acted as a windbreak and concentrated the sun.

If you have a partially walled garden, plan it as you would an open garden but bearing in mind the dictates of the wall and all that implies in terms of frost pockets and circular wind currents.

walled gardens

Walled gardens built for monasteries and the houses of the rich from the Middle Ages onwards vary in size from 250 square metres to two or three hectares.

A walled garden will probably have some form of greenhouse, cold frames and possibly even double walls with flues running inside them heated by a coal-burning stove, though none of this will be working. The magnificent octagonal garden at Lafuness House in East Lothian, built by French prisoners of war during the Napoleonic Wars, is unique in that as well as heated double walls, it has adjustable polished metal plates to direct the sun's rays onto particular parts of the garden.

If you are lucky enough to have a walled garden it may already be up and running, but if not, in the UK at least, there are grants available for restoration. There has recently been a revival of interest in getting them back to speed with a view to selling their vegetables into farmers' markets and to local community and restaurant outlets. A good way of getting help with the restoration of a walled garden is to enlist your local history group both for advice and volunteers, while your local council will be able to advise you on grants.

insect repellent

Early Egyptian gardeners daubed their garden walls with clay to keep insects out of the crevices. This is a ploy that is still practised in France to this day. It is not as pretty as ageing brick but is very practical and saves on the re-pointing.

planning

As with any garden, plan your garden on graph paper, starting with the permanent features and dividing up the rest of the garden to accommodate your other needs.

Allotments are good news and many towns and cities have an allotment scheme. If you would like one, contact your local council and put your name on the waiting list.

Douglas Wayne-Heapy, my mentor in all vegetable matters, grows the most amazing vegetables on a dry windswept Birmingham allotment. On my birthday last year his wife and I sat in the sun by the River Avon at Bridgenorth. Here we consumed a thermos of baby broad beans he had grown and which he insisted she bring me to celebrate the day. Everything he grows has wonderful flavour and with the aid of a freezer, he and his wife buy virtually no vegetables at all. So don't delay. If you live in a city and haven't done so already, get your name on that waiting list.

In a walled garden the shade cast by the walls is used by gardeners for retarding plants to avoid gluts. The walls also provide somewhere to grow fruit trees against but be careful when hammering in nails. It is a good idea to use cast-iron nails heated in a roasting pan in the oven until they are red-hot then thrown into cold linseed oil. This prevents the mortar sticking to them and pulling away. The French used to build sheep shanks into their walls and tied the trees to them. Today we use horizontal wires as supports but they still need to be attached to the wall. Remember, too, that walls have two faces so you can grow blackberries and hardier fruit on the outside of the wall as well as the more tender fruits inside.

Now we come to the centre of the garden. This will need to be divided into beds. These can be any size but smaller beds are easier to work (see page 16) and make crop rotation easier, so they may suit best.

If your garden is very large, internal cross-walls and plant dividers may have been erected to prevent wind damage, however, high internal walls will create their own wind-current problems and mini-frost pockets, not too mention too much shade.

home to wildlife

Of course you may want your garden to be a home to some wildlife too. If you wish to indulge in some beekeeping (see pages 130–131) you should place your beehives in a warm, sheltered south-facing spot.

Walled gardens are also useful for keeping poultry but seeing the damage the Bantams do to my beds when they are dust bathing and snacking, I would recommend keeping them cooped in a moveable run.

'Remember, too, that walls have two faces so you can grow blackberries and hardier fruit on the outside of the wall as well as the more tender fruits inside.'

looking after the soil

It is important to identify your soil type and whether it is acid or alkaline as this will affect what you can grow in it. Soil types range from sandy to heavy clay. To find out what you've got, take a small handful and rub it between your fingers and thumb.

Sandy or light soil: This will not stick together at all as there are large spaces between the soil particles. It makes it easy to work but sandy soils dry quickly especially in windy conditions. They drain well but are difficult to keep together and will need manuring and having compost added. Sandy soil warms up quickly so is good for growing early crops but nutrients leach out of it very easily. As this soil tends

to be alkaline, add lime and check its pH (see opposite) every couple of years as lime washes away. Alliums and all root vegetables like light soils, as do salad crops, chard and spinach. Apple and nut trees thrive in sandy soils too.

Clay or heavy soil: A clay soil has a shiny surface and when rubbed between your fingers and thumb, the very tiny particles cohere. This makes it heavy to work and the soil sticks together like glue. If allowed to dry, a clay soil sets and cracks like a piece of bad pottery, so mulch well in the summer to retain moisture. In cases of really heavy clay you may have to dig in sand. Only cultivate clay soil in dry weather and see

that your compost and manure are well rotted before you add them as decomposition will be slow due to lack of air in the soil. Turn the soil in the autumn where possible so the frost will break it up. Peas and broad beans, strawberries, raspberries, pears and plums all like clay soil.

Silt: This tests like clay but without the shine. A silt soil is easier to work than a clay one but it gets sticky when very wet and turns to dust when dry.

Loam: The most sought-after soil, loam is a mixture of small and large particles. It doesn't stick together or fall apart but is like perfectly made pastry crumbs. It is possible though to have a sandy loam or a clay loam. Loam holds moisture but also drains well. It is quick to warm and slow to freeze and all your fruits and vegetables will grow well in it.

Peat soil: This forms a brown springy ball between the fingers. It is formed from decomposed vegetable matter rather than rock, so it is very fertile but you need to watch the pH level (see opposite). Peat is slow to warm up and to freeze. It tends to be neutral or slightly acid.

Once you have identified your soil you can decide what to grow. Having said all this I have to confess that I have never used a soil-testing kit and although I count some legendary gardeners among my acquaintances, when I rang round neither had any of them. The most crushing rejoinder I received was from my friend Isabel who told me that she simply looked at the weeds to tell her about the acidity of her soil. This is a very good point and one I shall deal with opposite.

acid versus alkaline

Soil may contain lime and the more there is, the more alkaline the soil will be. Certain plants thrive in a more acid soil, others do best in an alkaline soil, while yet others are best suited to a neutral one. Acidity and alkalinity are expressed as the soil's pH level. You can buy an inexpensive pH testing kit at any good garden centre to check the pH level of your soil.

above pH8 really means you're in a semi-desert. Very little will grow in soil like this.

pH7 is alkaline and is usually found in hot dry areas. Most garden plants will survive but need regular cultivation with compost and manure. Brassicas, spinach, currants, apples, peaches and plums like an alkaline soil.

pH6–pH7 is neutral and most plant life thrives in it.

pH5–pH6 is fairly acid. This is typical of unimproved soil in wet areas. It is good for potatoes, tomatoes and fruit.

pH4–pH5 is acid. This is found in cold wet areas. There is little soil life or earthworms. Rhododendrons and azaleas do alright in it but it makes growing fruit and vegetables more difficult. You can add lime to make the soil more alkaline but take it easy, adding small amounts regularly rather than chucking heaps on in one go, which would scorch the roots.

mineral deficiencies

You will also need to 'read' your plants to discover what mineral deficiencies your soil may have.

Nitrogen deficiency: This is apparent when plants show small yellowing leaves and stunted growth. Check your soil's drainage – if you have land drains running away, make sure they are clear – and also make sure the subsoil is not compacted. If it is, dig it well and dig through plenty of compost and muck.

Phosphorus deficiency: The signs are small pale leaves with a bluish tinge that drop early. Add compost and check the drainage, as for nitrogen deficiency.

Manganese deficiency: The leaves fade as they mature. Add lime or chalk – but carefully.

Magnesium deficiency: The signs are green veins and yellow leaves. Add compost and/or Epsom salts.

Iron deficiency: You will notice that the leaves are yellow between the veins. Add compost and sulphur.

Potassium deficiency: The signs are brown-tipped leaves with yellow veins. Use comfrey slurry (see page 28) and dig in black banana skins.

weeds

The main problem with weeds is that they are competition to your carefully planted vegetables. The greatest threat is during the first four weeks after planting. If you can keep them away from newly planted seeds and seedlings during this time, you don't need to worry too much.

Some 'weeds' are actually quite useful, for instance stinging nettles, fat hen and dock leaves are all great to use as pheasant and chicken feed.

Dandelions provide a delicious addition to your salad bowl as does chickweed.

The latter, made into a tisane, acts to clean the blood, as does pennyroyal, a type of wild mint that was once used as a substitute for tea. You shouldn't drink pennyroyal though if you are pregnant as it was once known as 'the abortionist's friend'. Dried moss is another useful weed as it can be made into an effectiv bandage or poultice.

Weeds are also a good indicator of the state of your soil. So what to look for? Acid soils grow sorrel, plantain and knotgrass. Alkaline soils grow poppies and field parsley, whilst nettles of all types, chickweed, dandelion and borage all indicate fertile soil.

Cow parsley grows where there is an excess of nitrogen and where there is too little, look for vetches and clovers. Compacted soils sport grasses while all types of buttercups, docks, sedges and mosses are signs of poor drainage.

Many weeds contain minerals and if they are dug up before they seed and are left to dry on the ground, they are useful on the compost heap. The dreaded couchgrass, for example, contains potassium as does yarrow which also brings iron, copper, phosphorus, nitrogen and sulphur. Dandelions, nettles, mayweed, bracken and horsetail are full of useful minerals and can be used for green compost (see page 40).

Deep-rooted weeds such as nettles and docks have the advantage that they bring up nutrients from deep in the soil for more shallow-rooted plants. Their root channels also help break up the soil and aerate it.

Cow parsley

digging

If you possibly can, borrow a pig; if not, digging is a hard slog. If the ground is very hard and has been left idle, hire or borrow a rotovator. This will at least remove the hardship of double-digging in most cases. Remember, however, that digging is a much better and more long-term exercise for the muscles than going to the gym.

The trick with digging is not to rush into it willynilly and rick your back. Start gently and do no more than half an hour at a time until you have strengthened your muscles. And always buy the best and strongest tools you can afford. You needn't spend a fortune; at county shows and game fairs you will find stalls selling all sorts of secondhand garden implements. I have often found a cracking selection of spades, forks and trowels, many of them much stronger than the latest gimmicky ones.

Spit-digging

The most effective way of digging a plot is spit-digging or single digging. It enables you to incorporate compost or manure into each spit or trench as you go along and before it is filled in. The spade has been developed to the depth and width it is as a means of achieving efficient spit-digging.

You will want to do your digging in the autumn after the equinoctial rains but before the first frosts so that they will break up the manure you have dug into your trenches.

Divide your plot in half either mentally or with a stretched piece of string. Starting nearest the string and working at right angles to it, dig out a spade's depth and width of soil and place it on the other side of the string. Put manure or well-rotted compost into the trench you have dug then dig a second trench parallel to the first, putting the soil from the second trench on top of the manure in the first one.

Continue digging in this way the length of the first half of the plot. When you reach the end, dig in a reverse direction down the other half. The soil from your first trench will fill the one you dig last.

Double-digging

Double-digging is used to improve drainage and break up compacted sub-soil. It is particularly necessary when growing root crops. Mark out your plot in the same way as for spit-digging and dig your trenches in the same way, but make each trench 60cm wide. When you have dug out the first trench, use a fork to break up the soil and dig out another spit's depth. Manure as before and fill in the trench.

Non-dig method

As an alternative to all this back-breaking digging, there is a non-dig method. Simply cover your patch of earth with a thick layer of compost and plant your vegetables into this. You can continue like this for 2–3 years, but after that you will have no option but to dig.

Digging out a spade's depth and width

Using a fork to break up the soil

Putting manure into the trench

composting

This is the Holy Grail of the true organic believer. Indeed, Lady Eve Balfour (see page 12), the original organicist, had her spiritual awakening beside a compost heap in East Lothian, so it is very fitting – although they probably don't realise it – that East Lothian Council, where I live, runs a composting scheme to help and advise those who want to compost.

Once you have discovered the joys of composting you will never look back and will become quite obsessively boring (as I am) to those who haven't yet 'crossed the line'.

Composting is caused by the presence of bacteria which need air, light moisture and nitrogen. Your heap (or temple of fertility) must stand on the earth so it can draw nutrients out of the earth as well as worms. If you stand it on polythene sheeting, it will rot and grow mould and fungi.

The optimum size for a compost heap is a metre square and 1–1.2 metres in height. You can construct one quite simply with stakes at each corner and chicken wire between or you can build a fine version with wooden slats for the sides, but remember to leave some space in between the slats to allow the air to circulate. I am not a great fan of purpose-built composters but . . . 'chacun à son goût'.

Choose the site of your compost heap carefully. Don't put one under drippy trees or they will keep to wet, nor in full sun as they will dry out too quickly. It is advisable to have three compost heaps – one ready to take compost from, one maturing away nicely and one that you are building up.

Build it up in layers of 15–25cm and do not have a layer of all one type of material, grass cuttings or autumn leaves for instance, as this will slow the process.

Mix each layer well like a fruit cake, then cover with a thin layer of garden soil to supply the bacteria and, if your soil is acid, a sprinkling of lime to keep all sweet. When the heap has reached the right height, cover with a layer of old carpet to keep everything warm. Some people recommend plastic sheeting but I think that makes the heap too wet.

If the weather is exceptionally dry you may want to sprinkle the heap with water. A finished compost heap needs about six months before it is usable and after three months, if all your power sources fail, it's so hot you can cook in the middle of it, using the haybox principle. A compost heap in my village made only of grass cuttings spontaneously combusted once and burned, leaving the owner with nothing but ash!

Some people put autumn leaves on their compost heaps but I prefer to keep them separate and allow them to do their own thing and form leafmould. It takes about 2–3 years to make proper leaf mould from the leaves of deciduous trees but is worth the wait. You can speed up the process by keeping your leaves in plastic bags for about a year. Personally, I prefer the slower-matured variety.

do not put on your compost heap

eggshells as they will attract rats.
any vegetable waste attacked by blight, i.e. club foot in brassicas, alliums suffering from white rot, blighted potatoes etc., as the disease may stay in the compost and be disseminated.
woody vegetation such as clippings from trees, shrubs or fruit bushes, as this will slow down the decomposing process. If you have a proper shredder you can in theory add them, but I find the twiggy bits irritating when sieving the compost. Burn them instead, have a lovely bonfire, dance round it, roast potatoes in the embers and you'll have nice ash to use as well, which will help keep out slugs as well as providing fertilizer.

Something else you can do is to grow lots of comfrey round the edges of your vegetable patch. This makes a wonderful addition to you compost heap as it helps the decomposition process. And add a few earthworms to your heap as well as they are great for breaking everything down and encouraging the bacteria.

manure

Don't balk at the thought of manure; if it is well rotted it doesn't smell nasty or indeed very much at all. One of the problems in organic vegetable growing is obtaining organic manure, in other words manure from cattle or pigs that have been raised organically. As the organic movement grows this naturally becomes easier, but it is still quite hard to find and expensive.

Organic fertilizers used to be made of bone or fish meal which have now become pretty well illegal in the European Union. In any event organic fertilizer used to attract foxes who dug it up and ate it, thus ruining your planting.

You cannot use fresh manure in your trenches as it needs to rot down. If it is not well rotted it will burn the plants. If you have your own animals you will have a regular supply of organic manure after the first year but it is worth buying it in to begin with. You can obtain horse manure from a friendly riding stables. Although horses are not eaten as food in England and consequently are not raised organically, there is not much in their diet to offend, so unless you are going for commercial organic status I'd use bought horse manure in year one. Personally I have always found the finest manure is well-rotted pig manure.

You can use spent mushroom compost instead of home-produced compost. I once had a car that grew mushrooms when it rained as a sack of mushroom compost I had in the back leaked and wasn't completely spent. Chicken droppings are

another alternative. It makes a very good manure for vegetables. Don't dig it in fresh but keep it for about three to four weeks. Grass cuttings are yet another possibility. You can put them into a bed intended for potatoes. Lay them at the bottom of the trench and fill in on top.

watering and mulching

Never water in full sun as this will burn the leaves of your plants. Early morning is best before the sun has any heat. The evening is also good but if the plants stay wet all night this may promote disease. Water closely around the roots so that the water doesn't dissipate, and on the leaves as well. Water needs vary with the different plant; brassicas for instance need 10–15 litres a week in dry weather, whereas legumes don't need much watering at the seedling stage as this promotes leaf growth at the expense of flowers and pods. Once the pods are set however, they need watering to promote internal and external pod growth. Ten litres of water per square metre per week applied twice daily in dry weather is about right.

A good way of feeding the plants whilst watering is to fill a rain butt with water and throw in a good quantity of comfrey. Leave it to stand for a week or so and use it for watering. Use it in the ratio of about one part comfrey slurry to three or four parts water. You can also throw manure into your rain butt which gives a rich feed, but use this sparingly and do not water the leaves with it.

Mulching, the practice of applying compost or leafmould around the plants, is another good way of retaining moisture and keeping down weeds. Apply after the seedlings are well up. It is easy to remove any wind-blown weed seeds from the soft surface. Don't feel romantic about weeds; they leach both moisture and nutrition from the soil at the expense of your vegetables.

sowing seed

Unless you are sowing outside in the autumn, in which case the seeds lie dormant over winter, it is prudent to wait until the soil warms up a bit. The potato farmers of East Lothian used to pull down their trousers and rest their naked bottoms on the sod to see if it was warm enough to plant. It is all very well of me to say smugly that you should sow seed in March or April but if you have a year with late frosts and cold rains, it can hold back or arrest germination quite considerably. If the soil is too wet the nascent seedlings may drown. It is all part of the frustrating adventure of gardening.

preparing the soil

In general though, once winter has worked its wrath on your soil, spring winds will begin to dry it out and break

down any large clods of earth to give you a friable soil surface. Then you need to advance this process. Using a hand cultivator if you have one or a rake if you don't, produce a tilth, working the top 15–20cm of soil from both angles. Don't overwork the soil as you don't want the tilth too fine at this stage. If you are a cook you'll know what I mean by coarse breadcrumbs.

Evenly apply a base dressing of fertilizer, then use the head of a rake to break down any remaining clods. Only do a traditional foot shuffle on very fluffy soils.

Vegetable seeds can be sown directly into the ground or can be transplanted from seed trays (see page 32) in a greenhouse or cold frame. If you are planting directly outside, you need to cut out a drill to plant them in. To do this, put two pegs into the soil where you want the drill to be, string a line between them, then cut out the drill with a hoe following the line of the string.

sowing seed

Remember when sowing seed not to plant the seeds too deep. The bigger seeds like beans and peas will need to be dibbed in about 1.25cm. Make sure that the soil is firmed down but not compacted over them. Smaller seeds really only need a thin drill made with the tip of a rake. Don't forget to put strings with tied-on pieces of aluminium foil across emerging seedlings to save them from pigeons and other birds.

Cutting a drill

Sowing seed

Always sow seed as thinly as you can. This cuts down on thinning, prevents competition between seedlings, and gives sturdier plants. Large seeds such as broad beans, runner beans and sweetcorn can be sown individually in their final positions.

Sow the seeds and water, then rake the soil back over the seeds.

Don't forget to label your rows. At the earliest possible moment thin your seedlings (see page 32) and water the remainder.

Watering

cloches

Cloches (see page 42) are a good way to bring seedlings on. They are like portable greenhouses, concentrating the warmth and focussing the sun's rays. Remember to remove them however if there is a scorching hot day as the sun may burn the seedlings, rather on the magnifying-glass principle.

planting seed in seed trays and pots

If you are setting seeds in trays – and what is more exciting than watching the start of new life? – use fine potting compost. If your own compost is well rotted and friable it will do nicely but pass it through a fine garden sieve to make the finest possible bed for your seedlings. Put the seed trays in a warm place and keep them just moist but not wet. Depending on the species, your seedlings should start to show at ten days to two weeks.

Positioning of your seed trays is important. Some people like to put them in the airing cupboard or buy a heated propagator, which I don't think is really necessary. A warm windowsill or a shelf in the kitchen with good light is usually enough. If you have a cold greenhouse that is ideal.

I tend to plant the bigger seeds such as peas or beans straight into small shallow pots – allow 2–3 per pot – rather than seed trays.

When the seedlings are well above the surface you will want to harden them off before they finally venture outside. If you have a sheltered patio, this is perfect and unless the weather bodes very cold or wet, they can sit there until they are ready to transplant.

speeding up germination

When propagating seeds you may find a plastic bag comes in handy. My friend Douglas Wayne-Heapy, who grows better vegetables than anyone I know, will put three or four larger seeds in a small pot of compost, water them well and cover them completely with a plastic bag, which keeps the moisture in and helps them sprout. With all types of beans he lays a folded plastic bag on top of the compost to the same effect. Germination occurs much more quickly in this diminutive greenhouse.

thinning

One of the great questions is when to thin out your seedlings in their trays and really, like so many things, it's all a case of using your common sense. Remove any seedlings that show signs of deformity or weakness or don't straighten themselves out, and consign these to the compost heap. There is no place for sentimentality in gardening. Once your seedlings look strong enough and are showing signs of leaf growth, move them on to the next stage of their lives. If you are transferring them to individual pots, continue to use fine potting compost; if they are going to be planted outside, make sure that the soil is well worked.

My friend Douglas Wayne-Heapy says that when you have planted out seeds or are hardening them off under cold frames or cloches you must listen to the weather forecast continually. This season the frost was so bad in May in my area it actually got through the cloches and scorched the plants. Potatoes and most over-wintered plants will grow back if cut back by frost, but peas, beans and delicate or half-hardy plants won't, so it's a question of starting again. Douglas is a great believer in staggering germination to preserve against gluts. He sows his seeds at fortnightly or even monthly intervals so he can keep gathering his crops right through until October.

using seed you have saved yourself

One of the problems of saving your own seed is that it may have a low germination yield, either because you have taken the seeds too early or because they have not properly dried, so watch out for this when they are germinating. A good way of testing your seed in enough time to buy more if necessary is to put a few seeds in early and see how well they sprout.

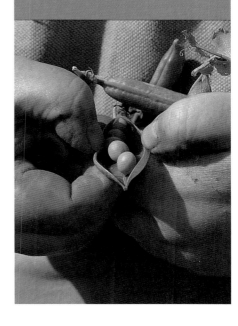

transplanting

This is the moment when a cold frame will really come in useful. Transfer your seedlings to their pots and stand them in the shelter of the cold frame until they have 3–4 proper leaves before planting out. This will give them the best possible chance of survival.

Obviously take the greatest care when transplanting seedlings to handle them gently. Hold the seedlings by the leaves rather than the stalk as leaves can regrow if damaged, but if you snap the stalk, you've had it. Make sure you allow yourself plenty of time when transplanting. Hurry or stress may not transfer to the plants but it will to your fingers!

trees

If you have the space you can grow a few useful trees, whether for wood, fruit or nuts. I am always amazed at townies who think trees just grow in the countryside any old how. I usually point out acerbically that if Charles II hadn't planted his oak plantation in the midst of the New Forest we would have lost the Battle of Trafalgar because we wouldn't have had enough oak trees to lay the keels of Nelson's fleet.

Different trees are used for different things; wood has very individual uses according to the species. Trees are also good for drainage if your land tends to wetness. One excellent tree that will grow straight and strong anywhere is the ash. I have two ash bookcases and an ash writing desk at which I am sitting at the moment, both made for me in Scotland. Ash is much used for furniture and has a lovely grain and a pleasing light colour. Because of its strength and flexibility – it doesn't shatter or splinter under pressure – ash is mostly used for tool handles.

buying your trees

You will need to buy young trees; when choosing them try and ensure that the roots have been trained using the Airpot method. This Australian invention is a device for training tree roots that prevents root-spiralling problems and produces a better root system. In addition, the Airpot system reduces the shock factor that is caused by travel and planting, which means there is less chance of you losing your rather expensive investment.

alder

Alder trees are also good for drainage and produce a hard, waterproof wood. In the days when people wore clogs, the soles were made of alder and boxes made from alder were often used for storing gunpowder. If you have alder containers in your kitchen you can be sure that they will be moisture-free.

sycamore

Sycamore contains an inbuilt antiseptic and should be used for rolling pins and kitchen containers. Food put in sycamore bowls will not go bad on you.

locust wood

The English writer William Cobbett raved about the properties of locust wood. It has the great advantage that it doesn't rot so is excellent for fence stakes, barn footings and indeed anywhere else where wood is set in earth.

beech

Beech is best for furniture. It is an easily worked strong wood, much used in country furniture. Of course its leaves make the best leafmould and if you're lucky enough to have a beech wood you should have bluebells and mushrooms and even possibly truffles.

sweet chestnut

Sweet chestnut of course produces nuts but is also coppiced for long straight poles. It was much used for traditional rood screens, fireplaces and minstrels' galleries as it carves very well.

oak

Oaks are always nice to have especially if you keep pigs, and I am told by the brilliant furniture-maker and designer Ben Dawson, whose work includes the inside of the Scottish Parliament and the Welsh Assembly, that oak is now back in vogue although most of it is currently sourced in central Europe.

nut trees

Whilst planning your tree planting you might give a thought to growing some nuts if your garden is big enough. I like to see nut trees growing. There is something primitive about their presence which brings out the hunter-gatherer gene. Johnny talks about the virtues of hazel for coppicing (see page 80) but remember that fresh hazelnuts are quite delicious eaten whole, or dried and grated for cooking, both for bread-making and in such delights as hazelnut meringues.

almond

Almond trees are elegant and have beautiful blossom in the spring. In most of the UK the fruit won't ripen but if you have a walled garden or live in the south-west you are in with a chance. For those of you who are reading this in warmer climes or have a second home in southern Europe, give them a go. Fresh almonds are delicious either plain or covered in sugar syrup or spices and dried in the oven, while ground almonds are a must in baking and a great help when cooking for a celiac.

walnut

There is a walnut tree in the garden where I live in Scotland and even though the fruit doesn't ripen most years, I am able to make lots of pickled walnuts and walnut ketchup from the unripe fruit.

(see page 80)

large-scale planting

If you are planning to plant a large plantation you should seek professional advice. If you simply want trees to act as windbreaks or simply for beauty, you can easily choose varieties that will offer a useful end product, though you may have to wait anything from seven to 30 years for the result. Aosta in Italy is one of the major tree-producing areas of the world, the others being Oregon and North Florida.

The wood of a good tree is valuable too. If you live somewhere warmer, you will have lovely walnuts to eat and if you cut a growing shoot of walnut on St John's Day, 24 June in the northern hemisphere or Christmas Eve in the southern hemisphere, and put it in a bottle of eau de vie, you will make a delicious liqueur.

brazil nut

Brazil nuts are an important part of a vegetarian diet but will only grow south of the Equator.

cultivation of fruit trees

Although you can buy container-grown fruit trees all the experts agree that it is best to buy dormant bareroot trees in the late autumn and early winter.

The care you invest in the planting of your tree will repay you many times over the years ahead.

planting

Make sure the hole is wide enough to spread the root system out. It needs to be at least 60cm across but not too deep and no deeper than the hole from which the root was removed. You will be able to tell by looking at your tree; the graft point, the swollen bit on the bottom of the stem, should be just above the level of the soil. Put well-rotted compost or manure in the bottom of the hole before planting. Only unwrap the tree once the hole is dug and if the roots seem in any way dry, soak them for a couple of hours in a bucket of water. Trim off any damaged roots as they may let in disease.

protect from attack

Don't let pigs into your orchard until the trees are well established or they will dig them up. To guard against bird predation hang old CDs in the tree or any glittery, tinkly items. Mothballs hung in the tree are good for keeping insects away.

Plant a treated stake alongside the tree and tie it to help support its early life unless of course it is against a wall or wires. Water well immediately after planting and in the early months, water often to help the tree establish itself. Fruit trees need pruning as soon as they are planted.

Keep a circle of soil round the base of the tree bare as a guard against disease for at least the first two or three years. After that if you are letting the grass grow, leave it longer around the trees as that conserves moisture better.

pruning

Pruning helps shape a tree and removes much of the risk of disease. It encourages fruit production and lets in light. Only prune in winter, except for apricots, nectarines, cherries and plums, which must be pruned when they are growing vigorously to minimize the risk of attack by silverleaf.

Always cut out damaged, diseased and cankered growth and burn the latter at once. Keep your cuts as small as possible. As a general rule, prune vigorous shoots lightly and weak ones hard, which seems bizarre but heavy pruning encourages vigorous growth. If removing larger branches cut at the collar – the swelling where one branch meets another. If the cut is particularly big you may need to tar it to prevent disease.

For cones, fans and espaliers, remember the principle of strong and weak shoots as you prune to shape the plants to fit along your wall.

spur or tip?

Before pruning an apple tree check whether it is a spur-bearer (the most common), a tip-bearer (more usual in pippins) or a partial tip-bearer, which includes Bramleys. Pruning tip-bearers usually requires the removal of old wood to encourage new shoots and tip-pruning branch leaders, which may otherwise break under the apple's weight, so that they form tip-bearing shoots.

For partial tip-bearers, cut back any strong lateral shoots that are longer than 25cm to 5–6 buds.

pruning after planting

When pruning fruit trees and bushes after planting, cut the central leader so it just tops the tallest laterals then reduce the laterals by two -thirds. In the tree's second winter, cut the laterals you want as your main branches back by half. Remove any crossing and misplaced shoots and prune everything else back to 5 buds. In the third winter look at your framework and remove a quarter of the leader's new growth, prune weak laterals back to 2–3 buds and strong laterals to 5 buds. Thereafter shorten weak leaders by half and strong ones by less than a quarter. Use your discretion.

thinning fruit

It is very important to thin your fruit once they are set. In midsummer the tree will shed some leaves anyway as nature's way of exposing the ripening fruit to the light. At this time go though the clusters of fruit removing any that are damaged or diseased and thinning out some smaller ones so that you will get bigger fruit. The remaining fruit should be 5–10cm apart, depending on the species size.

pollination

Most of the time clever nature does the work for you. The colour and scent of plants is all about attracting pollinators – just like short skirts and fancy hairdos or hipster jeans in clubs attract boys. However there are a few things you can do to help nature along.

Having your own bees (see page 130) is one possibility of course. Nothing beats a hive in your own garden for ensuring that there is always a roaming bee, but beekeeping is not always possible. There are however hives all over the place, even in London. A beekeeping friend of mine used to sit in the garden of her

planting to attract bees

One way to ensure pollination is to grow plants that will attract neighbouring bees. They will then wander among your plants carrying pollen on their feet or proboscis. But if you are trying to attract bees, remember all the precautions against drowning bees in you beer traps (see page 44) or otherwise damaging them.

Borage is a bee herb par excellence. It also happens to be a delicious salad herb and the leaves are good cooked as fritters in the same way as sage or comfrey leaves.

Also good is lavender, especially the cotton lavender varieties. You will notice there are always bees around lavender hedges. Borage and lavender are particularly beneficial because they flower during what we in England call the June gap – the barren period for flowering. Your barren flowering month may well be different; it depends where you live. In Scotland, for instance, the barren month is July.

Knightsbridge flat and watch the bees, as dusk drew in, streaming up to the roof of Harrods where someone kept several hives. The trick is to lure those bees to your plants.

problem pollinators

I have talked elsewhere of the difficulty of pollinating maize and sweetcorn (see page 73) due to the way the male and female tassels grow low down on the plant stalks. All wind-pollinated plants should be grown in blocks or at least close enough to cross-pollinate easily.

Fruit trees nowadays are usually self-pollinating but some of the older varieties may need a bit of help. Check from your plantsman to find out if any of your species need cross-pollinating, in which case you may need to plant two trees of the same variety. I have helped gardeners to cross-pollinate their trees using a soft sable paintbrush, but that is mostly a thing of the past.

Old varieties of fig trees needed a fig wasp for pollination. This is an insect which laid its eggs in the buds of the trees. The hatched grub would then eat its way out and cross onto another flower, thus pollinating the tree. This curious feature of the fig explains why trees of old fig varieties planted in areas where there are no fig wasps are frequently barren. This problem has largely been sorted out by hybridization but remember Christ's advice on the barren fig, and if you have inherited one, root it out and condemn it to the flames in a suitably biblical fashion.

'If the weather is very cold there may be an absence of bees and if rough winds are shaking your darling buds of May you may need to resort to using a paintbrush.'

cloning

Some plants, mostly airborne varieties such as orchids, can be cloned. This is done using centrifugal force but whilst it is quite fun to witness the machinery at work, it is a very expensive process and is not really that much use for growing vegetables in your own garden.

You must keep a weather eye when the blossom is out to ensure that cross-pollination is taking place. If the weather is very cold there may be an absence of bees and if rough winds are shaking your darling buds of May you may need to resort to using a paintbrush. Accept that some years have better conditions than others for fruit-setting resulting in variations in your fruit production, but if you continue to have low yields you may have to call in an expert.

cucurbit problems

The worst-case pollination scenario in your garden will be the cucurbits, especially melons and squashes. Usually these plants intertwine so that pollination does take place, but if you are having problems you may have to pluck a male flower and thrust it into the female flower and shake it about. Make sure that the sexual bits actually connect. It's just like sexual penetration in humans, but less fun. Remember to cook the male flower afterwards – a bonus we don't enjoy, at least not since pagan prehistoric times.

rotation of crops

In order to prevent disease it is vital to rotate your crops. Vegetables grown in the same spot year after year will take the same vitamins and minerals from the patch of soil they are grown in, which will weaken subsequent growth. Moreover if there is any trace of disease in the soil or of earth-bound pests such as eel and wire worms, these will stay in there and attack the same vegetables the next year.

'Apply muck before potatoes but not before root crops such as carrots.'

green nutrition crops

You may be wondering what I mean by overwintering nutrition crops in the table below. Let me explain. Any land that is left bare to rest is subject to erosion by wind and water as well as invasion by wind-borne weeds and rough grasses. These will leach nutrition from the soil and negate the reason for resting it. It is like the house in the Bible that is swept clean and waiting for more devils to move in. The best way to avoid such 'devils' is to sow green manure crops – alfalfa, clovers or winter tares. These can then be dug into the soil to provide feed for the next batch of crops.

the four-year plan

One common rotation plan that works best is a four-year plan. Divide the plot into four and plant as follows:

	Section A	Section B	Section C	Section D
Spring/summer	early and main-crop potatoes	carrots beetroot (chard and spinach are classed with beetroot) celery fennel parsnips	brassicas	legumes alliums
Autumn/winter	autumn-planted onions	phacelia or other overwintering nutrition crop	winter cabbage	winter tares (*Vicia villosa*) or other nutrition crop

Next year move everything around one space. Apply muck before potatoes but not before root crops such as carrots. Dig in the green overwintering nutrition crops before spring planting. Cucurbits, in other words courgettes, marrows, squash, pumpkins and cucumbers, will go in the beds where the green manure has been dug in as they like a good layer of muck.

the greenhouse and its satellites

The greenhouse is a wonderful tool for a gardener. It enables you to provide a winter growing season, improve ripening conditions for some plants, extend the length of the growing season, isolate rare species from cross-pollination and allow you to grow exotica.

Before we come to the greenhouse proper let us consider growing under cover, with one word of warning which is to make sure you are not enclosing a plant that needs insect pollination.

cloches

These are portable greenhouses, transparent covers made of glass or plastic which can be moved about as needed. Cloches can be used to cover planted-out seedlings until they are hardened and to place over tender plants if frost is about. They vary from ornate covers to cut-off clear plastic bottles. Even the plastic you see spread over fields of potatoes is really just a huge cloche. Use your imagination but make sure you give the plants plenty of room under them.

polytunnels

These are sheets of polythene placed over hoops, open each end and facing east to west for maximum light. They are simply a variant of the greenhouse. I don't love them but they are very useful. I once had a

Above left: Cloches; Above top: Horticultural fleece; Above: A cold frame

friend who ran a snail farm inside some on the Mull of Kintyre. The snails flourished, which says it all really.

horticultural fleece

Nowadays horticultural fleece is a translucent fabric that acts as protection against wind and pest damage. It is supported on hoops or sticks to keep clear of the plants. Originally it was a poor fleece that was not usable for spinning. Dig the edges of your fleece into the earth and/or pin them down securely.

cold frames

Cold frames protect from wind and frost damage and are excellent for hardening off seedlings between the seed tray and the real world. At Lennoxlove House we had wonderful brick-built cold frames with hinged glass lids, but this is the ideal and not necessarily the reality. A few bales of straw to prop up some old glass or windows will do. Lay out the bales in a square and place a wooden board on top. Put another layer of bales on the board and top these with the glass. Cover the board with compost and plant out seedlings in the compost.

hot beds and hot walls

Much used in more northerly gardens, hot beds – like cold frames but heated – and hot walls create extra warmth that enables you to force fruit or grow fruit, such as melons, that need a good amount of heat.

In the eighteenth century growers put walls of deal planks in front of the brick garden walls against which fruit trees were growing, and piled dung into the gap between the wood and the brick. The heat generated by the rotting dung helped to force cherries, peaches and other fruit.

In the nineteenth century a company in the Suffolk town of Bury St Edmunds patented a moveable glass wall to be used with fruit trees growing against a wall. A bracket with a cantilevered hook was screwed to the wall and this held the wall of glass in its wooden frame in front of the tree. The glass reflected the sunlight so the fruit tree benefited. Hot walls like these are still in use in heritage gardens around the world.

Although modern hot beds use electric cables, I prefer the green variety where the frame is placed on top of a bed of rotting manure. More manure is heaped round the sides. You can put these hot beds anywhere, even in a cold greenhouse or polytunnel. Hot beds give you the opportunity to grow some unusual plants if you fancy. The first pineapple grown in England in the seventeenth century was grown in a hot bed.

cold greenhouses

The principle of a greenhouse is that the sun heats the greenhouse and it cools slowly when the sun has gone. The same principle applies to a lean-to, so if you are building one against a house, make sure it gets the sun.

You can of course buy a greenhouse or you can make your own, which is easier than it may sound. Old glass doors salvaged from skips, old windows, sheets of glass or clear plastic and a little imagination are all you need.

You will need ventilation to admit insects and to prevent rot and moulds, and you will also need to water your plants regularly. At times of frost you may want to leave a small paraffin heater or a halogen light or heater burning overnight inside. Another way of introducing some heat is to store your rainwater in large black plastic tubs in your greenhouse. These will act just like night-storage heaters. Alternatively, you can build a hot bed (see above), which will give off a lot of warmth.

Inside the greenhouse use compost not soil for your beds, top-dress them each spring and autumn and practise crop rotation. Remove any diseased plants at once and observe the suggestions for tying back and stopping the various plants so that the foliage doesn't obscure too much of the light.

Tomatoes, cucumbers, peppers, aubergines and chillies will all grow well in a greenhouse if you can keep it clear of whitefly (see page 45). Winter crops that do well sown in the autumn are carrots, chicory, Chinese greens, endive and winter varieties of lettuce, including lamb's lettuce, peas and perpetual spinach.

heated greenhouses

From the late eighteenth century onwards there was a passion for large heated greenhouses. The mid-Victorians in particular went wild for them, priding themselves on growing grapes and new potatoes in time for Christmas. They even grew tender peach trees such as the white Italian varieties.

Their greenhouses were ventilated via windows that opened with rotating handles and were heated with coal- or charcoal-burning stoves with hot pipes running under all the raised beds. They also had water pipes running through, either half-pipes from which the water would evaporate into the air, or pipes with holes in them running above the beds. These operated with plugs that could be raised or lowered to open or close the holes – a sort of early sprinkler system. Nowadays you can heat your greenhouse with electric cable running under the beds or with heaters, but why not a wood-burning stove in the middle?

pests and diseases

Nothing will bring home to you your organic status more than growing vegetables. The minute you embark on a vegetable garden you are at war – pigeons will want your brassicas and legumes, song birds will be after your soft fruits, and there will be insect predators galore. You will have to marshal your troops and enlist your allies carefully.

Gone are the days when you could simply blast everything with chemicals. In fact, you are probably reading this book in order to protect yourself and your children from the systemic spraying of food crops. We perhaps don't have to go as far as the great Lord Coke of Holkham in Norfolk who, in the seventeenth century, turned 200 ducks into a field of cabbages infested with caterpillars. The ducks ate all the creepy crawlies and the cabbages were saved. Bear it in mind.

slugs and snails

Just as Coke turned to ducks, you might care to encourage hedgehogs. You will be delighted when you realise quite how many slugs and snails these spiky predators will consume. I have always been kindly disposed to hedgehogs ever since I read about Mrs Tiggywinkle and Fuzzy in the Little Grey Rabbit books. There was a tendency among country people to abjure hedgehogs as they believed they stole the milk from cows and brought bovine TB, allegations which have all now been proved to be untrue. Hedgehogs are fewer than they once were due to the growth of roads and car traffic, but they are still to be found. If, when the warm days begin and they are coming out

of hibernation, you leave out a saucer of milk mixed with a little chopped meat or dog food after dark, you may well lure them into your garden, especially if there is an early spring when there is not much about for them to eat.

You may also lure in the odd fox, in which case shoot it and make a nice hat like the one I'm wearing on the back cover. That one was shot by an urban Yorkshire butcher in his hen run.

follow the trail

Slugs and snails pose a major problem and they are your worst enemies early in the growing season. To locate them, follow the slime trails. Both these creatures need to feed to create slime, without which they die. They are hermaphrodite and therefore can impregnate their own eggs. If you

come across a batch of eggs, wait until daylight then remove the stone they are under and give the birds a caviar feast.

If you put wood ash, ground seashells or sawdust around your plants, this will help to deter slugs and snails. Copper wire and aluminium foil are also deterrents; use them to construct little fences around tender plants.

Slugs love beer, so sinking shallow containers of beer as slug traps is very efficacious, but hedgehogs are also partial to beer, so do make sure the traps aren't too deep for the hedgehogs to climb out of and leave a stick in for any beetles to climb out. (I'm not being 'fluffy' about this – beetles feed on soft-skinned insects so you need them too to help you in your fight.) And if you keep bees, don't use beer traps in early summer as the young bees are attracted to them and may get drowned.

snail hunt

Another way of dealing with slugs and snails is to seek them out. My grandmother in Singapore used to keep me out of mischief during the afternoon siesta by getting me to swat flies at a cent a fly. Apply the same principle to your children or grandchildren and send them on a slug and snail search. Slugs and snails prefer to come out in the dampness of evening so this is the time to mount your torch-lit hunts. Children may not want to pick the creatures up by hand so provide them with chopsticks, rubber gloves or tweezers as accessories. When you have located the enemies, drop them into a bucket of water to drown them, then compost them or feed them to your poultry.

eat your snails

Whilst slugs make chicken food, snails can provide a tasty dish for you. In order to eat them they need to be placed on oatmeal for 2–3 days to clean them out. Then boil them like whelks to remove them from their shells. After that you can cook them with garlic and butter or stew them with tomatoes in the Spanish fashion, or cook them in any other way you choose.

Most commercial snails come from Turkey but especially in chalk regions you find what country people call 'wall-fish' – the land snails transported throughout their empire by the Romans to supplement their diets. If you have African land snails (sometimes the size of a pudding plate) in your area, they are also good eating but are tough so will need to be marinated for a day or two in pawpaw or pineapple juice.

frogs and toads versus slugs and snails

Other allies in your fight against the slugs and snails are frogs and toads, so build a small pond in your garden if you don't already have one. You may have to borrow some frog spawn from a friendly neighbour to get your frogs started. Don't forget to plant a few water lilies to shelter the frogs from marauding birds. You may also have to acquire a toad. Find a nice damp, cool spot for it to shelter during the day and you will be repaid one hundredfold.

Ponds do, however, attract mosquitoes which lay their eggs on the surface. This is another reason to encourage frogs as they will eat the mosquito larvae. Build a proper pond lined with clay in the old-fashioned manner, not one with a fibreglass or plastic lining. You will find your pond life does better in it.

birdlife joins the struggle

Thrushes and blackbirds are also your friends in the slug and snail war but in order to ensure their safety and encourage them to breed, you will need to kill or remove crows, rooks, jays, magpies, jackdaws and squirrels, all of which prey on songbird eggs and chicks.

A Larsen trap or a small-bore rifle will do the job for crows and magpies. Jackdaws nest in chimneys, so sweep your chimneys as they are building their nests. This will destroy the nests before the eggs are laid and the jackdaws will quickly move elsewhere.

Squirrels are good eating in a stew with prunes and tomatoes. It's funny but once you actually start engaging with nature rather than watching it on televison or through your binoculars you very quickly become un-fluffy. Take all these steps and your reward will be glorious birdsong, to say nothing of fewer snails.

'Squirrels are good eating in a stew with prunes and tomatoes.'

keeping insects and other creatures at bay

There are many traditional ways of dealing with insect pests around the fruit and vegetable garden. To kill and prevent whitefly, I recommend a splendid remedy that was told me by my good friend Charlie. He cuts rhubarb leaves, puts them in a galvanized bucket, pours on boiling water and leaves them to rot down. Then he sprays with the rather smelly liquid that results.

Another friend in the war against greenfly is the ladybird. There are actually companies now that will send you ladybirds by post. Put them on those plants that are affected by greenfly and the ladybirds will do the work for you. Don't order too many ladybirds though as they will reproduce.

insecticides

Then there are insecticides. Botanical insecticides derive from plants and these are greatly to be preferred. Many work as well as synthetic insecticides and because they break down quickly, there will be less risk of residues on your crops.

There are, for instance, the nicotine-based insecticides deriving from *Nicotiniana tabacum* that work on the nervous systems of insects to kill them. Just be careful not to use them immediately before harvesting. Pyrethrum, made from the dried and powdered flowers of the daisy chrysanthemum, Cineranaefolium, is one of the safest of this type of the botanical insecticides, but make sure you get pure powdered pyrethrum as some formulas include piperonyl butoxide, which is not suitable for an organic garden. Derris dust is extracted from tropical and sub-tropical plants belonging to the legume family. It is a good general-purpose insecticide but is harmful to fish so don't use it near ponds or streams.

Soapy water is good against soft-bodied insects but must be sprayed directly on them. Spray when the adult insects are less active, either in the cool early morning or, if you have beehives, in the evening after the bees have gone to bed as the soap will hurt them. And only use soap, never washing-up liquid, which may damage your plants.

fighting plant disease

There is little you can do against fungal infections and leaf curls apart from spraying, but it is a general rule of thumb that the healthier your garden, the fewer the diseases. Composting, mulching and weeding are the tunes to which a well-kept garden marches. These basic tasks will all help combat disease as will regular inspections and removal of infected material as soon as you see it.

companion planting

For most of my life modern notions have scorned companion planting as foolish country lore. Holistic gardeners, however, have long known that growing certain plants close together complements and sustains them whilst some species detest each other. Modern scientists who dislike what they cannot explain poo-pooh the idea and forget the maxim 'there are more things in heaven and earth'. Repeatedly nowadays I come across some 'invention', 'discovery' or 'innovation' by some young Turk which was actually mooted centuries ago by Trusser, Markam or Culpeper. If Alexander Fleming had read his mother's Mrs Beeton he would have discovered penicillin a lot earlier: 'the mould that grows on bread and oranges is excellent in the treatment of boils, carbuncles and infested wounds.' Companion planting works, so do try it.

● Grow marigolds among your vegetables as marigold roots secrete a substance that destroys nematodes and eel worms. If your soil is badly infested, grow a solid block of marigolds for a season then dig them in as green manure. If you make sure that you grow the edible pot marigolds, you'll have an extra food harvest, too.

● Nasturtiums are irresistible to aphids so use them to distract the aphids' attention from your vegetables, but make sure you plant them well away from the vegetable plot. As a bonus, nasturtium leaves, flowers and seeds are all good additions to salads too.

● Alliums of all sorts exude enzymes from their roots which are toxic to many pests, so plant garlic among your lines of vegetables.

● Rue, mint, tansy, lavender, sage, rosemary and wormwood all deter a variety of pests so plant them among the rows, too.

● Nettles attract butterflies as well as the early aphids that provide food for ladybirds waking from hibernation. This means that nettles not only keep the aphids off other plants, but also encourage aphid predators to breed.

● If you plant nettles near your tomatoes they will help the fruit ripen, and remember that young nettles make good eating (see page 82) and are full of iron.

● If you are reclaiming field land for vegetables, there may be a real problem with click beetle so plant mustard for a season and dig it in as a green manure.

Another thing that will help is to keep some rainwater barrels. Use this purer water for watering and for mixing your sprays. If you look in the back of this book you will find the names of some providers of organic pesticides and plant sprays so you will be able to exercise control without breaching your organic principals. However, remember that, at the end of the day, you will never win completely. That is part of the adventure of gardening.

'If Alexander Fleming had read his mother's Mrs Beeton he would have discovered penicillin a lot earlier...'

fruit

cane fruits

It is a great joy to grow fruit canes as they only need a little attention – just pruning and watering in dry weather as the fruit begin to colour. You are also advised to protect the canes from birds with netting. It is very fulfilling – as well as filling – to pick your own berries and currants; pick one to eat yourself and two for the trug.

You can grow a variety of cane fruits, including raspberries, tayberries, loganberries and gooseberries and you can even grow thornless blackberries, although I prefer to pick my blackberries in the hedgerows. You might also like to grow red, white and blackcurrants. I always find that just as there are never enough raspberries, so there are never enough blackcurrants. All of these fruits freeze well and you can make jams, jellies and syrups with them also.

raspberries

Raspberries prefer a neutral, very well drained soil. Plant the canes from late winter to early spring, once the soil has dried out. Set them in shallow holes, about 5cm deep, and spread the roots out in the hole to encourage suckers that will form new canes. Plant the canes 45cm apart and the rows 2 metres apart. Once you have planted your canes cut them back to about 30cm above the ground, cutting to a good bud. Mulch well in the spring to conserve moisture.

Once the new canes appear cut out the old ones. Allow about 6–7 canes per plant

buying the canes

When buying your canes make sure that they are guaranteed virus-free. All of these plants, with the exception of gooseberries, which grow as a shrub, will need support. Grow them either against a wire fence at the edge of your garden or hammer in stakes and string wires between them to support the canes. If space is limited you can twist the canes round just one post. The raspberry variety Autumn Blissa will grow without any support at all and can be grown as a container plant.

but do not select your canes until late spring as this is when you will be able to choose the best. Cut out any that show signs of disease.

As soon as they are tall enough, tie them to the wires (see box above). Weed well throughout the season. Harvest as and when the fruit is ripe.

When the plants have finished fruiting, cut back the brown woody canes as next year's fruit will grow on new wood. There are a number of varieties you may like to grow; talk to your plantsman about what suits your area best. Plants should last for around 10 years.

blackberries and their hybrids

Blackberries and their hybrids prefer well-drained but not dry soil. They like full sun best but will do alright in partial shade. Dig in plenty of manure or compost before planting. Otherwise treat as raspberries.

gooseberries

Gooseberries are little shrub-like plants that do well if neglected. I have got the best fruit off stunted little bushes that I have totally ignored while I have had little or tasteless fruit off those that I've carefully nurtured.

currants

Tie up carefully to support the fruit bunches and to let the light get at them. Remember not to grow too many whitecurrants as they fruit best and you will find that you end up adding them to your redcurrant jelly in despair.

soft fruits

strawberries

So called because a layer of straw spread around the plants helps them to ripen and keeps back slugs and snails. I prefer to grow my strawberries in raised beds because it prevents the crawlies and saves backache. Strawberries also do well in planters or containers.

They tolerate most soils except heavy, wet ones. They prefer a slightly acid soil and if yours is chalky or alkaline, you may have to feed for iron deficiencies (see page 25).

Plant in late autumn or winter and remove runners – this is how strawberries spread themselves – as they develop to help the plant produce more fruit. The final distance between plants should be about 45cm. Harvest as soon as the fruit is ripe.

Plants crop best in their second year but should last four years. They benefit from a light dressing of ash, watered in. If you are careful in your selection of varieties you can have strawberries all summer and autumn. They do not store and do not really freeze well so unless you want masses of jam, aim for different varieties that will crop at different times.

wild strawberries

These make wonderful groundcover, are easy to grow and do not need straw. Grow them on a very well-drained bank and you will reap a wonderful reward.

blueberries

These are excellent if your soil has a high pH reading – they will even grow in soils that are above pH6. They are high in anti-oxidants so are very good for you, and even babies love them as they aren't tart. Mixed with either strawberries, raspberries or both, they make a visually attractive summer fruit salad. They love peaty soils, where they are found growing wild. Blueberries also do very well in tubs on your patio and are tolerant of either sun or partial shade. If you are planting them in a barrel mix well-rotted coniferous bark or crumbled peat in with your soil.

tree fruits

apples

Considering mankind gave up earthly paradise for an apple or, as Lord Byron put it, 'since Eve met Adam much depends on dinner', we should pay attention to this splendid fruit. It will be another joy to add to your new way of life. Supermarket apples are tasteless, horrible and have usually travelled around the world in heavily chilled conditions. An apple freshly plucked and ripe from the tree has a brilliant taste sensation.

choosing an apple variety

There are many great new apple varieties but I am fonder of the older types.

Worcester Permain – this is my favourite apple. I carry in my head the flavour of Worcester Permains picked from a tree in Sussex.

Costard – I wonder about this now-extinct apple from which the word 'costermonger' (fruit seller) comes. It was the definitive apple of the Middle Ages in England.

Flower of Kent – also now lost to us but this was the apple that fell on Isaac Newton's head and changed the world.

Api – another favourite of mine and the most likely contender for the apple of the Garden of Eden. It was beloved of the Romans and features in their poetry and prose. It is a small, very pretty apple with a sweet but sharp taste and it keeps very well.

Blenheim Orange – I suppose this is the apple many of us carry in our mind's eye as it is the most frequently painted of apples. It is red and yellow with a crisp sweet flavour – the perfect Christmas apple.

Cox's Orange Pippin, Discovery and any of the **Laxton** family are good keepers for winter eating.

White Joanetting – named for Joan the Fair Maid of Kent, mother of the Black Prince, this was the Elizabethan favourite. It ripens in early July and has a beautiful aroma as well as a sweet flavour.

Gladstone – another reliable summer apple with a good scent.

Allington Pippin – this is a good example of the 'pippins' – apples grown from a pip. Pippins usually keep well.

Bismark or **Granny Smith** – if you are reading this in Australia, South Africa or Chile, try either of these for tarts and fritters.

Egremont Russet – seldom seen nowadays but always worth growing as they are easy maintenance and good storers but are rustic rather than pretty. They are too misshapen for today's supermarkets. They vary from the largest, the Royal, a pre-seventeenth-century type, through to the Golden.

Cider apples – virtually inedible and intended solely for the making of cider.

Apples are entirely a matter of personal taste. There are currently over 5000 different species of apples to choose from so it is important to find a local plantsman to advise you. Ask about having a selection of early and late species. Or you can go to one of your local apple days – the Brogdale or Wisley apple days are some examples. Here you can taste a good cross section and make your choice. Remember too that apples need to be cross-pollinated so it is important that you choose trees that flower at the same time. Again take advice on this.

Early apples do not store well but are excellent eating. Later-ripening apples are picked as the first frosts come and are stored over winter. They become sweeter but less visually appealing as the months go by. You also want to include some cooking apples, though not necessarily Bramleys, which were developed by Victorian plantsmen to collapse when baked and are the best for purées and apple sauces. Instead you may want something that will make a splendid apple tart.

Rootstocks

Apples grown from seed rarely succeed and take a long time to mature so it is best to buy young trees. Apples are grafted onto a variety of rootstocks which really dictate their future growth, eventual size and what growth conditions the tree will need. Again seek advice.

For dwarfing trees M9 and M27 rootstocks are probably a good choice. M27 will produce a squat shrubby tree and M9, which reaches 2–3 metres at most, is very good for cordons, although it is quite high-maintenance. M26 is slightly taller and good for three-tier espaliers and cordons. MM106 gives a nicely shaped tree up to about 5.5 metres in height.

pears

In the Middle Ages they preferred pears to apples and the great monasteries of France grew and developed many varieties. There have been waves of pear mania at different periods of history, the last of which swept New England in the nineteenth century. Although there is no native American pear, these 'epidemics' have led to the development of over a thousand types of pears, both eaters and cookers.

Pears deteriorate very quickly and do not store that well, so they taste best when they are picked ripe, which is impossible for supermarkets to do.

Pears follow the same growing requirements as apples but unless you live in a very warm part of the world, grow them against a wall or, as I once saw in the late Lord Sefton's garden, as a chalice. This is a technique where the centre of the tree is removed and the leaders are trained to grow upwards to form an open bowl, allowing the sun to strike the centre of the tree. The lady gardener there was very proud of her achievement as it takes time, effort and

meticulous husbandry to avoid disease and destruction by pests during the formation period.

Apart from the obvious ways of cooking and storing pears, they are very good halved and dried (see page 204).

plums

It is a fine thing to have a plum tree in your garden. It is almost impossible to buy decent plums and there is nothing to compare with a ripe juicy one.

The main worry with plums is that they flower very early and the blossoms can be damaged by frost. If possible cover the tree with a fleece or burn smoke braziers nearby to keep frost off the flowers.

There are many varieties of self-fertilizing plums so if you are just having one tree, make sure you choose one of these.

Plant plums as for apples, exercising the same degree of care. They like a sunny position and damp but not wet soil.

All stone fruits are prone to silverleaf, a potentially fatal disease. Trees acquire a silvery sheen on the leaves which then spreads to the branches and then the tree dies. If this happens cut out the affected areas. Any diseased branch over 2.5cm wide will show a brown stain. Cut this wood out to well below the stained area and burn the prunings. Because of this tendency to disease, prune only where necessary and always in summer when the tree is growing strongly. Remember to thin your fruit at the midsummer shed (see page 37).

(see page 37)

plum predators

The worst predators for plums are wasps and pigeons. Other birds may strip the buds even before you have to worry about the fruit. Hanging discarded CDs and mothballs among the branches may suffice but sometimes the only answer is to net the whole tree or invest in a hawk. A wasp trap or a beer filler jar are also useful as deterrents but not if you keep bees.

Plums for small spaces
If you live in a cold place or if space is limited, grow your plum as a cordon, fan or espalier. For small gardens there is a rootstock called Pixy, which provides dwarf trees. These can be grown in pots. If space is limited you can also grow the single-stemmed Minarette.

other stoned fruit

The rules for plums apply to all stoned fruit. Cherries, including geans (wild cherries for cooking) are a joy. One of the best things I ever ate was a wild cherry crumble made by my friend Alaphia Bidwell. I also love the Hungarian wild cherry soup.

If you have the climate or a wall to ripen them on apricots are reckoned by some to be the taste of paradise. Damsons are happily making a come back. In the Lye Valley in Cumbria they have a Damson Day for admiring the blossom, much as the Japanese do with their cherry blossom. Be careful when buying damson gin as many commercial producers use imported sloe and damson juice from Poland rather than steeping the fruit.

mulberries

I would put in a plea that you plant a mulberry tree, although you will have to wait nearly a decade for the first fruit. It is an attractive tree in its own right and quite delicious. The fruit makes wonderful ice cream and is very good dried as the Persians and Afghanis do. And of course, if you want a totally new way of life you can always keep silkworms. I did this when I was young and although I never made much silk it was fascinating. I always love the story of how Napoleon, bored to tears during his brief stay on Elba, observed that black mulberry trees grow in profusion there and encouraged the establishment of a silk industry on the island.

melons

When I was at school at Brighton there was a splendid aged nun called Mother Peirquet who taught me Latin and Greek with a high Prussian accent and gardened magnificently. Her great pride was that in a good year she succeeded in growing melons outside. Hopefully many of you will be reading this where you can easily grow melons but for those of us in Britain it is possible, especially with a greenhouse or hot bed.

Sow your seeds 1cm deep in individual pots in mid-winter. They want to be at about 20°C/68°F. Re-pot the seedlings when they have about four true leaves. If you are growing them inside, transfer them to their final position at this point. If growing them outside, harden them in a cold frame and plant them after the frosts are finished. Melons like a lot of muck, so dig in plenty of manure.

Once the side-shoots have produced five leaves, pinch out the tips. Stop further side-shoots at three leaves. You may have to pollinate as you would for courgettes, thrusting the male flower into the female. If you are training your melons up a frame you will need hammocks to support the fruit. Netting is best but you can buy ferret hammocks at game fairs, which do very well. Old tights are alright too but aren't very elegant. If you are growing them on the ground, grow them on a small mound. To prevent the fruit rotting put a slate or wooden slat under the fruit. You will know when they are ripe from the smell; the musky, erotic smell of a ripe melon is unmistakable.

grapes

If you are living in Britain successful grape growing depends on where you live. There is a fair-sized English wine industry and the Romans grew grapes in Lincolnshire, but for table grapes you really need a hothouse. However my friend Henrietta Palmer, a descendant of the man who grew the first pineapple in Britain, grows a vine in her guest loo, a room with a lot of south-facing glass.

Grapes flourish on dried blood, either dug in around the roots of the vine or watered on. The great vine at Hampton Court, still thriving since the reign of Henry VIII, used to have the blood of an ox poured over the roots every few years. Today I believe they use the dried variety. When it comes to table grapes, Black Hamburg is my favourite.

citrus fruits

There is much theorizing that the fruit Adam plucked was actually an orange, just as people believe that Paris's prize to Venus was an orange rather than an apple. All of this seems pretty likely in the context of Mesopotamia or Greece.

If you are reading this in a hotter clime, picking the fruit in your own garden will always be a joy. I find nothing nicer when visiting friends in Spain than to go into the garden or even the street and pluck an orange or a lemon. On the Costa del Sol, the oranges grow in the streets as sycamores do in London. The silly ex-pat Brits step over the fallen fruit and go to the supermarkets to buy them instead. They look at me askance when I pick them up and take them home to squeeze for breakfast.

In the orange groves behind the hills on the Costa del Sol, you can get drunk on the scent of the trees but even a single one will give out the most lovely scent. If you live in the right place you can easily grow oranges, lemons, grapefruits or any of the many other citrus species.

When I was a child and visited relatives in Australia I loved the little kumquats that grow there. They make the most delicious marmalade, are very simple to grow and are a compact size, which makes them ideal for terraces and patios.

A warm enclosed space is a good place for citrus trees and growing dwarf

a bit of history

Henry VIII's romantic wedding gift to the homesick Catherine of Aragon was an orangerie and a salad garden in every royal palace. Orangeries in great houses in the British Isles have flourished ever since. The fruit most commonly grown was the China orange, which is better suited to our colder climate than the oranges of Spain.

varieties is a particularly good idea where space is limited. All the rules that apply to other fruit trees apply to citrus.

figs

Eating a ripe fig freshly plucked and warm from the sun is a truly sensuous experience. If you are reading this in a country where figs are easy to grow I will not need to tell you much about their cultivation – they just get on with it themselves. All the usual information on bird predation, training and pruning apply.

The most common fig grown in the UK is the Bardaic or Brown Turkey fig. It doesn't need caprification – a method of pollinating by a fig wasp – which many of the wilder varieties still require. Walled gardens sometimes have fig houses that are like vine houses, but figs can ripen perfectly well in a good year on a south-facing wall.

potatoes

Potatoes are in my genes. My father, a true gourmet, writing an introduction to a celebrity charity cookbook chose, of all things, to write about the potatoes of his childhood, while my mother's comfort food was new potatoes eaten with a bowl of double cream. It is such a joy to grow your own potatoes. You will taste the difference once you try.

In England, potatoes are classified as: 'earlies', which are ready in June and July having been planted in March; 'second earlies' for eating in August and early September; and 'main crop', maturing in September and October. You will immediately have grasped that any supermarket selling British 'new' potatoes other than Jersey Royals earlier than June is palming you off with last year's chilled, irradiated, small salad potatoes!

'...any supermarket selling British "new" potatoes other than Jersey Royals earlier than June is palming you off with last year's chilled, irradiated, small salad potatoes!'

vegetables

cultivation

To grow, manure your ground the previous autumn. Be careful not to plant potatoes in frost pockets and remember they need a deep tilth. Your seed potatoes should be about 30g in weight and the size of a pullet's egg. Dig drills 60cm deep and 75cm apart and place you seed potatoes with the rose end upwards in the drills. Plant 'earlies' 30cm apart and all others 40cm apart. Cover immediately and draw up the soil to make a ridge 10–15cm high.

Water 'earlies' at the rate of 5 litres per square metre over a 14-day period and once they reach the size of a marble (check this by gently digging around in the soil) increase this to 5 litres per square metre every 10 days. Main crops should be watered at this rate only at flowering time, as this will increase yield and will prevent scab; otherwise water when the weather is very dry.

Potatoes are ready to harvest after three months, when the flowers are fully opened. Leave potatoes on dry soil or anywhere dry for 2–3 hours before storing. Lift all potatoes to prevent future disease. Store only undamaged tubers in a frost-free building and keep them in the dark or under black plastic to prevent greening. For large quantities, store in an outside

clamp. This involves removing the leaves after lifting, heaping the potatoes under straw and, after they have sweated for two or three days, mounding up the earth over them. Do not underestimate the danger of eating green potatoes; all solanums are quite poisonous in certain conditions and there is a direct link between green potatoes eaten by pregnant women and spina bifida.

potatoes for small spaces

Don't worry if you live in a town or city; potatoes grow perfectly well in pots. To grow them this way, you must first chit them in early February by placing a single layer of seed potatoes 'rose' end up in a box or tray in a light airy spot such as a cool greenhouse. By late March you will have strong, sturdy shoots. Take a large pot, at least 30cm wide, and fill it with garden soil. Plant 2–3 chitted potatoes in the pot and keep in a slightly heated greenhouse until the frosts are past.

There is a fashion for urban gardeners to grow potatoes in planters made from old tyres; personally I think this makes your garden look like a tinker's bothy but there is no doubt that it does work. In fact, many other vegetables can also be grown in this way. Put down your first tyre and fill it with well-rotted manure or compost. Add another tyre and fill with soil; add a third tyre and put in a thin layer of manure or compost and more soil. Three tyres will probably do you. Don't completely fill the last tyre as you will need to leave room for plant growth. Bury your chitted potatoes in the soil and cover with sacking or black plastic to promote growth.

When the time comes for harvesting, break down the tyre structure, removing the potatoes as you go. This method works surprisingly well and offers the benefit of pest protection as slugs can't climb that high. It also avoids a lot of digging. Remember when planning crop rotation (see page 40) that potatoes, tomatoes and aubergines are all from the same family.

onions

You can never grow too many onions and in fact we could be facing future shortages. A few years ago there was a major onion shortage in India, which caused rioting in the streets. The soil for an onion bed should be finely tilled, reasonably fertile but not freshly manured. Onions like a sunny sheltered spot and can be grown successfully from seed or from sets.

cultivation

Double-dig your onion plot in the late autumn or early winter and lay a 5–7.5cm layer of manure in the bottom. A week before sowing top-dress with twice as much potash as nitrogen. Onion bulbs sown the previous autumn do not require this; instead dress them sparingly with chalk in February. Sow the seeds thinly in drills 1.5cm deep and 25cm apart and if the soil is dry, water. Thin out the seedlings to 5–7cm apart once they have straightened. Onions shouldn't need more watering unless the weather is dry in May and June, when you may need to water sparingly. It is however important to keep them free of weeds. In mid- to late August or early September, the stalks will flop over and turn yellow indicating that they are mature. In a wet summer you may have to bend the tops by hand to assist bulb maturity. Once the tops are yellow and withered, try to pick a dry spell for harvesting then you can leave the onions on top of the dry soil to dry for a day or two. You will notice some onions are bull-necked and will not bend; never store these as they will rot, so eat them first.

growing from seed

Choosing the dates for sowing over-wintering onions is important as you want the seedlings to be strong enough to survive the winter and you need the

warmer soil for germination, but if they are sown too early, you will suffer attacks of bean fly. I find the first week in September best as there is usually a spell of good weather then. Sow the seeds thinly so that you can leave the thinning until early spring to produce bigger onions. If you sow seed in a greenhouse, sow in January, then harden the plants under a cold frame in March so that you can transplant to the bed in April.

growing from sets

'Sets' are partly developed onion bulbs stored over the winter and planted in the spring, when they grow rapidly. This method is most useful in areas with a short growing season. You can buy sets, but they aren't cheap, or instead you can keep back some of your own from the previous season, choosing firm onions about 60mm in diameter. Plant your sets in fine tilth in late March or early April in rows 25cm apart. Your onions should be separated by 7.5–10cm and only the tip should be visible. Firm the soil round the plants. If birds or frost should pull them out of the ground replant at once.

onion pests

Onions' main pests are onion fly, which lays its eggs around the onions in early May, and eel worm. That is when you should treat your seedlings. If you are gardening organically, the best protection is a layer of ash both on and around the base of the plants. Be very careful to rotate your onions as pests will stay in the soil for a year or more.

onions for small spaces

If you have a flat or small town garden you can grow shallots, which take up less space for more gain. Spring onions (aka salad onions or scallions) will grow quite happily in a pot on your windowsill or in a window box. These are sown from seed and don't need thinning except as you pick them for eating. The other type of onion for small-space gardening is the Welsh or tree onion which is a perennial and, as it grows up rather than out, does not take up much space. Tree onions are particularly good for companion planting, as like all alliums they emit a substance that is abhorred by aphids and many other pests.

storing onions

When you have lifted your onions lay them on newspaper in a dry place until their stalks are completely dry and straw-like. Turn them every 3–4 days to ensure proper drying then sort them and retain the perfect ones for storing over winter. Any with signs of fly, rot, mould or bull necks should not be stored but used as soon as possible. In my drinking days, dear friends used to invite me over at the time of onion harvesting, as the fascinating (to me) task of sorting onions kept me off the gin somewhat, hence I was better company. I would then make large quantities of onion soup for eating or freezing with the 'must use' ones.

When you have sorted out your storing onions, rub off any excess dry skin and plait the stalks together, reinforcing them with thin string, and then hang them by the string from hooks in a dry place. I think they look very gratifying hanging in a kitchen or larder. Small onions and shallots can be stored in nets; old tights or stockings are good for this. A good onion crop should see you through the winter and when they start sprouting in the spring you can eat the green tops in salad as an anti-scorbutic. If you don't want to string them or hang them in nets, lay them in boxes in a cool, dry place and check them from time to time. When storing shallots you may like to separate the bigger bulbs as this will stop any tendency to rot.

garlic

Garlic is a true gardener's friend and is good for your health. In the sixteenth century, Culpeper, the herbalist, wrote that 'garlic burns away the fat that is stored around the heart' so eat it as a cholesterol-controller.

Garlic likes sunny conditions and will grow happily in plots, pots or windowboxes. Plant your garlic from bulblets separated from the main bulb in February or March. If planted in a plot among other vegetables, it will help with pest control but don't plant next to any legume. Harvest as for onions and store in nets in a cool, dry place. The bulbs are frost-hardy so can be left in the ground throughout the winter.

leeks

I live in Musselburgh, the land of the leek. Indeed the finest standard leek bears the name of my 'honest town', a name registered by the great botanist, Mr Scarlett, who lived at the end of my street. The Romans, who were great leek eaters, raved about our local leeks and one of the duties of the soldiers on the Antonine wall in Scotland was to guard leek shipments to Rome. By the church near me there was a Roman cavalry fort and there is a temple to Mithras in our park, so I often muse over our Roman ghosts and their affection for our leeks. Leeks like a well-drained soil and not too much food as that makes them grow lush and floppy, which is fatal. They also do not like heavy or clay soils that hold the wet during winter months.

cultivation

Leek seeds mature very slowly, so it is best to sow them in trays in a warm greenhouse and harden them under cloches. Sow in trays in late January to early February and prick out to other trays when the seedlings have straightened. Outside, sow seeds in drills 1.25cm deep and 15cm apart in late March.

Leeks should be planted out when they are as thick as a pencil and 15–20cm high. Make a hole 5cm wide and 15cm deep with a dibber, insert your seedling, then do not put the earth back, but instead fill the hole with water. If you are sowing seed, you will need to mound up the earth round the rows to aid blanching. Leeks are virtually pest-free. Harvest them as needed from Christmas onwards. They can remain in the ground until May when they begin to sprout.

companion planting

Plant leeks with carrots, onion and celery, but not with legumes.

carrots

Only for you dear reader would I write this section. We all have something we hate in this world and, long before Mr Blair, my hatred has always been reserved for the carrot. So much so that Johnny's wife Mary teases with me carrot gifts. I have a magnificent handbag with a bas-relief of carrots on it, I have a carrot pepper grinder and many such other joys. I love the gifts but continue to hate the vegetable. When I was a little girl my father would pull them from the soil, dust them off and make me eat them slugs and all. Today I would probably fry the slug in garlic and butter but the carrot remains a black spot in my soul. I know, however, this is irrational and I don't condemn you for liking them, so here we go.

cultivation

The carrot likes a light sandy soil which has not been manured for a year. Soil that is too rich will cause it to fork and heavy clay will make it rot. If carrots are deprived of water while they are growing, they become coarse and woody, but too much water encourages leaf growth which draws in the deadly carrotfly.

From early March sow the seed thinly in drills 1.5cm deep and 15cm apart, then cover with fine soil. Thin the seedlings regularly throughout the summer as they are ready to eat. Young and tender carrots I'm told are delicious! When weeding take care not to damage the shoulders of the plants as this will encourage disease.

Harvest your main-crop carrots in October, cut off the foliage and clean off the soil. Pack in boxes of dry sand, ensure the carrots are separate, not touching, and keep in a cool, dry, frost-free place. They should last until March. Don't attempt to store damaged or diseased roots; burn the latter and compost or eat the former.

carrot pests

The carrotfly is attracted by the smell of crushed foliage, so thin in the evening and do not leave the removed leaves lying about. The carrotfly has two main seasons, May and August, so bear this in mind. Apart from planting onions as companions, the only organic remedy is to liberally sprinkle the leaves and shoulders with wood ash, replacing the ash during fly seasons if it is washed away by rain. The ash deters the fly from laying its eggs. Don't even bother growing carrots south of the River Tamar as the damned fly flies all the time. That's why traditionally Cornish pasties should not contain carrots.

carrots for small spaces

If you live in a town you can happily grow carrots in a growbag on your balcony or in shallow pots.

companion planting

Plant carrots with onions, peas, herbs, tomatoes and radishes. Strangely, they dislike dill but this herb eats well with carrots! I do hope you have a good crop but don't invite me to share it!

parsnips

Soil for parsnips must not have been manured before sowing; if it is too rich they will fork. They require little nitrogen and like a sunny spot, although they will tolerate light shade. Unless you are growing a short-root variety of parsnip, you will need to dig deep to prepare the soil for planting as parsnip roots can go down as much as 60cm. Dig a spade's depth and loosen the soil below this with a fork.

Two weeks before sowing in late February to early March, apply a dressing of general fertilizer. Try to avoid sowing in cold, wet weather but if the soil is dry, water before sowing. Use new seed each year as parsnip seeds lose fertility quickly and plant 3–4 seeds together. Then, when the first true leaves appear, leave the strongest plant in each grouping.

The seeds take anything from 10 days to 4 weeks to germinate, depending on soil temperature. Don't let your parsnips get dry throughout the year as this will cause splitting, and when hoeing the rows, take care not to damage the shoulders of the plants as this can let in disease.

You can harvest when the leaves die back in late autumn or early winter, but they are much improved by frost. Leave the plants in the ground throughout the winter and harvest at will. If you have to lift them, you can store as carrots but they tend to go soft and are only really useful for soup once that happens. Lift any remaining in March to make way for other vegetables.

parsnip pests

Parsnips are also prone to carrotfly so treat as for carrots.

parsnips for small spaces

In a town garden parsnips can be grown in tyre planters or in deep frost-proof pots.

the secret of borstch

In Russia and other parts of central Europe the beets are stored in barrels on the roof where the cold causes them to ferment. I firmly believe this is what gives true Borstch its special flavour.

beetroot

A wonderfully versatile cropping vegetable, sow beetroot any time between February and June. The small, round-crop varieties will be ready in 12 weeks to adorn your summer cold table and salads. Plant on well-drained ground that isn't freshly manured or intersperse between rows of other vegetables or even, in a town garden, between other plants. Plant and thin as for parsnips.

Protect the seedlings from sparrows with black thread and take care when hoeing or weeding as damaged roots will bleed badly. Your main crop can be left in the ground through the winter, covered with straw against frost, or it can be harvested in October and stored in sand boxes. Inspect regularly for deteriorating roots.

companion planting

Beets love onions and cabbage or other brassicas but dislike beans.

'...long before Mr Blair, my hatred has always been reserved for the carrot.'

brassicas

This large family covers a huge range of vegetables – cabbages, Brussels sprouts, cauliflower, kale, swedes and turnips, broccoli and, my favourite of all, purple sprouting broccoli. I am torn between this and asparagus for my funeral; debating the merits of each as the seasons come and go will probably keep me alive forever.

cultivation

There are certain key principles involved in growing brassicas. Plant them in a seedbed and transplant them at 5–7 weeks, or buy established plants. They like a fertile soil and should not be planted in the same plot more than one year in three. For preference, grow them to follow legumes as they benefit from the nitrogen in the soil.

All brassicas like a firm ground so cultivate and manure early in the winter or, if for some reason you must cultivate later, feed the soil and firm it down well. How? you ask. Use your feet.

The seedbed should preferably be open, sunny and sheltered. Manure it well in the autumn and rake over before using. Water if dry. Firm the soil and rake again to produce a fine tilth. Sow in drills 15cm apart and 4cm deep. Germination takes 7–12 days. Thin to 5cm apart as soon as possible, keep weed-free and water if dry. Firm the soil down after weeding or thinning and remember to label the rows if you are sowing different varieties at the same time.

Double-dig your permanent main bed to between 45cm and 60cm. Brassicas get

companion planting

Rosemary, sage, thyme and mint planted among all brassicas deter their pests. No brassicas like tomatoes, with the exception of red cabbage, which don't mind them

very thirsty and this will allow deep, well-formed root structures, which aid water intake and are more resistant to disease. Transplant your seedlings when they have 3–4 leaves and are about 15cm tall. Take care not to damage the roots when transplanting, water with a rose and, if it is very dry, make puddle holes and plant into them. Remember to firm down the soil; a gardener we had when I was a child said brassicas are just like small children, they like to be tucked well into their beds.

brassica diseases

The main reason for moving your brassicas to a fresh plot most years is the danger of club root infection; should this occur, carefully root up and burn infected plants and do not grow brassicas again on that spot for at least seven years.

> 'I am torn between purple sprouting broccoli and asparagus for my funeral...'

cabbages

Never underestimate a gardener's passion for cabbage. I remember when once we were staying in Barbados, the West Indian gardener who had all the lovely Caribbean plants at his command would present us proudly with his cabbages, which I am ashamed to say we rather spurned. Having said that, I am very fond of cabbage when cooked properly, and cooked with partridge, it is a delight.

spring cabbage

Sow in late July or early August, to transplant between mid-September and mid-October. Plant 30cm apart for hearted plants or 10cm apart for spring greens. You can get the best of both worlds by removing two out of three greens in February and dressing with soda, then with sulphate of ammonia or wood ash in early March. Plants will keep in the ground until June.

summer cabbage

You may not bother to grow summer cabbage as there are lots of alternatives to eat at this time of year and summer cabbage is the most prone to club root. If you do want it, sow between February and May for transplanting between April and May, and for harvesting between July and autumn. Be particularly careful at all stages of sowing and transplanting, as damaged roots are more prone to disease. To my mind, the main reason for bothering to grow summer cabbage is to eat sauerkraut.

cauliflower

This is the most difficult of the brassicas to grow successfully as it is very demanding in its soil, moisture and food requirements. It is less hardy than other brassicas and in a bad winter even the over-wintering varieties will be damaged or killed by adverse weather. I suspect this is a gardener's vegetable, grown for pride – a head of mature 'curds' looks impressive – but it is not a cook's dream as it is difficult to cook interestingly and tricky to store. However, if you are a vegetarian and aren't too worried about appearances, it is a godsend as it holds flavours well and has a different texture to other vegetables.

winter cabbage

Savoys and other winter varieties are the hardiest and thrive better on poorer soils than other brassicas. Sow in May and transplant in July. Water frequently and harvest from October onwards. In August, as they begin to heart, tie up the outer leaves with raffia.

red cabbage

Grow as spring or summer cabbage, cutting mature heads well before any frost. Take care not to grow too many red cabbages as a little goes a long way even if you are pickling.

storing cabbages

Red and white cabbages will store well in a frost-free area. Dig up the whole plant, cut off the roots and the coarse outer leaves, and store so they the cabbages are not touching. Inspectthem from time to time to make sure they are no rotting.

brussels sprouts

In your new green world, you will want to grow the older varieties of Brussels sprouts which mature irregularly on the same plant so that you can keep picking throughout the season. The new hybrids are designed for the freezer or for the farmers' market where you will see whole stalks being sold. Brussels sprouts freeze well on the stalk. I remember picking them with frozen fingers and they went tinkle plonk into the pan as we threw them in.

Sow in March or early April to transplant in May or June. A week before transplanting, dig over the site and rake in fertilizer at 75g per square metre. Hoe and weed regularly, but only water if very dry. Pick the sprouts as they mature from the bottom up, and when all are picked, cut the tops as greens. Dig it up as soon as you have finished with it as the plants draw heavily on nutrients in the soil. Dig up the woody stalk and burn it (don't compost it as it won't rot down well and may cause disease).

cultivation

A deeply dug, fertile soil, rich in humus is essential and a heavy dressing of manure helps to provide food and retain moisture during growing. Cauliflowers should never be allowed to dry out as this will produce poor heads. During dry periods they need 5 litres of water per square metre per day. If other brassicas don't heart you still have top greens, but with cauliflowers you are left with diddlysquat!

Dressings of sulphate of ammonia or wood ash should be watered into young plants before the curds form to promote vigorous healthy growth. Sow summer cauliflowers in March or early April to transplant in June and harvest in August and early September. Unless you live in a mild, dry area, don't even think about winter cauliflowers as they hate heavy soils and bad weather.

broccoli

Unlike cauliflower, purple and white sprouting broccoli are very hardy and happy with the poor soils and cold areas that other brassicas disdain. Moreover they are totally delicious and are among those gratifying vegetables that you really have to grow yourself as the short season means the supermarkets avoid them. Sprouting broccoli matures from January to May and in very mild areas you may even get them for Christmas. Their main predator is the pigeon, who can decimate a crop, but with a gun and a little luck, you can have a perfect dinner. They are also useful plants to intersperse in an ordinary garden as they are out of the way quite early.

cultivation

The seeds are planted in April or May for transplanting in June and July. Harvest the plants as they mature, picking the central spear first at about 10cm long but before the flowers begin to open, then picking the side shoots as they mature. Pick every two days and you will harvest for several months. The white variety crops later and is less prolific.

calabrese

I rather sided with President Bush when he said that he would never serve calabrese at the White House. I'm sure it is clever American marketing that, in order to tackle the damage he did, has persuaded the health-obsessed that calabrese is better for you than any other brassica. Why this is, no one has explained or as far as I know proved. The large green head is in season from August until October and takes 12–14 weeks to mature, although with a mild autumn it will crop until the first frost.

cultivation

Sow in April and May and transplant in June. The seedlings should be planted in rows 45cm apart with 45cm between the plants. Harvest as the head's seven side-shoots mature. An ideal plant for freezing.

kale

This is an extremely hardy and useful winter plant, tolerant of club root, root fly and poor soils. It is also beloved of pheasants so the old poachers' trick of using brandy-soaked raisins to lure pheasants into the kale will supply your whole meal. The old Scots expression, 'Have you had your kale yet?' meant 'Have you eaten?' and the Highland vegetable plot was known as the 'kale yard'. Kale soup is delicious; it was a staple of the Scots' diet before the Industrial Revolution, and is far healthier than the Scots' current obsession with deep-fat frying! Remember, the fashionable cavalo nero is only black kale! The larger leaves of kale can be bitter but are good for soup or for slow-cooking with other vegetables. Kale is happy with an open site but in areas of high, cold winds some windbreak is advisable, though having shot pheasants in East Anglian kale fields with the wind arriving straight off the Siberian steppe, I suspect it is not vital.

cultivation

Sow kale in April and May to transplant from late June to early August. Plant 40cm apart in rows the same distance apart. Harvest after the first frost, selecting young shoots and discarding woody or yellowed stems. Inspect from time to time.

legumes

This group of plants is vital to a green garden as they are the best providers of nitrogen for your soil. They should not be grown on the same site two years running and after cropping has finished, cut back the plants to 10cm above the ground and compost the vegetation, then dig or rotate the rest back into the ground. All legumes have little tubers attached to the roots which will restore nitrogen.

french beans

When I was a child, these were regarded as a delicacy and my mother, who loved them, was viewed as rather eccentric for growing them and serving them at dinner parties. Now they are fairly

commonplace and easy to grow. We used to call the round ones bobby beans, but now they all tend to be classed together.

French beans do not thrive in cold soils and will rot if too wet. They grow best in a well-drained, fertile soil but I find that farmyard manure or compost dug in the winter before is usually enough, with no top-dressing needed. Don't grow them in the shade and choose dwarf or climbing varieties to suit your garden.

cultivation

Don't sow before early May and protect under cloches until they are established. Continue sowing until July and you will have beans all summer. Sow dwarf beans 45cm apart, space the seeds 5cm apart in drills 5cm deep, and water the bottom of the drills. Sow climbing beans with a 60cm gap between the rows and plant 8–10cm apart.

In June, give the plants a good mulching. Once established, unless it is very dry, do not water until the flowers appear, then water well allowing 5 litres per square metre per week during flowering and pod-setting. This will give a good crop. Regular picking ensures a continuing crop, so pick whilst they are young and tender and snap cleanly off the plant. Protect against aphids and burn plants infected by mould – never save seeds from diseased plants.

beans for small spaces

They grow very well on terraces, balconies or decking, twining happily round the trellising and providing the sweet smell of bean flowers. In eighteenth-century England, Londoners used to walk among the bean fields of Chelsea to smell the lovely scent.

support for climbing beans

Climbing beans will grow up virtually anything – bamboo poles, tepee frames made of poles or just some string strung between poles.

'In eighteenth-century England, Londoners used to walk among the bean fields of Chelsea to smell the lovely scent.'

runner beans

Cultivation is as for French beans but runner beans will need stronger supports. Twist the plants anti-clockwise round the supports and they won't need much tying. They are insect-pollinated, so remember this when spraying. Sow in a sheltered, sunny spot, after the frosts are over. During cropping they will need picking every day.

broad beans

These were sacred in ancient Greece. I think I love young broad beans more than anything. You cannot buy really good broad beans; they are so much better when you pick them young and eat them at once.

The birthday beans from my friend Douglas (see page 22) were from overwintered plants sown the previous November. More usually they are sown under cloches in February for picking from late June. Remove the cloches when the seeds reach the glass. Whilst they tolerate relatively poor soils, a better yield is obtained from rich, well-drained soil. Avoid cold, wet soils especially over winter, as the seeds will rot.

cultivation

Broad-bean seeds are very large and don't need a finely prepared bed. Plant them in 8cm holes in double rows, 12cm apart with 45cm between the rows. The plants are quite frost-resistant and will germinate at soil temperatures of 5°C. Successive sowings will ensure beans throughout the summer.

When the plants are in full flower pinch out 10–15cm of shoot to reduce the danger of blackfly and aphids and to produce a more uniform pod. These pickings are delicious cooked up in a little butter with salt and pepper.

From mid-June pick the pods whilst young and supple. After harvesting cut to 10cm above the soil, compost the cut material, then dig the stem bases and roots into the soil to add nitrogen.

When you have shelled the pods, cook them and put them through the mouli or stew them whole in their pods. They also freeze very successfully.

peas

This group includes garden peas, marrow-fat peas, petit pois, mange tout, sugar snap peas and asparagus peas. For me, garden peas fall into the same category as broad beans: they are only really wonderful when freshly picked because the sugar in them turns to starch really quickly so even when bought in farmers' markets or the best vegetable shops, they are less than perfect.

cultivation

Peas must be grown on fertile, well-drained soil. Any waterlogging and the seeds will rot. Peas can be grown as 'earlies', 'second earlies' and main crop. From sowing to picking, 'first earlies' take 12 weeks, 'second earlies' 13–14 weeks and main crop 14–16 weeks. You can also plant 'late earlies' in early July for picking in early October if you live in the warmer south.

> ### a choice of peas
>
> **Petit pois** – best for bottling so are worth growing for your larder.
>
> **Marrow-fat peas** – these dry well and were used to provide a useful staple for soups and stews as well as for mushy peas throughout the winter.
>
> **Mange tout, sugar snap peas** and **asparagus peas** – fine if you have the room. I would go for the asparagus peas as they are more unusual.

Sow early peas in November for overwintering, then sow successively from early March until the end of April. Peas will germinate at 5°C but an intrusion of cold weather will knock them back and may lead to fungal disease.

Manure the ground the winter before planting. Pick when the pods are 2.5cm long; if they are left until they are too big, they become fibrous and inedible.

pea support and protection

The taller varieties of peas give a better crop. Traditionally they are grown up pea sticks which are thin hedgerow twigs, but if you don't have access to these, grow them up netting instead.

Seeds and seedlings are prone to attack from birds and mice so use a guard of netting against the birds and sprinkle liberally with white pepper to keep the mice at bay. This tip was discovered accidentally by my mother, who didn't want to put down poison because of the dogs we had. It works very well against cats and foxes too.

soya beans

These are an excellent source of non-animal protein. Take particular care to plant when the frosts are past, and harvest in the autumn when the leaves turn yellow. The beans can then be threshed and dried.

tomatoes

You can grow tomatoes anywhere that has access to the sun – in greenhouses, on balconies, on windowsills.

cultivation

Sow the seeds thinly into seed trays and cover with finely sieved compost. Keep moist but not waterlogged. Ten to twelve days after sowing, when they have true leaves, transplant the seedlings to individual pots. Water to firm them, then water little and often. Liquid-feed the plants before planting out when the plants are 15–25cm tall and the first flowers are just opening. Water well before and after planting. Do not plant out any diseased plants. Alternatively you can buy ready-grown plants at this stage.

Snap off any side-shoots that develop or cut off with a sharp knife. When the plants are 120–150cm tall, cut away the lower leaves with a sharp knife to allow light into the bottom of the plants and to guard against the risk of fungal diseases. In hot weather, water little and often, 3–4 times a day for pot and growbag plants, mixing feed in with the water.

If you have difficulty pollinating, spray with a fine spray of water or shake the cane or string gently to disseminate pollen. Stop your plants at the fourth truss by pinching off the plant two leaves above this point. In greenhouses, the plants should be stopped when they reach the roof, usually the sixth truss. For whitefly, use the rotted rhubarb cure (see page 45) and if the leaves turn yellow, water in a pinch or two of Epsom salts.

Pick the fruit as it ripens, but if you have unripened tomatoes in September you can either de-stake the plant and lay it on straw covered with a cloche, or pick the tomatoes and lay them in a dark drawer to ripen, or put them in a brown paper bag with a banana. If you have small green tomatoes, you can crystallize them or even make chutney.

tomatoes for small spaces

In small spaces tomatoes are best grown in 22cm pots or in stone circles with a polythene base. Lay out your polythene to protect your terrace or balcony, lay a circle of stones around the edge and pile soil in the middle of the circle. They can even be grown on bales of straw with the aid of a little compost. They always need feeding with liquid manure (think back to your comfrey slurry – see page 28) and also need to be staked securely and protected from the wind.

marrows, squashes, courgettes and pumpkins

All of this family of plants, though different in appearance, have roughly the same habit and produce from June (early courgettes) until September. They all need well-drained soils and preferably a sunny sheltered position.

Do not plant outdoors before mid-May or once frosts are over. Dig your holes 150cm apart for trailing varieties and 90cm apart for bush varieties. Fill the holes with well-rotted manure or compost and replace the soil to form a mound over each hole. Sow 2–3 seeds in each mound and when each seedling has 3–4 leaves, remove the weakest seedlings leaving just one. They can also be chitted (see page 55) and transplanted later.

If growing early in pots, transplant one plant to each mound. Keep well watered and feed as the plants start to swell. Pinch out the growing points of laterals at 60cm and train them at will.

You may need to pollinate them early in the season. The male flower is smaller and only produces pollen, so pluck these and brush the female flowers with them before frying the males in batter or stuffing them.

squashes for small spaces

In town gardens, squashes can be grown up trellises while one courgette plant on a balcony will keep you supplied all summer. A single pumpkin plant on a terrace is dramatic and productive, especially if you plant a miniature variety. Custard marrows look like tiny flying saucers, so they are fun to grow as well as delicious.

cucumbers

Cucumber seeds germinate erratically, so put them on moist kitchen towel in a plastic container, then cover and place in the airing cupboard for 2–3 days. After that, transfer to their individual compost-filled containers.

In the greenhouse, grow as for tomatoes and stop your laterals after two leaves. Remove any male flowers as pollinated female cucumbers are very bitter. New strains only produce female flowers. Cut with a sharp knife when ready.

Ridge cucumbers and gherkins can be grown outdoors. They need pollinating so you should keep both sets of flowers. Sow the seed directly into well-manured ground and feed with liquid fertilizer. Gherkins are best for pickling and can be grown in pots.

salad greens

All types can be grown in troughs, pots or outdoors. Sow thinly after frosts have passed and keep well-watered. Feed the hearted varieties 7–10 days before maturity. Rocket grown in soil is a hundred times better-tasting than any commercial hydroponically grown types. I won't eat salad unless I or a friend grow it. I can't stand the thought of all the chlorine gas you get with commercial salads, which taste of nothing. Protect from slugs by putting grit or wood ash around the plants.

aubergines, peppers and chillies

These can all be grown in pots in a greenhouse or on a sheltered terrace or windowsill. Grow as for tomatoes. Remember aubergines are solanums so they must be ripe before you eat them or they are bitter and poisonous.

artichokes and cardoons

You will remember, gentle reader, that I owe my career to the stately cardoon. I was first seen on television with my friend, Stefan, and our cardoons in his Lincolnshire field.

Artichokes are part of the Cynararia or edible thistle family. They have a three-year growth cycle after which they should be discarded. In the first year, 4–5 seedheads are all you can expect but in the second and third years, anything from 10 to 12 seedheads are normal. They grow by way of side-suckers, which you cut from the main plant in March or April with some root still attached.

All Cynararias like well-drained sandy soil.

Intersperse your plants among other plants as they are useful to fill gaps in the garden.

Cardoons need a lot of watering in dry weather, preferably with comfrey slurry (see page 21) or they will bolt. Unless you are a cheese-maker (see page 180) you don't want them to produce a seedhead which they will do if they dry out and think the end of the world is nigh. In late August or early September, wrap the whole plant in cardboard or black plastic to blanch for at least three weeks.

Pick artichokes when the heads are still tightly closed or they will be unpalatable. When your plants have finished for the year, cut them right back and cover with straw over the winter. Cardoons are not frost-hardy so protect them well.

herbs

'The crusaders believed it gave you courage and drank a borage cup before they rode out to fight.'

Sometimes herbs are all you have, but they are enough. If you are poor without even a windowsill to call your own, as I have been at times in my life, you will always find some herbs if you roam the streets. You might find a large rosemary bush overhanging a fence or one planted for remembrance in a quiet churchyard. And who would begrudge you a few sprigs to enliven your lamb breast or your pork belly, especially if you offer a prayer? Or you might find a sprig of lavender in a park for your apple turnover or a bay leaf from a tree outside a smart house. No one will miss it but it will enrich your life.

Herbs are so easy to grow. They begrudge you nothing when planted on the poorest and stoniest soils. They dry easily in their bunches to perfume your winters and your soups and stews. They heal and nurture you for no more than a few pence. Seeds, heel cuttings, rooted slips – whichever way you get started, thank heaven for herbs. You can grow herbs for balconies, terraces, gardens, windowsills, even a doorstep on a quiet street.

Herbs for immediate use can be dried above the stove. For longer-keeping herbs dry them in a warm well-ventilated place. If they are seed herbs like coriander or anise, hang them with their heads in a paper bag so that the seeds will drop into the bag as they ripen fully.

If you are freezing herbs, lay the sprigs flat on trays in the freezer until they are frozen then transfer them to a large freezer bag so that you can pick out sprigs at will. The herbs I freeze are dill, fennel and tarragon.

Harvest your herbs for storing on a warm morning just before they begin flowering and when the oils are flowing to the sun.

angelica

A vital source of vitamin C, this large Umbelliferate was once the main export of eleventh-century Iceland for use as an anti-scorbutic. When we think of angelica, many of us think of the bright green candied stalks used in cake decoration. Think again; a piece of raw or dried angelica stalk cooked with tart fruit overcomes the tartness and negates the need for sugar, a fact much overlooked in recipes for diabetics. Grow only from fresh seed in the spring and harvest at high summer.

anise

This annual should be grown from seed. It needs a lot of sun to ripen. Pick the seeds in late summer and dry them before storing. It has been used as a digestive since Egyptian times. The Romans made spiced cakes with it to be eaten at the end of the meal. The Greeks filled a cockerel with the seeds and seethed it for broth to give to those with weak or damaged digestions. It is the basis of a number of digestive liqueurs and the crushed seeds can be made into a tea. It is very good for dry coughs, catarrh and hiccoughs. My great Uncle Bertie once used aniseed to cure a Chinese mandarin of a bout of bad hiccups that would respond to nothing else, and was well rewarded for his efforts. Aniseed mixed into food for fowl or pheasants stops them from straying.

basil

Basil grows indoors from seed or on a warm terrace. Every good Hindu goes to his rest with a basil leaf on his breast as his passport to paradise. The plant is sacred in that religion to Krishna and Vishnu and the ancient Greeks regarded it as the plant of kings, hence its name, from the Greek *basileus*, meaning 'king'. In Greece it is known as the herb of welcome but be careful for ladies of easy virtue as they use it outside their homes instead of a red light. Keep a pot of basil in your kitchen and the flies will avoid the room. It is delicious in salads, cooked with pasta or in soups. We used to rub basil oil round the horses' heads in summer to keep off the flies and bruised basil leaves draw out the sting of wasps or biting insects.

melissa

This is also known as 'heart's delight' or lemon balm. It is easy to grow from slips or heel cuttings. Melissa soothes the nerves, improves memory, prolongs youthfulness and prevents hardening of the arteries. John Hussey of Sydenham, who lived to 116, and Llewellyn, Prince of Glamorgan, who lived to 108, both breakfasted every morning on a tea of lemon balm sweetened with honey. Melissa is extremely good as a tisane or cooked with fish. I always stuff a white fish with lots of it or put a bunch of it under the fish on a barbecue.

french tarragon

Tarragon is also know as 'little dragon' or, in France, as *herbe au dragon*. First time round buy plants and protect against the

Sweet basil

frost. To propagate, grow from cuttings, strike slips and lift your roots in the autumn to overwinter. Do not confuse with Siberian tarragon, which is much coarser. Grow in poor, well-drained soil in a warm place. It is delicious with chicken or fish, is a must for sauces and is the only correct flavouring for tartare sauce. Make tarragon vinegar by immersing sprigs in white wine vinegar. The oil is used for insect bites.

flower fennel

In France this plant is called quatre épices. It should not to be confused with the vegetable Florence fennel. Sow seeds in the spring and ignore them until late summer when you harvest the seeds. You can also freeze the leaves. Fennel is a good digestive, it encourages the production of milk in feeding mothers and if the seeds are laid among linen, they will keep away insects. The leaves are good with fish, chicken and pork. The seeds will flavour curries and stews and are good for baking.

borage

This annual grows particularly well on chalky soil. The crusaders believed it gave you courage and drank a borage cup before they rode out to fight. It is now proved that borage stimulates the adrenal gland. It is good cooked in the same way as early spinach, is delicious in salads and of course is vital to Pimms, to which it adds a cooling cucumber taste. It is also a good sweetener in baking and when cooked with tart fruit, it reduces the need for sugar.

hyssop

Hyssop is grown from seed. It is a good flea herb and used to be used strewn among the floor rushes to keep the fleas away. It can also be used as a tisane against colds and hyssop tea is good for asthma. Country people believe that it is an effective cure for rheumatism.

coriander

Sow the seed directly into the ground in spring. The main use of coriander seed is in cooking and baking, but it is also an anti-colic herb and is good against stomach cramps.

caraway

Seeds can be sown either in early spring or in autumn and left to overwinter. It is a wonderful anti-flatulent and shifter of mucus when drunk as a tisane, and is also good for baking or for cooking with fatty meats. It is the main ingredient of the liqueur Kummel and is also great cooked with cabbage. What is more, it is a vital ingredient in love potions! If a piece of caraway dough is baked and left in a pigeon loft it will stop the birds from straying.

summer and winter savorys

These were Elizabeth I's favourite herbs. When cooked with beans they counter any flatulence, and they are good with pork, stews and in soups, but use sparingly as they have a strong flavour. Both are sown from seed and summer savoury is an excellent pot herb that can be used to add an unusual flavour to salads. The plant also makes an efficacious eye-wash.

lavender

This was known in the past as spikenard. It may be grown from slips, roots or seeds and is an undemanding plant provided it doesn't get too wet. The plants last about 5–6 years after which they begin to deteriorate. Lavender looks pretty in the garden and the dried flowers will keep your linen fresh and free of moths and silverfish. It main use is for the distillation of lavender oil which is good for headaches and lifts depression. A small bag of the dried flowers under your pillow relaxes and

Black peppermint

aids sleep. The flowers make a good ice cream and can be used in baking but be careful because the volatile oils anaesthetize the taste buds; you will be unable to taste and may bake a biscuit that is overpoweringly strong and quite hallucinogenic!

lovage

I always feel affectionate towards this plant. A boyfriend of mine called Graeme once dragged his botanist aunt into the fields around Wick to find me a lovage plant as in the late 1960s it was virtually impossible to buy either plants or seed. It was the stock cube of the Middle Ages. Indeed the German company Maggi used to use it for their sauce. It gives body to soups and stews and is good in salad though use it sparingly. The seeds can also be kept for cooking. The food writer Annie Bell has a good recipe for lovage ice cream.

mint

I grow peppermint and Moroccan mint for tea but there are many other varieties. Rats hate mint and rat catchers used to soak rags in peppermint oil and leave them near the rat holes to save blocking them. They could then drive the rats through the remaining holes with ferrets. Mint in all its varieties is great for teas, for cooking with gooseberries and for making sauce for lamb. Mint sauce is, I believe, the last one of the dishes brought back by the Crusaders to England from the East.

parsley

There are three types of parsley grown for food, flat (or celery-leaved parsley), curly, or Hamburg parsley, which is grown solely for its root. They say of parsley that it goes down seven times to see the devil, which is a reference to its slow germination. I find you can overcome this by soaking the seeds in hot water before planting. They also say that where parsley grows well, the woman wears the trousers in the household. Parsley sauce with ham is a must but the plant adds colour and flavour to many dishes. However please avoid it solely as a garnish. I once stayed in a hotel where the chef was so mad on the stuff that I even found a sprig on my breakfast porridge! It freezes well and if frozen chopped, can be sprinkled on potatoes straight from the freezer. Hamburg parsley roots are cooked like parsnips and have an unusual but pleasant flavour.

Rosemary

pennyroyal

This is the smallest of the mints and is great in a tisane for cleansing the blood and sorting out menstrual problems. Do not drink it if you're pregnant as it is an abortant and was banned by the Victorians for this reason. The women of Mile End in east London, where it grew profusely, would gather it and bring it to the London markets to sell. When tea was heavily taxed it was much drunk as an alternative.

rosemary

My rosemary bush lasts all year round in sunny Scotland but rosemary bushes can die on you quite suddenly, in which case never replant in the same spot. Grow from slips or heel cuttings. The leaves are great for cooking with meat or fish. Rosemary is also a very good shampoo ingredient for those with dark hair.

sage

'He that would live for Aye, let him eat sage in May.' As the saying implies, sage is a great preserver of health. My father was a great fan of it and adopted the country habit of eating it between slices

Variegated rue

of buttered bread. He also gave everyone sage tea when they had a cold on their chest and I still drink it to shift the mucous. Add honey as the tea is rather bitter. There are many types of sage and they are all good with fatty meats as a digestive. Sage fritters made with the mature leaves are a good addition to any dish. Cut back your sage plants each year to encourage new growth.

thyme

Thyme was originally burnt as incense by the ancient Greeks. The name means 'to fumigate' – burning thyme on a shovel will rid a room of any horrid smells. There are many varieties, including the rare orange thyme, which is much nicer than its lemon brother. In medieval times ladies would embroider a bee hovering over a thyme plant on a kerchief to give to their knights as encouragement in battle. It is good in soups, stews and finely chopped in salads and stuffing. Traditionally a joint of beef was rubbed with thyme before roasting. Plant it as a companion herb with lavender.

rue

Rue was another brilliant flea herb that was once strewn in the rushes on floors to deter fleas. Rue water sprinkled on flea-infested rugs or rubbed into cats and dogs will do the same trick. Rue was known as the Herb of Grace because bunches of rue were used to sprinkle holy water in church and the touch of it was said to bring about repentance.

The Italians eat rue sparingly in salads and a leaf chewed is a good remedy against headaches and tiredness. Be careful when cutting it because the oils can cause burns on the skin in high summer. It is good to grow rue among your vegetables as it wards off many garden pests.

sweet cicely

This is a type of chervil that is native to Britain. The leaf is good in salads or in sauces for fish, while the liquorice-tasting stalk makes a delicious addition to an apple or gooseberry pie.

Sage

grain crops

If you have the space you can grow a few grain crops, and if you don't, you can always sprout them. I once worked on a charter yacht in the Caribbean and learned that if you wanted fresh salad stuff, your best bet was to sprout grains in the fo'c's'le. Most grain crops, such as wheat, barley and alfalfa are capable of sprouting and all make excellent and healthy food.

barley

I am a 'Horlicks baby', so owe my good health to early consumption of barley, Horlicks being malt-based. When I was a child we were often given Radio Malt – a health-food product of the 1940s and 1950s – on a spoon if we were peelyweel or under the weather. It was delicious.

Barley has a variety of uses and is the easiest of the grass-grain crops to grow as it does not need as good a soil as, for example, wheat. Barley is the earliest cultivated grass and the one that was the most sacred to the Earth-Mother and to other gods. It is also arguably the most beautiful of the grain crops, with its long bearded heads waving like silk in the breeze. Endless songs and poems have been written about this.

In spring, the ancient Egyptians would put barley seeds in a clay dish in the shape of the god Isis. The dish with its seeds were planted in Nile mud and when they germinated it was a sign that the god was reborn. The ever-determined Vikings grew barley in their settlements on Iceland. Why? The answer lies in barley's popularity for making beer.

cultivation

Barley is planted either in spring or autumn. Autumn-planted, or winter barley as it is called, remains dominant until the spring and gives higher yields but poorer quality grains. It is harvested in July and is mostly rolled for animal feed. Spring barley is harvested in August. It gives lower yields of better quality grains and is malted for the food, brewing and whisky industries, where it fetches a good price.

If you want to grow barley in your field you must plough the land, cut the drills, then plant the seed and roll it. It can be grown as a continuous crop but is more usually found as a three-year rotated crop in a cycle beginning with wheat, then barley, then sugar beet or peas. If you have the space it is a rewarding crop to grow. If you grow a lot, send it away to be milled otherwise you can let it dry and make yourself a quern or stone handmill.

Barley straw is tougher and less brittle than wheat straw and at a pinch can be chopped for animal fodder.

barley as food

Barley as food is very diverse. Bere flour made from barley was the main grain of the Highlands of Scotland and of much of Scandinavia and Northern Russia. Barley bannocks were cooked either on a griddle or in the embers of the fire. The flour does not leaven much.

Two types of food barley exist. There is pot barley, also know as Scots barley or, in Italy, as faro. It is used in soups and stews.

Barley

Polished barley, which has had most of the husk removed, has less flavour but is used in baby food and porridge.

Barley porridge is more digestible than oats and was traditionally made with milk and fed to invalids as gruel. The Sephardic Jews celebrated the cutting of a baby's first tooth with a dish called belita which is a sweetened barley porridge with nuts and fruit. Barley can also be cooked with ale to make a thick savoury porridge, which is very good as a staple instead of rice or potatoes. There was a trend a few years ago among chefs for barley risotto; I am glad to say it has sunk without trace.

Malt vinegar for pickling and sprinkling on fish and chips is also made from milled barley.

malted barley

Malted barley is largely made commercially nowadays. The process involves soaking the grains until they chit, in other words until the roots burst through the skin (remember potatoes). Heat is then applied in a kiln to kill the embryo and the grain is either milled for brewing or distilling, or is left whole or cracked for baking.

I know nobody now who malts their own barley but that doesn't mean you can't do it. Gervaise Markham, the great horticulturalist of the seventeenth century, tells us to steep the barley in fresh water for three days. On the fourth day it is drained and allowed to drip for a day. The barley is then piled into a heap on a dry barn floor for three more days to sprout. The sprouted grain is then spread thinly over the floor and turned, either with a shovel or by hand, two or three times a day for fourteen days. It is then dried in a kiln over a gentle fire of sweet straw for any other fuel is too hot or would taint it. The result is then polished and milled.

Barley

maize and sweetcorn

Zea, or maize, in all its forms is native to the American continents and was allegedly brought back to Spain by the conquistador Pizarro, who found it in Peru. It is the staple grain of southern and central America and of the southern states of America. The pantheistic Amerindians saw it as a young and fertile warrior.

cultivation

In the UK maize will grow south of the Mersey-Humber line on sites lower than 125 metres. Although there are hybrids that will grow further north, this is uncommon. It prefers rich, loamy soil but will do quite well in drier soils. It will not grow in compacted soils and dislikes heavy wet clays.

Grow maize in a corner of your vegetable garden where it makes a splendid windbreak for delicate plants. The same applies to sweetcorn cultivation as to maize, especially when it comes to pollination problems (see right), but the ears ripen earlier and should be picked when almost ripe.

Plant in spring 100–125cm apart and in deep drills. Obviously this can be done by machine if you have a large field. Keep the rows free of weeds until the plants are well established.

In the northern hemisphere the corn is harvested in late October to early November and because of the climate, it must then be dried in a warm dry barn by being spread out and turned. The stalks are cut and the ears stripped by hand.

The grains can either be ground for cornflour or eaten as hominy grits or

Maize

polenta. The liquid in the stalks is made into corn syrup or liquid glucose but unless you have a press, this is not for domestic production. Alternatively, the head can be eaten as a vegetable, as corn on the cob, or the stripped grains are eaten as niblets. Don't cook corn on the cob with salt as this will toughen it.

pollination problems

Maize must be grown in a block as the ears grow low down and are covered and surrounded by fleshy leaves, with male and female plants quite far apart. This means that the wind may not catch the pollen and there may be pollination problems. It is due to this as much as dehydration that maize doesn't thrive in seaside or windy sites. There are no self-pollinating Zeas and due to the proliferation of GM maize in the USA there is a good market there for organic maize.

'Grow maize in a corner of your vegetable garden where it makes a splendid windbreak'

oats

This is the grain which the misogynistic Dr Johnson said is eaten by men in Scotland and horses in England. Poor old Dr J. It has now been proved that the presence of beta glucan in oats dramatically lowers cholesterol, especially LLD or 'bad' cholesterol, reduces blood pressure and is a cancer-deterrent, so eat your porridge every day. And as well as its health-giving qualities, it also guards against adhesions on operation scars and is good in the treatment of non-insulin dependent diabetes.

Wild oats have grown in Asia and the Middle East for thousands of years and were first cultivated for food in the first century AD. Only 5 per cent of the oat crop worldwide is now used for human consumption; the rest is fed to animals. Oat straw is a very good straw to use for animal bedding.

cultivation

If you have the right climate and the land, and want to grow oats, it is a rewarding crop. Nowadays people in towns can buy wild oats for the patio; they look pretty, attract wild birds and are an endless source of jokes!

Oats grow well in marginal soil and cool damp climates but will tolerate cool and dry. They dislike copper deficiency in the soil but will endure everything else, but don't plant them where the pH in the soil (see page 25) is above level 7.

The plant, which grows to about 1 metre tall, is sown as either winter oats in the autumn or spring oats. In either case it should be sown as early as possible in the growing season.

Oats

wheat

Basically don't do it! It's more trouble than it's worth to grow wheat in a small plot and this book is not about wheat farming. Wheat is the world's biggest staple crop. Huge areas are given up to its cultivation and it's not even as good for you as the crops described above.

There are two types: the hard flinty durum wheat, which grows in hot climates and is used for pasta and other noodles, and the soft variety grown for bread-making. There is quite enough of it about and you can buy organic stoneground flour quite easily.

If you do want to grow it, you make your drills and sow it in either spring or autumn just like barley, and you pray for a sunny summer to ripen it. You then harvest it and send the grain away to be ground for flour. But it's far less bother to just buy the flour.

protect your apples with wheat

You might consider growing your wheat among newly planted apple trees. Scientific research shows that where you plant new trees to replace old apple trees in an established orchard the trees won't flourish without the use of chemical anti-microbe treatments. However, if you plant wheat between the trees, an enzyme in the wheat kills the microbes and the trees flourish.

the wheatgrass craze

One grain crop that you might want to grow, especially if you live in a town, is wheatgrass. Wheatgrass juice is the latest craze. It is said to be a cure-all remedy, largely because a woman called Mary Wigmore had a gangrenous leg which she refused to have amputated. It was miraculously cured, a fact that she attributed to eating wheatgrass.

History is full of incidents of the body healing itself. It is also full of dubious miracles and I speak as one who does believe in miracles, however I would like to see some medical proof of the benefits of juiced grass for humans.

What I do believe in is the benefit of wheatgrass for cats and dogs who we see eating grass when they aren't feeling well. In New York people are now growing wheat in ceramic dishes in 2–3cm of soil and letting their animals eat it when it is 10 days old, with great benefits to their health. Why then don't I believe it benefits humans? The human appendix can no longer deal with the cellulose in grasses, so we can't process it. That's why.

What is good for humans however is wheatgerm and also sprouted wheat, which contains vitamin C not present in the whole grain.

Wheat

Wheat

diseases of cereal crops

All these cereal crops are subject to a variety of diseases ranging from rust and dwarfing to ergot. Ergot is a parasitic plant that grows on the ear of grasses. It looks rather like mice droppings and is poisonous. Or rather, it is a hallucinogenic drug and an abortant that causes the eater to go mad and suffer from a syndrome called St Anthony's Fire – an excruciating inflammation of all the body's nerve endings. The mystery of the Marie Celeste is believed to have been the result of ergot poisoning, which caused the entire crew to leap into the sea. If you get ergot, your crop will have to be burnt. It is most prevalent in wheat, which is another good reason not to grow that crop!

wild food

Despite centuries of agricultural reclamations there are still hundreds of thousands of square kilometres across Europe, North America, Australia and New Zealand that are covered in natural woodland, hedgerows, moors, wetlands, heaths, scrub, salt marshes and shore line dissected by rivers, streams, lakes and ponds. These are the natural habitats of a wide range of wildlife, and are where edible wild plants, berries, nuts and fungi grow. Much of this land is easily accessible and, depending on the game and conservation restrictions in the different countries, many of these delicacies are available to pick, shoot, trap or fish. Here are a few tasters, which I hope will wet the appetite of those who are looking for a greener life.

food from wild plants

It is perfectly feasible to obtain all that one needs in the way of vitamins, trace elements and minerals from wild plants without recourse to cultivated vegetables and fruit. As the saying goes, 'Anything green that grew out of the mould was an excellent herb to our fathers of old.' In fact, for many country people, wild plants were the mainstay of their existence through all but the coldest months of the year.

late winter

By February, people longed for signs of spring growth. Common sorrel (*Runex aretosa*) is always one of the first wild plants to make an appearance and country people eagerly looked for it on heaths and acid soil during February. Its young, arrow-shaped leaves were mashed with vinegar and honey to make a sauce for cold meat and in many areas it was boiled together with nettle (*Urtica dioica*), dandelion (*Taraxacum officinale*), chickweed (*Stellaria media*) and ramsons (*Allium ursinum*), then mixed with eggs and potatoes.

Then there are the leaves of fat hen (*Chenopodium album*) and good King Henry (*C. bonus-henricus*), common orache (*Atriplex patula*), pigweed (*Amaranthus retroflexus*) – an import from America – and bladder campion (*Silene vulgaris*). These are full of iron, vitamin B and calcium, and were eaten boiled like spinach (see page 82). Similarly, the fiddleheads – the coiled, crozier-shaped tips – of bracken fern, which now have something of a cult following in North America, were eaten boiled like asparagus, or fried. The rhizomes were also dug up, dried and made into flour.

spring to summer

Many other green-leafed plants were also eaten through the spring and summer, for example the cresses, such as watercress, which was once cultivated in great quantities. Women selling watercress were a common sight in nineteenth-century London. There was also wintercress (*Barbarea vulgaris*), lady's smock (*Cardamine pratensis*) and shepherd's purse (*Capsella bursa-pastoris*), these last two being types of cress also. In addition there was ground elder (*Aegopodium podograria*), lovage (*Levisticum officinale*), and the roots of pignut (*Conopodium majus*), which were dug up, boiled and peeled.

late summer

As summer moves to autumn and the leaves begin to turn, hedgerows hang heavy with ripening berries and the serious business of picking for bottling and jam-making can begin. Parties of pickers with children, their faces smeared with berry juice, used to be seen on the outskirts of towns and across the countryside, filling their baskets with rosehips, blackberries, dewberries, wild raspberries, blackcurrants and redcurrants. In the hills above my farm in southern Scotland, we look for small round black bilberries growing amongst deep heather and we pick rowans from the tree planted to ward off evil, that grows beside a ruined shepherd's cottage. All of these fruits and berries make wonderful jams or jellies (see pages 211–213). Rowan jelly is particularly good with venison or mutton.

Wild cherries are the first to ripen; these little fruits will happily adapt to any cultivated cherry recipe, provided enough extra sugar is added to compensate for their tartness. Elderflowers come next: the clusters of black berries make a strong dark wine (see page 222) as well as delicious syrups. The Germans make a

Elderflower

purée called Holdermus of elderberries, milk, flour, lots of butter and honey, which they eat piping hot with cubes of bread fried in butter. Regency bucks were very partial to Pontac, a well matured, peppery sauce made with elderberries stewed in claret, peppercorns, ginger, mace and onions. And there are any number of recipes for damsons, which ripen in October. Damsons, heated till they burst open, the stones removed, then sieved through a coarse colander and baked for several hours until the pulp thickened into a 'cheese' was a popular nineteenth-century relish, eaten with cold meats.

Sloes, the bitter dark blue fruit of the blackthorns that grow in every hedgerow, are best picked after the first hard frost. In the heyday of port drinking, tonnes of sloes were made into wine that was sold as port. Nowadays, most go to make sloe gin, but a jelly can be made by boiling them up with sugar, or they can be made

into a 'cheese', similar to damson cheese, by mixing them with apples.

Little yellow, rock-hard crab apples are ready to pick in October. Once highly prized by our ancestors, crab apples were mixed with wild honey to make a type of cider and were the essential ingredient in the pagan ceremony of wassail. Originally part of a winter fertility rite intended to hasten the arrival of spring, wassail was hot spiced ale, sweetened with honey, in which roasted crab apples floated. It later became part of the Christmas ritual of goodwill to mankind, with toasts drunk on Twelfth Night from beautifully carved wassail bowls. Verjuice (see page 151), the juice of crab apples and similar in taste to lemon juice, was much used in early medieval cuisine. Some continental chefs still prefer it to lemon juice. We pickle crab apples in red wine cider and sugar for eating with our Christmas ham – the tart flavour offsets the ham – or we mix crab apples with rowan berries to make a jelly.

coastal plants for eating

People who lived near the sea and salt marshes had a range of delicious, healthy coastal plants at their disposal. Sea kale (*Crambe maritima*), a cabbage-like plant, was once sold by the cartload in London's Covent Garden. The bitter-tasting common scurvy grass (*Cochlearia officinalis*) is rich in vitamin C and its anti-scorbutic properties were recognized by sailors centuries before scurvy was fully understood. It was also grown commercially at one time and made into a tonic for sickly children. Sea purslane (*Sesuvium portulacastrum*), sea beet (*Beta vulgaris* ssp. *maritima*) and wild spinach are also good to eat.

One of my favourites is marsh samphire (*Salicornia europea*), a delicious thick-stemmed plant that grows on the tidal reaches of saltings and mud flats. In early summer, when the plants are young and thin, they make a refreshing addition to salads or can be cooked and served as a vegetable. Later on, when the plants are plump and fully grown, they are best eaten like asparagus. In Norfolk, marsh samphire is harvested during August and September and is pickled in vinegar for eating through the winter. Marsh samphire is in fact so rich in vitamins and minerals that when I farmed on the north Kent marshes, which ran up mto the Thames Estuary, if we had a sickly ewe, we would carry her over the sea wall and leave her to feed on the marsh samphire. She would inevitably improve.

Among the rocks on the seashore, particularly in Wales, people would regularly harvest the purple-fronded laver (*Pophyra umbilicalis*), a type of seaweed. This same seaweed is grown artificially in the Far East for the restaurant trade. When I was an agricultural student, doing a year's practical on a sheep farm in Carmarthenshire, we often bought a laver purée from the fishmonger and ate it, rolled in oatmeal, with bacon and eggs, or as an accompaniment to mutton.

nuts

The other autumn harvest is nuts. In the days when coppicing was still a rural industry, there were many more nut-bearing trees and 'nutting' meant extra income for many country people, with sacks of nuts going to be sold in the cities. There are still plenty to be had for those who take the trouble to look for them.

Hazel, which was once one of the principal coppicing crops, is abundant throughout Europe in woods, hedgerows and scrubland. Clusters of three nuts in a thick green husk ripen in late September and, once picked, should be stored in a warm dry place. Hazel nuts are very rich in protein and can be added to muesli, ground up and added to milk, or just enjoyed in their natural state.

Sweet chestnuts are enormously versatile, which is no doubt why the Romans introduced them to Britain. They can be pickled, boiled, peeled and repeatedly dipped in hot syrup to make marrons glacés, my favourite Christmas treat. They can also be cooked with cabbage, made into a soup, puréed, ground into flour, or simply roasted on the fire.

Walnut trees, with their wide spreading branches, are not only a beautiful sight on the landscape but the nuts are delicious ripe or pickled when green in July. I am envious of anyone who has access to such a tree.

Beech mast, which lie in brown carpets under stands of beech trees, contain four little fruits which are worth the trouble to pick, peel and eat. They can be squeezed to produce an oil and are cooked with sugar in North America to produce a treacle. By contrast, I always think it a shame that the mighty oak only produces a fruit that is palatable to pigs or, in times of desperation, like the last world war, that can be used to make a particularly offensive form of coffee.

poisonous plants

One rule of the countryside is never eat anything, particularly a berry, unless you are absolutely certain what it is. It is especially important, if you have children, to find out exactly what is edible and what is dangerous. When I was a child, my sister and I were taught to recognise poisonous plants when we were taken on the seasonal wild-food harvesting expeditions that were so much a part of the life of every rural child. The following are a few of the more common poisonous plants that can be found in most temperate climates.

Black and white bryony (*Tammus comunis* and *Bryonia alba*)
These thin, twining, climbing plants found in hedgerows have either black or translucent berries which rapidly turn red. Children find them irresistible. The berries give off a sickly smell when squeezed and are poisonous. The plants grow from large tubers which have a variety of homeopathic uses. The root of white bryony is called 'mandrake' and was used to treat leprosy. It is rare in northern Europe but is frequently found elsewhere in Europe and has been introduced to parts of the United States.

Buttercup (*Ranunculus acris*)
This innocuous-looking glittering yellow plant that grows in old permanent pasture is to be avoided. Belonging to the same family as baneberry (*Actaea spicata*), which is seriously poisonous, the leaves of the buttercup easily raise blisters on little hands and would make a child ill if eaten. Once used as an alternative to Spanish Fly for its aphrodisiac effects, it is common across Britain, Europe, Asia and North America.

Deadly nightshade (*Atropa bella-donna*)
This is the belladona of old, whose bell-shaped purple flowers add a sinister colour to hedgerows during June and July. Unlike most poisonous berries, which have a bitter taste, these are like small black cherries and are intensely sweet. However, every part of the plant is extremely poisonous and contains the toxin atropine, which affects the nervous system. One of the symptoms of nightshade poisoning, apart from lethargy, is loss of voice. Monks used to use belladona as a form of anaesthetic. It is common across Britain, Europe, Asia and the Americas.

Henbane (*Hyoscyamus albus*)
Another of the narcotics used by the ancients, this grey-green, hairy plant, grows to about 60cm on waste land. It has dirty-yellow, bell-shaped flowers covered in purple veins. Every part of the plant is poisonous. It is found in Britain, Europe, Asia, and North and South America.

Hemlock (*Conium maculatum*)
Even the name 'hemlock' sounds poisonous. This graceful plant, which appears to be a finer version of cow parsley (*Anthriscus sylvestris*), is another that affects the central nervous system. Curiously it was widely used in the nineteenth century as an antidote to poisoning. It is widespread across Britain, Europe, Asia, and North and South America.

Meadow Saffron (*Colchicum autumnale*)
This purple-flowering plant, sometimes known as autumn crocus, is found in meadows, particularly on limestone. It was used to treat gout. It is rare in northern Britain but common in other parts of Britain and Europe, and can also be found in North America.

fat hen and good king henry

Chenopodium album and *C. bonus-henricus*

These stemmy, drab plants are considered invasive weeds but from Neolithic times until the middle of the last century, they were greatly prized for their anti-scorbutic properties. Both have a higher proportion of vitamins A, B and C, calcium, potassium, phosphorous and protein than most cultivated vegetables. Picked in early summer, the leaves are an exciting alternative to spinach and make a delicious broth. Added to beans, their carminative properties help suppress flatulence.

As a rather freckly small boy, I have particular reason to remember fat hen. There was a belief among country people that leaves vigorously rubbed into the face would remove these unsightly blemishes, and I can still feel their mealy texture. Both plants grow wherever man has built or cultivated and they particularly like a fresh dunghill, hence their other names 'Midden Myles' or 'Dirty Dick'. Fat hen seeds can be made into flour and both seeds and leaves are often included in game crop mixtures.

The leaves of fat hen or Good King Henry can be adapted to any spinach recipe, but I prefer them in their simplest form.

SERVES 4

900g leaves fat hen or Good King Henry
110g butter
salt and pepper

Wash the leaves in several changes of water. Dry well. Fill a large saucepan with the leaves. Fix the lid firmly and set over a low heat. The leaves will provide their own moisture and, as soon as you hear movement in the saucepan, remove the lid and turn up the heat. Stir to avoid leaves sticking to the bottom. After 10 minutes, drain and keep warm.

Just before serving add butter and seasoning and warm through, stirring to ensure the butter is well distributed.

stinging nettle

(Urtica dioica)

Nettles, which grow in such abundance and once had a wide range of different uses, are now a tragically under-utilized plant. Fibres from mature nettles were used by early man for thread and, later, to make a variety of different grades of cloth. As Germany ran short of materials during both world wars, enormous areas of nettles were cultivated as a cotton substitute. During the same period, Britain harvested tonnes of wild nettles to extract a khaki dye for camouflaging. Nettles also have a very ancient culinary history and if the leaves are picked young, they can be eaten boiled with butter, made into soup, puréed or as a traditional Scots dish – nettle pudding.

Nettles also have a number of medicinal uses, particularly in relieving rheumatism. Joe Botting, our elderly gardener was, like so many people in agricultural employment in those days, a victim of 'the screws'. He would brew many litres of nettle beer in the early summer to help him through the winter, and on cold days he would rub his swollen hands with handfuls of nettles.

nettle beer

MAKES 4.5 LITRES

1 kilo young nettle tops
zest and juice of 2 lemons
25g cream of tartar
500g demerara sugar or honey
4.5 litres water
15g brewers yeast

Wear rubber gloves to pick the nettle tops. Wash and drain them. Place the lemon zest and juice, cream of tartar and sugar or honey in a large container, preferably an earthenware fermenting vessel. Put the nettles and water in a large saucepan and bring to the boil. Boil for 15 minutes. (This can be done in two batches.) Strain the liquid into the lemon juice mixture. Stir well. Allow to cool to around 21°C/70°F. Remove a little of the liquid and make a paste with the yeast. Stir into the large container. Cover with a layer of thick cloth, tied down so that it doesn't sag into the liquid.

Leave in a warm place for three days to help the yeast to activate. Strain into bottles and cork loosely. Store in a cool, dark place. It is drinkable in one week, but as Joe used to say, 'the longer you keep it, the better it be'.

rosehip

(Rosa canina)

The scarlet fruit of the dog rose that adds such vibrant colour to the hedgerows in autumn are the vitamin C-rich ingredient for jams, jellies, marmalades and syrup. As a child, gathering rosehips down country lanes and along hedgerows was a major part of every autumn's berry harvesting. The baskets of hips were tipped out on the kitchen table and divided into piles, for the laborious process of halving to remove the seeds and pith before boiling them down for syrup. Rosehip syrup has been made for centuries by country people as a cough mixture and children's tonic, but it was during the war that a commercial initiative was started by the Government, which remains with us today. In America, they boil rosehips and eat them as a vegetable with butter.

rosehip syrup

MAKES 2.5 LITRES

2.5 litres water
1 kilo rosehips
500g sugar or honey

Boil 2 litres water. Mince the rosehips in a coarse mincer or food processor, and put immediately into the boiling water. Pour into a crash (coarse cotton or linen) jelly bag and allow to drip until the bulk of the liquid has come through. Return the residue to the saucepan, add 1 litre boiling water, stir and stand for 10 minutes.

Pour back into the jelly bag and allow to drip. To make sure all the sharp hairs are removed, put back the first half-cupful of liquid and allow to drip through again. Put the mixed juice into a clean saucepan and boil down until the juice measures about 1 litre, then add 600g sugar or honey and boil for a further 5 minutes. Pour into hot, sterile bottles and seal immediately.

If you are using corks, boil them for an hour previously and after insertion, coat with melted paraffin wax. Use small bottles as the syrup will not keep for more than a week or two once opened.

ramsons or wild garlic
(Allium ursinum)

After the snowdrops have died back, a thick carpet of wild garlic appears beneath the alder and willow trees growing along the banks of the stream that runs through the farm. From late spring to early summer, beautiful white flowers appear on stems protruding from the clusters of broad green leaves. These give a very powerful acrid scent that can be smelt from a considerable distance. The bulbs are too tiny to be of any use but the leaves, which one can pick as soon as they appear in early spring, have a delicate garlicky flavour, which we sometimes eat with steak, fried in the pan juices, or added to a salad.

wild garlic to serve with steak

SERVES 4

100g butter
steak juices from the pan
24 wild garlic leaves
150ml double cream

Warm the butter in a pan with the steak juices, stirring well. Tear up the leaves to release the flavour. As the butter begins to bubble, add the leaves. Stir well and when they have gone soft, remove from the pan. Allow to cool slightly, stir in the double cream and serve.

mushrooms

Nothing evokes the period of mists and mellow fruitfulness and the musty smell of fallen leaves more than fungi. There are several thousand different species of fungi worldwide, of which only about 50 are deadly. Around 150 or so are good to eat and it is symptomatic of the lack of knowledge about the countryside that most of these are wasted.

Much of this is to do with fear. Fungi, by and large, look sinister: some resemble decaying human body parts – ears, sexual organs and bits that one knows exist, but would rather not think about. Others have the reputation for being spectacularly toxic, like death cap (*Amanita phalloides*) and destroying angel (*Amanita virosa*), or for having hallucinogenic properties – fly agaric (*Amanita muscaria*) and liberty cap (*Psilocybe semilanceata*) or magic mushrooms are examples. Furthermore, fungi require other plants – usually dead ones – to supply them with carbohydrates, so they tend to grow in dank places among the rotting vegetation of mature woodland or in old pasture. They do, however, more than reward the time spent learning to identify them and the effort in searching for them.

My advice is to learn to identify positively twenty or so of the most common edible species and stick to them. Always remember to take a knife when you go foraging for fungi and cut them off at the bottom of the stem. As always in nature, don't take everything. Next autumn's crop is in the spores of those you leave behind.

some common edible mushrooms

● Field mushrooms (*Agaricus campestris* syn. *Psalliota campestris*) and the larger horse mushrooms (*Agaricus arvensis*) – these are the most recognizable mushrooms and the earliest to appear, often on pasture that has been grazed by horses.

● Ceps (*Boletus edulis*) – these bulbous, brown, thick-stemmed mushrooms grow in conifer woods, especially spruce. They used to be harvested and sold in fruit and vegetable markets in Britain and still are in many other parts of the world. Ceps are one of the most popular fungi in Europe, with large quantities dried for winter additions to soup and stews.

● Yellow chanterelles (*Cantharellus lutescens*) – exquisite and found in leafy woodland, particularly among beech trees.

● Horns of plenty (*Craterellus cornucopiodes*) – these are graveyard-grey and, like the chanterelles, are found in leafy woodland.

● Giant puffballs (*Lycoperdon giganteum* syn. *Calvatia gigantea*) – these pop up where you least expect them, on the edge of woodland or in the corner of a field. They must be picked while they are still vibrant white.

● Hedgehog fungi (*Hydnum repandum* syn. *Dentinum repandum*) – these are delicious and creamy coloured. They come from coniferous and deciduous woodland, and are commonly sold at farmers' markets in Europe.

● Shaggy ink caps (*Coprinus comatus*) – these are found all over the place, by the roadside, among garden rubbish, or on lawns after a spell of rain. They are best while the gills are still white, and they make a delicious base for oeufs en cocotte.

● Chicken of the woods (*Laetiporus sulphureus* syn. *Polyporus sulphureus*) – these are a great delicacy in North America, Germany and Poland. They are thick, fleshy and yellow and grow at the base of deciduous trees, particularly oak, sweet chestnut and cherry.

● Wood blewits (*Lepista nuda* syn. *Tricholoma nudum*) – these are lilac-coloured and are found in deciduous woodland, at the bottom of hedgerows and in rings in old pasture land. They are strongly scented and are excellent fried in butter.

● Field blewits (*Lepista saeva* syn. *L. personata*) – these are lighter coloured than wood blewits and are found in the same habitat.

● Parasol mushrooms (*Lepiota procera* syn. *Macrolepiota procera*) – these are sweet tasting and buff-coloured with a flaky skin.

● Oyster mushrooms (*Pleurotus ostreatus*) – these are fragile, blue-grey mushrooms that grow in clumps on the stumps of beech trees.

'...don't take everything. Next autumn's crop is in the spores of those you leave behind.'

wild mushroom pancakes

(MAKES APPROXIMATELY 10)

This is a good dish for mushroom hunters. If you find lots of mushrooms you can have lavish pancakes, and if you don't find any then you can just have pancakes.

For the batter
175g self-raising flour
2 medium eggs
200ml milk
salt and pepper to taste

50g unsalted butter
350g wild mushrooms
a little oil for frying

Mix all the batter ingredients together and leave to stand for 1 hour. Meanwhile, melt the butter in a frying pan and fry the mushrooms until they have softened and all the liquid has evaporated. Keep back a little batter as the first pancake is always for the dog. Let the mushrooms cool slightly and mix in with the rest of the batter. Heat a small frying pan, smear with a little oil and cook the first, plain pancake. Discard. Add more oil to the pan if necessary, then pour in enough mushroom batter to coat the bottom of the pan. Cook for a minute or so, turn, then cook the other side. Serve immediately or stack the pancakes between greaseproof paper and put in a very low oven to keep warm while you make the rest.

mushroom pies

(MAKES 6)

450g shortcrust pastry
450g wild mushrooms
1 shallot, peeled and very finely chopped
50g Cheddar cheese, grated
pinch dry mustard
2 tbsp olive oil
1 egg, beaten, to glaze
salt and pepper

Line 6 deep patty tins using ²/₃ of the pastry. Chill. Preheat the oven to Gas Mark 6/200°C/400°F. Heat a pan of boiling water and dip your mushrooms into the water for 2–3 seconds. Drain and pat dry on kitchen paper. Put the mushrooms in a bowl and mix with all the remaining ingredients, except the egg.

Fill the patty tins with the mixture, cover with rounds made from the remaining pastry and seal. Glaze with the egg. Make a small incision in the middle of each patty. Bake until the pastry is golden, about 15 minutes.

Eat warm.

trapping, shooting and fishing

Current agricultural policies in Europe and America are geared towards landscape enhancement and away from food production, so there have been substantial grants for tree planting and much land has been allowed to revert to nature. This has created a habitat that encourages all bio-diversity, but game in particular. Game has always been a harvestable natural food source. It is intrinsically organic, low in fat, high in protein and has never been more accessible to both urban and country dwellers than it is today.

Most game that comes to the larder has been shot. If you are a novice who wishes to shoot, no matter what your age, you should join your local association for shooting and conservation. In Britain this is the British Association for Shooting and Conservation (BASC). They offer advice on all aspects of wildlife management. If you are planning on going wildfowling or shooting winged game or pigeons, or deer, such an association will be able to assist with everything from applying for a shotgun certificate and purchasing a shotgun, through to offering tuition on safety and accuracy. Similar organizations exist in other countries where the game laws are different.

Remember that in Britain all game and vermin belong to the landlord on whose land they live, so access to them has to be by permission. Most farmers are only too pleased to allow responsible people access in order to shoot pigeons or assist in controlling the rabbit population, and both wild pigeons and rabbits provide delicious and underrated meat. In Britain

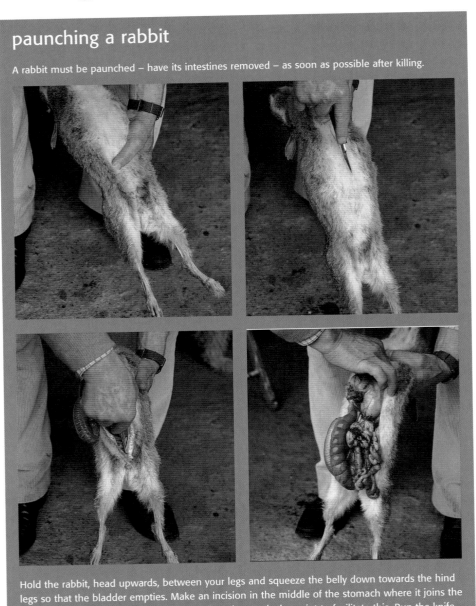

paunching a rabbit

A rabbit must be paunched – have its intestines removed – as soon as possible after killing.

Hold the rabbit, head upwards, between your legs and squeeze the belly down towards the hind legs so that the bladder empties. Make an incision in the middle of the stomach where it joins the brisket or sternum. A skinning knife is scalloped towards the point to facilitate this. Run the knife straight down and over the pelvis, trying not to puncture the intestines. Insert a couple of fingers and remove the intestines.

the BASC can assist with obtaining permission from landlords too.

In America anyone can shoot what they want on national parkland subject to acquiring the necessary licenses relative to the different game species. In most of Europe, game is accessible to everyone, but you need a licence for the different firearm categories.

rabbits

As well as shooting them, rabbits may also be snared, provided the snaring regulations are complied with. For example in Britain snares may not be left unattended for more than twelve hours. You should check your local regulations.

The first task is to find your rabbits. They like to establish their burrows in rough ground, and they venture out at dusk and dawn to find better grazing. They invariably follow the same route, leaving a distinct track through the grass and under fence wires. You can trap them using snares made of strands of copper wire formed into a noose. These are set beside one of these tracks. One end of the wire is tied to a small stake pushed firmly into the ground while the other is looped over the track and supported by a twig. The loop, or noose, must be at rabbit head height and it must be the diameter of its neck.

The other way to catch rabbits is by bolting them out of their burrows into nets with a ferret. Ferreting is a wonderful way for children to learn about the countryside and to become a provider for the household before they are old enough to have a shotgun licence. Unless you intend to breed from your ferrets, I would recommend having a hob (male) and a jill (female), both of whom have been neutered. Ferrets should be kept in as big an area as you can spare but they must not be able to get out of it. They love to run about and play. I used to

skinning a rabbit

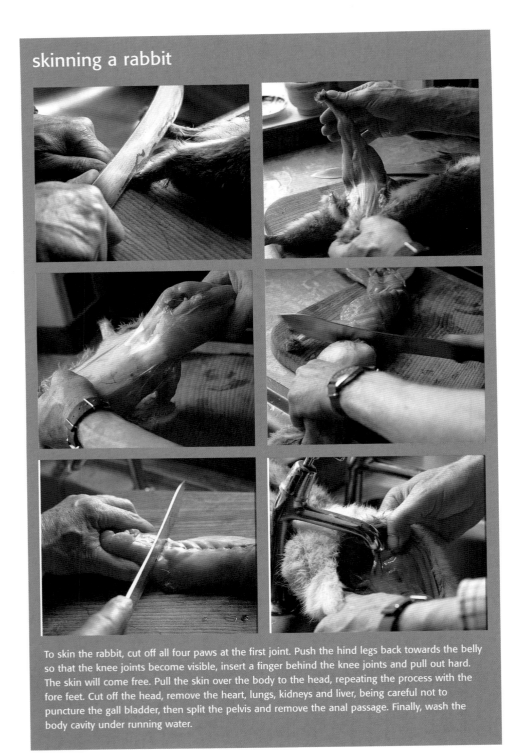

To skin the rabbit, cut off all four paws at the first joint. Push the hind legs back towards the belly so that the knee joints become visible, insert a finger behind the knee joints and pull out hard. The skin will come free. Pull the skin over the body to the head, repeating the process with the fore feet. Cut off the head, remove the heart, lungs, kidneys and liver, being careful not to puncture the gall bladder, then split the pelvis and remove the anal passage. Finally, wash the body cavity under running water.

dung through as they are very clean animals. Properly handled, ferrets can become enchanting pets.

Again, your local association for shooting and conservation will be only to happy to give advice on ferreting, but the basics are as follows. Once you have located an area – usually an earth bank – where there are a number of burrows, approach quietly and peg out the purse nets. These have a drawstring running round the edge that enables them to be stretched open and spread over the rabbit holes. The end of the string is attached to a wooden peg, firmly pressed into the ground to the side or above the holes. Once you have the net in place, slip the ferret into a burrow. His subterranean hunting will make the rabbits bolt above ground and, as they come rocketing out, they become entangled in the net. Then take hold of the rabbit by its hind legs, remove the net and hit it hard across the back of the neck with the side of the hand. This 'rabbit punch' dislocates the neck, killing the rabbit instantly.

Another very effective way of catching rabbits is with a long net. Rabbits often graze a considerable distance from their burrows and the long net is set up, rather like a tennis net, near their burrows while the rabbits are out feeding. Once the net is in position, the rabbits are driven back towards their burrows and become entangled in the net.

deer

The change in agricultural policies worldwide has benefited all bio-diversity, but deer in particular. In Britain we have the majestic red deer, once a forest animal, which live in herds on the open moors of Exmoor, parts of Cumberland and across the highlands of Scotland. We have other species too, fallow and roe deer – which were almost extinct in the late nineteenth century – sika, muntjac and even Chinese water deer, all living in increasing numbers throughout the rest of the country.

keep mine in an old stable with a sleeping hutch filled with hay and all sorts of tubes, balls and some branches for them to amuse themselves with. If you live in an urban area, a hutch measuring 1.5 x 0.5 x 0.5 metres will

suffice if the ferrets are taken out and handled often enough. The hutch should have a wooden sleeping box at one end, weld mesh sides, a hinged waterproofed wooden lid and a wooden floor with a 30cm area of weld mesh for them to

Europe has the same species as well as great herds of elk in the northern forests. North America has white deer, tail deer, mule deer, wapiti, little prong horns and moose, while New Zealand now has so many deer that the government is considering another national cull.

Deer are no respecters of agriculture or forestry and have to be controlled, not just to protect crops and young trees, but also to ensure that a reasonable balance is maintained between deer numbers and available grazing. As with any other form of stock, old and ill animals have to be removed as part of normal animal welfare procedures and the correct ratio of males to females must be preserved.

In Britain, stalking the red stag in the Highlands is considered the sport of kings and is priced as such, but there is any amount of hind, roe, fallow and sika stalking to be had at very affordable prices. Muntjac are such a pest that farmers would probably pay you to come and shoot them.

The situation is the same across Europe, North America and New Zealand. In America, the population of each species is assessed by the wildlife departments in each state and licences are issued to reflect the number that need to be killed. In Britain, the BASC are the best people to contact for information on deer stalking and there are similar organizations in America, Europe and New Zealand.

Once a deer has been shot, it should be gralloched, or disembowelled, bled and the guts buried on the spot. Gralloching is done in the same way as when dealing with a rabbit, in other words, by cutting the deer open from the brisket to the pelvis. This is done to lighten the carcass for carrying and to avoid the risk of internal damage tainting the flesh. Your local association for shooting and conservation will almost certainly run deer management courses which include instruction on skinning.

pheasants, grouse, pigeons

The same expansion of wildlife habitat has led to an increase in the number of pheasants, partridges, quail, woodcock and the different species of grouse. The pigeon and dove populations, on the other hand, increase most where there is agricultural expansion, particularly with the planting of winter-sown crops. The famous red grouse population of Scotland and northern England relies on the management of heather through rotational burning every year to provide them with the habitat and food to sustain their numbers. All these species are available for the pot depending on the regulations and laws governing wildlife in each different country.

fishing

Angling is globally the most popular participant pastime and, like all other field sports, is a vital contributor to the economy of countries worldwide as well as a key part of the socio-economic fabric of many rural areas. For example, rod-caught salmon from the river Tweed is worth £10,000 to the economy of Roxburghshire. The fish itself is only worth a few pounds a kilo, but its total value lies in the money spent by the anglers and their families who come to fish on one of Scotland's great salmon rivers.

Three and a half million people, encompassing all ages and social backgrounds, fish in Britain alone. Some three and a half billion pounds are spent by anglers in an industry that employs over six thousand people. Similarly, in excess of ten billion euros is generated by expenditure on field sports across the EU countries with fishing as a principal contributor. The thirty six million anglers in North America spend thirty-four billion dollars each year on their sport and provide employment for over a million people. But then, North America has some of the best and most varied fishing in the world.

There are three forms of rod fishing available in Britain and these are basically the same worldwide. The only difference is in places such as America and the Falkland Isles where the fish are bigger and there are more of them. The first is coarse fishing, which uses a bait, for the fifteen species and numerous sub-species of freshwater fish, from carp to pike, other than the members of the Salmonidae family. These fish are found in canals, ponds, lakes and sluggish rivers. The second is sea fishing, from boat, beach or pier, for the 24 saltwater species, which range from bass to conger eels and their sub-species. And finally there's game fishing, which is fishing with a fly for grayling, salmon, brown trout, rainbow trout, sea-trout, whitefish and char. These species of fish live in fast-flowing rivers and rely for their food on insects that settle on the surface of the water.

The opportunities for becoming involved in any of these sports and filling the freezer, is limitless. Possibly no other sport induces such passion among devotees from Iceland to New Zealand and a novice will find no shortage of helpful advice in getting started.

livestock

Of all the elements of a home producer's life, none is more satisfying than rearing one's own livestock and eating one's own produce. There is something cathartic about being governed by the reproductive cycle of the animals – spring for birth, summer for growth, autumn for harvesting and winter for mating – and about experiencing the highs and lows, exhilarations and dramas that are part of every livestock farmer's daily existence. Your choice of livestock will be limited to the size of your holding: bees, a few chickens or some pigeons can be kept in an average-sized garden while only a few hectares are needed for a more adventurous enterprise. I hope my simple advice on keeping a cow, sheep, goats, pigs, rabbits, ducks, geese, chickens, and bees, how and when to kill them and the best way to get rid of unwanted pests, will entice the new home producer to embark on this rewarding and enjoyable experience.

animal health

Anyone wishing to keep animals, whether it is a chicken, horse, or pig, must appreciate that they have complete responsibility for their welfare. Livestock are a total commitment. They wake with the dawn and, in the wild, start to feed soon after. Domestic animals are the same, but if you keep animals it is you who must be prepared to be up and about early to see that they are well and to feed them when necessary. You will have to know what, when and how much to give them and will need enough basic veterinary knowledge to carry out an annual health plan. Making a soil analysis to determine what minerals may be deficient is an important first step.

I would not advise anyone to try and keep stock without first going on one of the many courses that are available to the home producer at agricultural colleges. It is not fair to the animals, it will be counter-productive to you, the producer and, if things go wrong, which they almost certainly will, lack of knowledge could land you in court. What is more, lack of knowledge is no excuse for the ill treatment of animals.

some signs of animal ill-health

You will need to be able to spot signs of animal ill-health and react to them immediately. Most of these are a matter of commonsense.

● Loss of appetite is the most obvious. A healthy animal is a hungry one. Why is it off its food? Are there signs of discoloured scour (diarrhoea)? Is it hunched up indicating internal pain?

● Is it lame and is this lameness an injury or due to joint pain?

● Mucous around the nose and wheezing indicate pneumonia.

● Frothing at the mouth means it has eaten poison.

● A dull, staring coat – one that is lacking in bloom – could be caused by internal worms or a lack of essential minerals. Stockmen refer to a healthy animal as being 'bloomy'.

● An animal standing alone with its head down in the corner of a field is a sick creature. .Animals are, by and large, gregarious, so this is a sign there is something wrong.

● Pale, anaemic gums indicate a worm burden or ticks.

● Long, overgrown feet or hooves will lead to lameness and foot rot.

● Scratching or rubbing against a fence or tree suggests lice or worse, the debilitating scab mite.

● A dry hot nose in a dog is a sign of ill-health.

'Livestock are a total commitment. They wake with the dawn and, in the wild, start to feed soon after.'

choosing a breed

If you want a house cow, your choice of cow will be influenced by the quantity of milk you require as a family and how adventurous you wish to be. There is little point in going for a high-lactation dairy cow like a Friesian as that would give far too much milk for the average family and the carcass quality of the calf makes for poor beef. A Jersey is a lovely choice, with her superb butter-rich milk, but again, the calves have poor carcasses.

There are several alternatives to choose from among the old dual-purpose breeds. Devons, Welsh Blacks, Shorthorns, Red Polls, Herefords and even Highlanders all are good milkers and produce a nice calf, but my personal choice would be a long-legged Dexter. Dexters, which originate from the wild Celtic cattle of Ireland, are the smallest breed in the British Isles: even the long-legged Dexters only stand around 105cm at the shoulder. I wouild recommend that you go for the long-legged variety as the short-legged ones are quite difficult to milk. Dexters are hardy, low-maintenance and docile, and will easily become a family pet. These dual-purpose cattle will provide 3.5 litres of milk a day and will rear a calf. A steer will fatten off grass at 24 months and the small-jointed, well marbled Dexter beef is some of the best I have ever tasted.

COWS

'Dexters, which originate from the wild Celtic cattle of Ireland, are the smallest breed in the British Isles: even the long-legged Dexters only stand around 105cm at the shoulder.'

For most of my life, I have been fortunate to have had access to fresh milk straight from the cow. As a small child, we kept a house cow, as most farms did in those days, and I remember being taken to watch her being milked. Matthew, our retired ploughman, sat on his three-legged milking stool with his cap twisted round so he could press his head into the flank of the venerable Ayrshire cross, chatting to her as if she were a human. The rhythmical munching as she chewed hay from the rack and the 'splooshing' sounds as warm milk shot into the stainless-steel pail are still fresh in my memory. Once, bored with my chatter, Matthew squirted a jet of milk right across the milking parlour to catch me full in the face. When Matthew and the cow both went, we got milk in cylindrical aluminium containers with a lid from a neighbour who, in the 1960s, was making a decent living from twenty cows. Later on, when I farmed in lowland Scotland, my neighbouring shepherd kept a house cow and we collected fresh milk from him.

keeping cows

To keep a small cow and calf, you will need half a hectare of land and a suitable dry building, with water and electricity, to milk her in and house her overnight during the winter. Unless there is some form of natural shelter, a three-sided open shed is also important.

Ideally, you are looking to buy a four year-old, in-calf cow with a calf at foot, early in the spring. To find one, contact the secretary of the cattle society of the breed you choose. They will have a register of cattle for sale and addresses of all their members, one of whom is bound to live within reach. They also have enormously helpful local field officers. Once you have located an animal that sounds about right, ask the owners to show you how to hand-milk her if you don't already know how to do so. This is an opportunity to discover if the cow can be handled and whether there are any bumps or lumps in the udder indicating mastitis. If you buy her, ensure that you have her pedigree certificate, and a certificate of guarantee that she is in calf, that she has been tested for tuberculosis and is brucellosis-free. She must also posses the necessary passport documents.

When you get your cow and calf home, they will be stressed after the journey, so tie the cow up in the cowshed and give her lots to drink and a good feed. Spend some time with her, letting her get used to you. The following morning, after she has been milked, let her out into the paddock. She will rear her own calf and supply ample milk but it would be worthwhile teaching the calf to drink from a self-feed bucket with a rubber teat, containing a mixture of three parts mother's milk and one part warm water. This will keep the calf occupied and contented while you are milking the mother. After a few weeks, offer the calf some decent meadow hay and then a little palatable concentrates in pellet form. By the time the calf is six months old it will be fully weaned.

milking

Your cow must be milked twice a day every twelve hours without fail. It should be a pleasant experience for both of you. Tie her up so that she has access to some good hay or cattle cake and where she can see her calf. Thoroughly wash any dung off her tail and hindquarters and gently wash her udder and teats with warm, soapy water, then dry carefully. Make sure your own hands are clean and dry.

Sit down beside her on a stool facing towards her hindquarters, with a sterilized stainless-steel bucket beneath her udder, and gently take the two forward teats in either hand. Encircle the top of the teat where it joins the udder with thumb and forefinger and squeeze. This is to stop the milk inside the teat from going back into the udder. Bring the other three fingers round the teat and in towards your palm. Milk will squirt out of the end of the teat and when it does, release your fingers, allowing milk from the udder to seep down into the teat. Alternate all four teats until the flow stops. It takes a few days to get the hang of hand-milking and it pays to practise on a rubber teat before starting on the real thing, but from then on, you will do it without thinking.

feeding your cow

Half a hectare of permanent pasture is more than enough summer grazing for a small breed. It is advisable to divide it with a couple of strands of electric fencing and alternate her between the two patches. Apart from giving her a little hay and cattle cake while she is being milked, the pasture is all she will need from spring to autumn. If she goes down in condition – losing the shine to her coat is always a sign – or the milk yield drops away, you may need to increase her diet. If poor condition persists, call the vet.

For winter feed, your cow will need four kilos of good meadow hay a day and the calf will need two, making a total of about 1000 kilos over six months. They will also both need a concentrate supplement of one kilo for the cow and half a kilo for the calf – a total of 250 kilos through the winter. Keep them in overnight after the evening milking during winter as there is no feeding value in grass at that time and keeping them off the ground for twelve hours saves it from getting poached, or broken up into wet, muddy patches. It is also less work to have the cow already dry and undercover for the morning milking.

calving

A cow has a gestation period of nine months and the trick is to calve her in late spring so that she and the calf benefit from summer grass growth, or in autumn, when it will be up to you to feed her but the calf will wean onto grass. She needs to 'dry off', or cease being milked, at least eight weeks before calving to allow her to put on condition. Remember to freeze enough milk to cover you for this period.

A four year-old cow should calve without any assistance from you but be vigilant around her calving date and be sure to

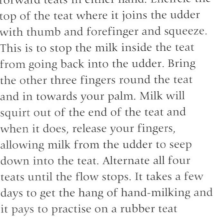

see that the calf is suckling well for the first three days, while the cow is producing the all-important yolk-like colostrum – the mixture of antibodies and organisms essential for the calf's survival. There will be an excess of this colostrum, also known as beistyn or beestings, which can be used to make the most delicious custard tarts. Once the colostrum is clear, normal milking may continue.

A cow comes on heat every 21 days and should not be inseminated until her second cycle, to give her time to recover from calving. In the absence of a local bull, insemination is done artificially. The breed's cattle society can provide details and will advise on specific bull semen.

A cow has one pregnancy a year which may be either a bull calf or a heifer. Either will require to be ear-tagged and registered as soon as possible after birth. In the case of a bull calf, castrate him by fitting a rubber elastrator ring over his testicles. A heifer can be sold at fifteen months or may be kept to breed from. It pays to halter-train her from an early age.

A bull calf has got to be for the deep freeze. He will be ready at two years but could be kept for another six months. It rather depends on whether he is a spring-born calf, in which case he would have another six months to fatten off grass. If he is autumn-born, the extra six months would be on expensive winter feed. When you decide to slaughter him, make sure you are properly prepared for the sudden influx of meat and that you have sufficient freezer space.

It is simply not feasible to risk slaughtering a valuable stirk (yearling) oneself. Ask around other owners of the same breed for a convenient local slaughterhouse where they would be prepared to hang your beast for at least four weeks and butcher it according to your specifications. And don't forget to ask for the hide back. Slaughtermen regard this as part-payment for killing and butchering a beast. Some leather is always a valuable commodity to have around the place to use for mending a strap or making a belt.

castration using an elastrator

The elastrator is one of the many innovations in animal husbandry to come from New Zealand. It resembles a four-pronged pair of pliers with a very tight rubber ring attached to the prongs. When the handles of the pliers are squeezed, the prongs open and the ring is stretched wide. The stretched ring is placed over the scrotum of the animal, after ensuring that the testes are contained in the scrotum.

The handles are then released and the prongs removed with a downward flick of the wrist, leaving the rubber ring in place. The rubber ring contracts to its original size, constricting the flow of blood to the testes. Eventually, the testes wither and drop off.

By law, the elastrator must be used within one week of birth.

'...be sure to see that the calf is suckling well for the first three days, while the cow is producing the all-important yolk-like colostrum...'

guyanan beef casserole

(SERVES 6)

In hot countries it isn't possible to hang meat (neither of course do supermarkets) so one must do something to compensate for the meat's toughness and lack of flavour. This is a really good dish I learnt in the Caribbean.

6 x 225g steaks cut from the rump or sirloin
250ml orange juice
4 tbsp oil
4 small onions, finely chopped
4 garlic cloves, finely chopped
sprig of thyme
3 tbsp beef stock
salt and pepper

Leave the steaks to marinate overnight in the orange juice in a shallow dish.

Remove the steaks from the dish, reserving the orange juice, then dry them. Heat a heavy lidded pan and seal the steaks quickly on both sides. Season then remove them. Heat the oil in the pan and sauté the onions, garlic and thyme until the onions are soft and just coloured.

Place the steaks on top of the onions, add the stock and the orange juice. Cover and cook gently for 90 minutes or until the steaks are tender.

Serve with mashed sweet potatoes.

brisket pot roast with almonds and anchoid chillies

(SERVES 6–8)

This is a Mexican dish given to me by a school friend Lydia Garcîa who lives in Chihuahua. My friend Jan McCourt at Northfield Farm in Leicestershire produces beautiful beef and often cooks brisket. Last time I dined there he added chickpeas so I have stolen the idea and added them to this dish. Anchoid chillies are large dried chillies with a smoky flavour. They are not that hot and are much used in Mexico.

1.5 kg brisket of beef
1¹/₂ tsp blanched slivered almonds
115g green ham or bacon
3 large anchoid chillies
sprig marjoram or oregano
6 crushed peppercorns
4 peeled garlic cloves
2 tbsp red wine vinegar
half pint water
85g lard or bacon fat
450g chickpeas soaked overnight

With a sharp knife make slits in the beef and insert the slivered almonds and slivers of ham or bacon. Set aside.

Toast the chillies on a hot pan then cut them open and soak them in water for half an hour. Drain the chillies and transfer them to a food processor or blender, or to a mortar.

Add all the other ingredients except the lard or bacon fat and the chickpeas. Blend or mash to a smooth paste. Melt the fat and brown the meat all over. Set the meat aside.

Cook the chilli paste in the fat for 5 minutes, stirring as you go. Put the meat in a casserole and scrape over the chilli mixture. Cook at Gas Mark 3/170°C/325°F for 2 hours. Add the chickpeas after 1 hour and baste the meat. At 2 hours turn the meat and baste again, adding more water if necessary. Return to the oven for another hour.

Serve with rice, potatoes or corn dabs (see page 189).

pigs

Nothing is better suited to the home producer than keeping pigs. At one time, virtually every farm and cottager across Europe and Britain kept a fattening pig, and pig meat dominated the rural diet. Colonists from Britain and Europe to the New World took pigs with them, which is why there are so many feral pigs in Australia, New Zealand and North America. Throughout the summer, piglets born in the spring suckled their mother and then rootled happily among grass and weeds, their diet supplemented with excess milk from the house cow, with household scraps and with garden waste. In the autumn they gorged on windfall apples or were turned into woodland to feed on acorns or beech mast.

With the approach of Christmas, there was great activity as preparations were made for butchering the pigs. Journeys were made to the nearest town to buy all the ingredients – salt, spices and sugar – to cure the meat, and glazed stoneware crocks were scrupulously cleaned in readiness. Many people kept a beehive just for honey to use as an alternative to the sugar for curing.

Pigs graze when there is a full moon and so were killed when they were at their heaviest, on a night when the moon was on the wane. Every village had its pigsticker, a highly skilled craftsman, who killed and bled the pig, the blood being saved for black puddings.

The pig would be hung for 24 hours and the following evening the community would gather to help with butchering the carcass. First, it would be covered in a layer of burning straw to remove the long stiff hairs, or it would be scalded and scraped. While it was being butchered, the cottager's wife would start a great fry-up of the liver, kidneys and sweetbreads to keep the company going through the night. Nothing was wasted. Pots bubbled as lard was rendered down; trotters, head and tail were simmered to make brawn; trimmings were chopped and mixed with sage for pies; tripes were cleaned and turned inside out then soaked in salted water for 24 hours before being stuffed with sausagemeat or blood and oatmeal to make black pudding.

The carcass was jointed for bacon and hams and the pieces were strewn on stone or slate salting shelves and covered with dry salt mixed with herbs and sugar, or placed in stoneware crocks and covered in a wet pickle brine. Great care was taken as the meat represented the bulk of the family's food for the following year, with them eating the black puddings, pies and sausages in the early part of winter, and moving on to hams and bacon for the rest of the year. Rabbit, eggs, the occasional fowl, produce from the garden and seasonal wild food was all there was to vary the diet.

housing pigs

Once you have chosen a breed, look for advertisements for them in your local paper or on the breed website. Pigs are gregarious creatures and I would recommend buying two so that they keep each other company. If at all possible, try and see your piglets before buying them and buy from registered stock. They may be more expensive, but they tend to be healthier.

The first step in pig-keeping is housing and it is a false economy to try and take short cuts. A comfy pig is a happy pig and

choosing a breed

The main decision a home producer has to consider is whether to become involved in breeding or to buy in weaners and fatten them. Since breeding will pretty well dominate your entire home production enterprise, I would advise starting by buying in weaned piglets at about eight to ten weeks old and fattening them on to slaughter weight.

The next decision is which breed to choose, from the many hundreds available. If you are going to go down the weaner fattening path, you can have a fascinating time experimenting each year with a different breed. Gloucester Old Spot is a dual-purpose breed that was originally developed over 200 years ago for grazing orchards. Berkshires are a stocky descendant of the medieval pig that foraged in the forest and scavenged in towns and villages. It was a popular colonists' pig in the nineteenth century and hundreds were exported to Australia, New Zealand and North America.

Tamworths are a hardy old breed, unadulterated by crossing with the Chinese breeds that were introduced to Britain in the nineteenth century to improve fat content. Tamworths are slow-maturing, but the hams and sides of bacon they produce are unbeatable. Essex are even older; they are descendants of the wild swine that rootled in the great forests of East Anglia and were domesticated by the Saxons. They, too, are wonderful dual-purpose pigs. Oxford Sandys are another truly dual-purpose pig with a nice nature, and one that is increasing in popularity with home producers worldwide, is the New Zealand Kune Kune – a little stubby pig that was probably brought to New Zealand from Polynesia by whalers and is a quick fattener.

a happy pig puts on weight. Temporary housing made out of straw bales and tin will suffice but if you intend, as I suspect you will, to make weaner fattening a regular part of your home producing enterprise, it would be as well to do the job properly and build a permanent sty and run. These can be elaborate – I have seen magnificent porker palaces made of thatch and dressed stone – or completely simple, as long as they are dry, wind- and waterproof, have a gently sloping concrete floor and running water. The design of the cottager's pig sty, in which thousands of pigs were fattened in Britain over hundreds of years until a law was passed in the 1950s banning the keeping of pigs within a certain distance of human habitation, still remains the best.

It is important to build the sty facing south so the pigs get the morning sun. For two weaners being taken on to fatten you need a sleeping pen with a floor area of 1.8m x 1.8m, 1.5m high at the front with a stable door, dropping to 1.2m at the back. The walls should be of heavy wood planking, stone or breeze block and the floor should be concrete. Inside there should be a sleeping ledge 15cm off the ground.

You will also need a 3m run attached to the sleeping pen. This should have a concrete floor and solid walls 1m high. It needs an 8cm fall to a drain or sump. Your final requirements are running water and a feed trough next to a gate leading to a small, stoutly or electrically fenced paddock, where the pigs can graze on dry days. I would suggest that the gate to the paddock is large enough to get a small trailer through for the day when you come to load your pigs for the slaughterhouse.

bringing your piglets home

When you get your piglets – or 'guffs' as we call them in Scotland – home, shut them up in their sty for a few days and feed them twice a day before letting them out to graze in the paddock. In hot weather, give them a mud wallow to roll in by digging a shallow pit and pouring a few buckets of water into it. Weaners should be fed a mineralized 18 per cent organic growers pellet twice a day, morning and evening, when you let them out and when they are put back in their pen at night. Don't give them more than 0.75 kg for the first few days, but then increase the ration to 1.25 kg until they are sixteen weeks old. If you have chosen a small breed like Kune Kune's, halve these amounts. Increase the ration to 1.75 kg of pig nuts for the next two months if you are fattening for porkers, but stick to 1.25 kg ration for baconers, until your piglets are the size you want them. During this feeding period, they will be delighted to eat any leftovers from the vegetable garden, orchard waste or excess milk from the house cow.

slaughter

Unless you have taken a course on butchery, I would recommend speaking to a butcher at the slaughterhouse and asking him to cut the carcasses to your exact specification. Ham and bacon joints are butchered differently to pork. Alternatively, you can arrange for the carcass to be delivered to your friendly local butcher and you can have him butcher it for you. When you have taken your pigs to slaughter, clean and disinfect the pig sty, buy another couple of guffs and start all over again.

pig diseases

Like any other domesticated animal kept for human consumption, pigs are prone to a variety of debilitating diseases. Weaners are less vulnerable than breeding sows and piglets. The main problems will be ecto- and endo-parasites – worms, lice and mange – which nowadays can be controlled by a simple injection every two months. As with other animals, check for signs of animal ill-health, which with a young pig will be obvious. Look for lack of appetite, loss of energy, lameness and scouring, or diarrhoea, and if any of these persist for more than 24 hours, call the vet.

Most plants that are poisonous to humans will affect pigs too, so if you are grazing them on rough ground, be aware that rhododendrons, yew and laburnum will make pigs very ill. So will foxgloves, which contain digitalis, a cardiac stimulus that causes a brief but alarming period of hyperactivity followed by death. Young bracken is also poisonous to all stock and although the root system is edible through the winter, dust from the dry leaves causes dreadful eye problems.

There are stringent regulations designed to control epidemics like swine fever and foot and mouth disease, and these concern the registration, movement, transport and slaughtering of pigs. Anyone owning a pig in an EU country must have it identified by an ear tag or tattoo and must register it with the relevant Animal Health Office. You also require a movement licence to transport pigs from one place to another and the transport vehicle must conform to welfare standards. All pigs must be taken to an abattoir for slaughter. The days of home slaughtering and making sausages and blood puddings with the intestines are a thing of the past. You will, however, get the kidneys, heart and liver back if you ask for them.

pork knuckle with sauerkraut

(SERVES 6)

This is a universal German dish. In Berlin they use salt pork knuckle, in Hamburg they use smoked and in Bavaria they use fresh, but it is always served with sauerkraut and all are good. If the knuckles are salted you will need to soak them in water for 2–3 hours.

30g lard
1 onion, finely chopped
750g sauerkraut
1 bay leaf
6 juniper berries, crushed
2 pork knuckles

Melt the lard in a large casserole and cook the onion until soft but not coloured.

Add the sauerkraut, bay leaf and juniper berries and about 150ml water to stop the sauerkraut sticking. Put the knuckles on top and cook at Gas Mark 3/170°C/325°F for 2¹/₂ hours, turning the knuckles once and checking to see that the sauerkraut isn't sticking.

In Berlin they serve this dish with pease pudding and fried onion rings.

pork with apples

(SERVES 6)

This German dish is good cooked in a clay pot if you have one. Otherwise use a heavy casserole.

2 garlic cloves, crushed
salt and pepper
dried mustard
1 kg boned pork loin or shoulder rolled and tied
100g butter
1 onion, coarsely chopped
2 sticks celery, chopped
2 medium-sized potatoes cut into cubes
2 large cooking apples, cubed
200ml stock
200ml dry white wine
2 tbsp cider or apple brandy

Mix the garlic, salt and pepper with a generous amount of dried mustard and rub firmly into the meat.

Melt the butter in a large frying pan and brown the pork thoroughly. Meanwhile, put the onion, celery, potatoes and apple in the bottom of the casserole with the meat on top.

Pour the stock and alcohol into the frying pan to deglaze it then pour this liquid over the meat. Cover and put into the oven (not preheated) and turn to Gas Mark 6/200°C/400°F and cook for 2 hours. Serve with the cooking vegetables and juices.

goats

I always feel that goats are underappreciated. They are in fact very noble beasts of great antiquity. Before cows became our main milk source, they were kept for milk in every town and village. Their medieval status is reflected in the ancient breed brought back to England from the Crusades by King Richard II and given to Sir Richard Bagot, in gratitude for a memorable day's hunting at the end of the 1390 season. Pure descendants of Bagot goats are still with us today.

Goats breed earlier than sheep and kids fatten quickly, therefore, in the days when food availability was strictly governed by the seasons, kid was the first fresh meat people could eat in the year. Fresh goat's milk was also essential to any long sea voyage, which is why there are so many feral goats in places like Australia and New Zealand, brought there by sailors.

Goats do not only provide us with milk and meat. Goat leather is extremely fine and was often disguised to resemble shagreen, the very finest leather made from shark skin.

breeding

Female kids will come into season in their first autumn and, with proper care and attention, can be bred from then. Billy kids reach sexual maturity, with all the attendant smell, at three months and unless you particularly want an 'entire' goat to breed from, it should be castrated with an elastrator (see page 99) as soon after birth as possible. Young wether (castrated male) goats make excellent

choosing a breed

In many ways, a goat is the ideal milk provider for a self-supporter, particularly if the land is taken up with other enterprises. There are a number of high-yield milking goat breeds – little Toggenburgs, loppy-lugged Anglo-Nubians, British Alpine, and Saanens. The goat I would recommend is the Toggenburg This is a low-maintenance medium-sized goat found worldwide. It is considered to be ideal for the home producer as it will convert average grazing into a reasonable milk supply over a long period, without the need for large amounts of concentrate food. A Toggenburg doe will yield around 3 litres of milk during a 300 day lactation on marginal grazing. It is also a nice-natured goat and suited to most climates other than the tropics.

Goats are browsers and are destructive anywhere near trees, but they make good use of land grazed by other animals and would do well in with Shetland sheep, cleaning up behind them. If you let them browse on a tether they can also be extremely useful for controlling growth on rough unfenced ground, as long as they have access to water and are moved daily.

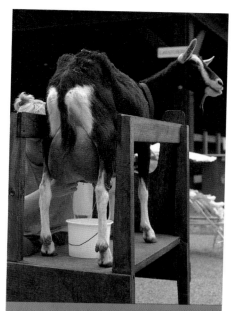

milking

Goats are milked exactly as you would a cow (see page 98), but a goat has only two teats. You will need a little milking parlour, either purpose-built or in a converted building and it should have lighting and water. The doe should be housed and fed at night and turned out to graze between milking. Unless you are a contortionist, I would advise building a 60cm stand to milk her on. This needs a small ramp for her to walk up, a hay rack at the far end and a barrier on the side opposite the side you milk from, to stop her falling off.

eating. They have more flavour than lamb of the same age and used to be known as 'poor man's venison'.

Assuming you have the one doe purely for milk and unless you have access to a Billy, I would recommend artificial insemination. This has become extremely refined recently and gives you the option for a choice of sire. A Boer, for example, would give a kid of much improved carcass conformation. The doe can be taken to a registered inseminator or they can come to you.

Signs of oestrous are pretty clear. The doe becomes noisy and unsettled, her tail wags from side to side, the vulva swells and there is fluid round the tail. Sometimes a Billy Rag, a piece of cloth reeking of male goat and kept in a hermetically sealed container, is used to hasten the oestrogen cycle. Gestation is around 150 days, give or take a week either side.

During the winter she should have half a kilo of good hay and a small amount – 125g – of mineralized goat nuts if she is being milked. As the foetus grows, her hay ration should be reduced slightly and the concentrates gradually increased to 200g.

Goats usually lamb themselves, but be prepared to assist with a difficult birth and ring the vet if you find yourself confronted with a problem that is beyond your range of experience. And don't forget that the kids must be tagged, recorded and registered.

Once a goat's productive life is over – usually after about six years – it must go to the abbatoir for slaughter. Deal with the skin as you would the skin of sheep and cattle.

Basic health care for goats is pretty much the same as that for sheep. Feet and internal parasites are the main concerns. As your commonsense will tell you, loss of energy, lack of appetite, dull coat, stiffness or lameness are all obvious signs of animal ill health. As with any livestock, you should go on a course at your local agricultural college before embarking on keeping goats.

sheep

'Of the sheep is cast away nothing,' is the opening line of a thirteenth-century verse extolling the virtues of sheep, the animals whose wool made Britain the most powerful country in medieval Europe. For centuries, nothing of the sheep was cast away. As well as wool and meat, the sheep provided bones that were made into protein meal, horns and hooves used for glue, and lanolin from the fleece used as a softener in skin creams. In addition, casings for sausages, harp strings and contraceptives were made from the intestines, sheep dung was used as a fertilizer, the hide provided soft leather, and the fat was used for tallow, essential for lighting until the advent of gas and electricity.

It is said that the value of a sheep's carcass is in the four quarters and until BSE in Britain, the head, the hooves, the hide and the innards were known as the fifth quarter, and were of equal value. This, sadly, is no longer the case and valuable natural products, like blood and bone, are now simply incinerated. To be fair though, it was AIDS that brought an end to the lucrative market for 'natural' protective sheaths. Unlike rubber, condoms made from a sheep's caecum are not impervious to the AIDS virus.

'Of the sheep is cast away nothing...'

choosing a breed

A little flock of sheep is ideal for a home producer with a small acreage. It will provide both wool and meat, and even milk if you want to be really adventurous. The pros and cons of the hundreds of different breeds need to be carefully assessed. Having farmed sheep all my life, I am, of course, a devoted fan, particularly of hill sheep, but I am equally aware that given sheep's determination to die at the least excuse, having a small flock can be problematic.

The main drawback to most breeds is that they must be shorn once a year and as there is a general shortage of shearers, it can be very difficult to find anyone prepared to shear a small flock. You could of course enroll on a sheep-shearing course, but it takes a great deal of experience to shear without causing the sheep and oneself considerable distress.

For this reason, the breed I would recommend is the Shetland sheep. They are small, hardy, wonderful mothers, and easy to keep and lamb. Their flesh is close-textured and full of flavour. Their wool is a variety of different colours, which traditionally went to make Fair Isle sweaters and 'ring' shawls – shawls so delicate they could be drawn through a wedding ring. It is one of the finest wools, much prized by hand-spinners. Best of all, you don't need to shear Shetland sheep. In the summer, from late July onwards, when the new wool begins to grow, the old wool loosens and can be pulled off. This is called 'rooing'. The wool fibres are of a better quality for spinning than some other wools, since they have not been cut.

Shetland sheep benefit from old rough pasture grazing with a good variety of herbage – on the Shetland islands they more or less live off seaweed – but they will adapt to improved pasture. Half a hectare of

pasture will keep six ewes through the summer, but you would need to divide it with an electric fence and graze each side for three weeks at a time. During the three weeks when the sheep are not grazing, any internal parasites that live in the pasture will complete their lifecycle and die without attaching themselves to a host, in other words, the sheep will be less prone to internal parasites if you graze each side for three weeks in this way.

You will also need a set of mobile handling pens or a shed to run your sheep into, for the various health procedures such as checking for foot rot, fly strike and drenching (see opposite) for internal parasites. The more Shetland sheep are handled, the easier they become to handle.

breeding

A flock of six ewes and a ram is an ideal number. The ram is something of a problem since he needs to be kept separate from the flock from the time the oestrogen cycle starts until you wish to use him, otherwise lambs could start appearing when they are least wanted.

The oestrogen cycle, which lasts seventeen days, is activated by diminishing hours of daylight and is influenced by body condition. In the northern hemisphere, ewes on good grazing come into heat from mid-September onwards. The gestation period is about 140 days or five months and I would advise aiming to have your ewes lamb when there is spring grass growth for them and their lambs. In the northern hemisphere therefore, the ewes would 'go to the tup' at the beginning of November or December ready for spring grass in April or May.

Three weeks before he goes in with the ewes, check that the ram is sound and that his pizzle, or penis, has not been damaged. The two most important parts of the ram for the next few weeks are his pizzle and his hind legs. Give the ram 250g of sheep nuts daily during tupping, or mating and, if you want, you can put a harness on him with a coloured wax crayon fixed to his brisket. If you change the colour on the ninth day, it will help indicate the week when individual ewes will lamb.

Your ewes should be neither too fat nor too lean. If they are in good health, they should all take within that period.

lambing

Feed the ewes with 250g hay or as much as they will eat until a month before lambing when they will benefit from a few nuts, building up to 250g of nuts just before they lamb. If there is sufficient grass and decent weather, run them into the handling pens every month through the winter to check their condition and let them out through a formalin foot bath. A fortnight before lambing, inject them with an anti-clostridia serum. This protects the lambs via the mother's milk from a number of soil-bound diseases.

Shetland sheep are easy lambers and should be left alone to get on with it. They are prolific on good ground, so expect twins. If you have never lambed, attend one of the lambing courses available at your local agricultural college. In the event of a problem call the vet.

Ram lambs ought to be castrated with an elastrator (see page 99) as soon as they are dry and suckled or within 24 hours. For the first ten weeks of their life, lambs should be drenched with a broad-spectrum anthelmintic or vermifuge to protect against intestinal worms during the months of grass growth, and protected from maggot fly using one of the oil-based, pour-on fly deterrents every six weeks. You should also check regularly for foot rot and run them through a foot bath. Your flock has to be registered and all lambs tagged and recorded.

after lambing

From June onwards in the northern hemisphere, beware of ewes becoming 'couped' as their fleece gets heavy. On hot days or after a fall of rain, their backs itch and they roll over to scratch. The fleece can prevent them from getting back onto their feet. Once they are couped, their digestive system ceases to work, gas from fermenting grass builds up and pressure on the lungs suffocates them.

In August, pluck the ewes and ram of their wool and drench the lambs at the same time, as by then they will be weaning themselves off milk. If any wool

remains firm, pluck what you can and leave them for another week, plucking them again and so on until they are clean. Ewes, the ram and any flock replacements must be injected against scab in October.

Lambs are ready to kill at between sixteen and eighteen weeks. Your little flock should have produced between six and ten lambs, each now weighing about 14–18 kilos live weight. You will need to keep some ewe lambs to replace old ewes, but bear in mind that in the northern hemisphere these will not breed until the following November.

It is illegal to home-kill in Britain nowadays, so your lambs will have to be taken to an abbatoir for slaughter, after which they can either be hung and butchered to your instructions or you can collect the carcass and bring it home. With the variation in temperature that we have through the winter, it is as well to have this hanging done professionally.

If you have a use for the skin, which the abbatoir might otherwise pay for, retrieve it and follow suggestions for the bullock hide (see page 99).

mutuk or armenian lamb stew

(SERVES 6)

Armenian food is delicious and I know some wonderful Armenian cooks. One must remember that Armenia once had a great empire, although this delicious dish is rather more populist. It is very heartening in cold weather and has an interesting combination of flavours.

225g breast of lamb or lamb chops
1 tbsp oil or fat
2 largish onions, sliced
2 tomatoes plus 1 tbsp tomato purée
1 tbsp chickpeas soaked overnight
2 largish potatoes, sliced
4 fresh damsons (you can use plums or even dried prunes instead)
4–5 chestnuts chopped (if available)
large sprig thyme
1 pint stock
half a glass red wine
a few threads saffron soaked in water (reserve the water)
1 tbsp each fresh coriander and parsley (if dried, only use ¹/₂ tbsp)
salt and pepper
sour cream to serve

Heat the oil in a frying pan. Trim excess fat from the meat and brown the meat. Set it aside. Fry the onions until soft, add the tomatoes and purée, season and cook 2–3 minutes longer.

Transfer the meat to a heavy pan, add the onion and tomato mix and all the other ingredients except the saffron and fresh coriander and parsley. If using dried herbs, add the herbs. Adjust the seasoning. Bring to the boil and simmer until the meat is tender, about 90 minutes. Add the saffron threads and their water and the fresh herbs and cook for 5 minutes longer.

Add a spoonful of sour cream when serving.

devilled lamb cutlets

SERVES 4–6)

I suppose the eighteenth-century passion for devilling meats was a forerunner of the twentieth-century passion for curry. I love devilled cutlets, especially for breakfast.

12 thin lamb cutlets
2 tbsp mustard powder
2 tbsp walnut ketchup (see page 202)
50g butter
50g very finely chopped shallots
1 tbsp soft brown sugar
1 tbsp Worcestershire sauce
150ml dark beer or stout
1 tsp cayenne pepper
salt and pepper

Mix the mustard to a smooth thin paste with the walnut ketchup. Smear all over the meat and leave to stand for at least 1 hour. Season.

Put the butter and all the other ingredients in a small pan and cook gently to a thick syrup. Spread half of this over the chops and cook them in the grill pan (not on the rack) under a hot grill for a few minutes. Turn them over, spread on the rest of the mixture and cook for a few minutes more. Eat with a good cup of coffee for breakfast

horses

In the first decade after the Second World War, it began to look as if many of the hundreds of different breeds of horse and pony were going to become at best, endangered species and at worst, die out altogether. Apart from ceremonial duties, the cavalry – the arme blanche – of the world's armies had all become mechanized. For farm, dray and forestry work tractors and lorries had largely replaced heavy horses, and though we still had a pair of Suffolk Punches on our farm, we were an exception. There was little place for any of the magnificent driving breeds – the Cleveland Bays, Norfolk trotters, Hackneys and the hundreds of different types of vanner that used to pull tradesmen's carts. Apart from the few animals kept for hunting, show jumping, eventing, racing and polo, horse and pony numbers worldwide seemed to be in a terminal decline. As someone who grew up with horses, I am delighted to say that nothing could now be further from the truth.

why have a horse?

Owning a horse opens up a huge range of possibilities and such is the love between man and horse that every discipline in the history of equitation has its devoted following. There is the complicated and ancient art form of Haute Ecole as well as polo, polo crosse, eventing, show jumping, dressage and endurance riding. Heavy

'Owning a horse opens up a huge range of possibilities...'

horses are now used for timber extraction once again and, occasionally for ploughing and pulling harrows and other farm implements, and there is a worldwide resurgence of interest in carriage driving. Hunting, the bedrock of all racing, is as popular now as it ever was, despite the political bias of the current British government.

children and horses

Any child wishing to own a horse or pony and to learn to ride would do well to contact their local branch of the Pony Club. Founded in Britain in 1928 and now an international organization with membership around the world, it is responsible for encouraging the ever-growing interest in riding among the young. It also encourages them to learn equine welfare and the broad spectrum of equine skills, from hunting, tetrathlon, show jumping and polo to eventing and dressage. In Britain alone there are nearly 400 branches organizing programmes of competitions, paper trails, training days and gymkhanas, and culminating in the annual pony club camps. One of the beauties of the club is that it encompasses children from urban as well as rural backgrounds and you don't even need to own a pony to be a member. Apart from gaining riding skills and a knowledge of horses from experts in the field, the Pony Club has provided generations of young people with a unique social experience, based on fun, friendship, training and the priceless responsibility of looking after an animal. Most of the British Olympic equestrian team members of the last 50 years started their careers as Pony Club members.

global horsiculture

Horsiculture is a global growth industry, with riding holidays, ranging from basic trekking holidays in beautiful parts of the British Isles, Europe and North America to mounted adventures in Africa, South America, Mongolia and unexplored parts of eastern Europe, becoming increasingly popular. In Britain, a recent survey showed that the equine population exceeded one million, of which 65,000 were owned professionally in the racing industry and by riding centres, with the rest privately owned. These figures may be replicated across Europe, North America, Australia and New Zealand.

adults and horses

There are equally as many opportunities for adults to learn to ride and become involved in a variety of equine sports, including driving, as there are for children. Internationally, there are any number of riding clubs and equestrian associations that can provide help and advice on choosing a riding school. In Britain, the British Horse Society is dedicated to pointing anyone interested in horses in the right direction, offering a list of recommended riding schools and livery yards and giving advice on such matters as equine passports. In Britain alone, there are hundreds of spectator events throughout the year – point to points and hunter trials, run by the 350 or so foxhound packs, one-, two- and three-day events, the great international spectacles of the Badminton and Burghley horse trials, polo tournaments and carriage-driving competitions such as the famous Lowther driving trials.

choosing a breed

Britain

● The British thoroughbred is the world's most famous and valuable horse. Its ease of action, speed, stamina and courage have underpinned a racing and breeding industry which is now multinational.

● The thoroughbred evolved from stallions imported from Syria, Turkey and Egypt during the late seventeenth and early eighteenth centuries.

● Three exceptional stallions – the Byerley, Turk with the Darley and Godolphin Arabians – are considered the foundation of all racehorses.

● The thoroughbred's superb qualities are used worldwide to improve many other breeds. A classic example were the hunters and eventers bred by my father. He took Welsh Cob mares to the Queen's Cleveland bay stallion, Mulgrave Supreme, and crossed the progeny with a thoroughbred. The Welsh Cob provided hardiness and common sense, the Cleveland, size and jumping ability, and the thoroughbred, quality and ease of action.

France

● The Selle Française is another famous competition horse using thoroughbred blood. The rather common all-purpose light draft Norman was crossed with an Arab and then with a thoroughbred to produce this excellent show jumper.

● The white horse of the Camargue, a very ancient breed improved with Moroccan Barb blood in the Middle Ages, is one of France's most famous breeds.

● The Landais and the Pottock are two indigenous French pony breeds that have been improved with Welsh and Arab blood.

Germany

● The Holstein, originally a carriage horse, has been improved with blood from the famous Yorkshire Coach Horse and the thoroughbred, to produce a first-rate show jumper and cross-country horse.

● The Oldenburg, particularly suited for driving and dressage, evolved from a cross between the French Norman, the Friesland and the thoroughbred.

Spain

● The Andalucian or Spanish horse was the most influential improver across the whole of Europe until it was superceded by the Arab.

● These are the horses used in the famous Spanish Riding School and were the foundation stock for the white Lippizaners.

● Andalucians were bred from the native Sorraias crossed with Barb stallions during the Moroccan conquest of Spain.

Australia

● Australia has the splendid Waler or Australian stock horse. There are a number of different categories – pony, light, medium and heavy.

● Walers originated when thoroughbreds were exported to Australia in the 1830s and were crossed with the hardy light draft horses that were already in the colony of New South Wales. This resulted in a tough, stylish stock horse with a bit of quality and a good temperament.

● Walers provided most of the cavalry horses for the British army in India and today. They are still used for stock work but are also popular as polo ponies, for endurance riding, show jumping and dressage.

The Americas

● The foundation of many South and North American horses were the Spanish horses brought over by Cortés in the sixteenth century and from which hardy breeds like the Rocky Mountain Pony, Criolla, Appaloosa, Mustang, Palomino, Quarter Horse, Colorado Ranger, Paso and Pinto descend.

● Crossing with thoroughbreds produced very stylish riding horses like the Saddlebred, Narragansett Pacer, Missouri Fox Trotter, Tennessee Walking Horse and the supreme stock horse, the Quarter Horse.

● One of North America's most famous breeds, the Morgan, evolved from a Welsh cob crossed with an Arab and a thoroughbred.

Top left: thoroughbred cross child's riding pony
Centre: Suffolk Punch mare and foal
Bottom left: A pair of Shire horses

riding for the disabled

Since the 1960s, independent bodies have been offering riding as a form of therapy for disabled people, particularly for those from an urban background. My mother, among others, was much involved in this movement and in 1969 the charity Riding for the Disabled was formed. This, and its sister organization, Driving for the Disabled, now have around 700 member groups run by nearly 15,000 volunteers. There are similar organizations, offering institution-alized people a new perspective on life, in every country where there is a vibrant horse culture.

looking after a horse

Looking after a horse or pony is an enormous responsibility and no one should keep one without first acquiring a thorough knowledge of equine welfare. Centuries of breeding have resulted in horses suitable for carrying riders or pulling wagons and carts. A horse may be compared to a superb athlete and, just as any athlete must take care with his or her diet, exercise and health, so the same applies to caring for a horse. The British Horse Society or a similar national organization will be able to advise you and there are, of course, societies for specific breeds who can also offer help.

In general you will need to ensure that you can offer proper stabling and grazing and you will also need a tack room and feed store. In terms of time and money, it is a big commitment, but the rewards and broadened horizons are incalculable, and who knows, you might start breeding to help cover some of your costs.

chickens

I would thoroughly recommend a few fowl to any would-be home producer. It takes a lot to beat a free-ranging brood of hens, or even a paddling of ducks (see page 124), a gaggle of geese (see page 126) or a rafter of turkeys. They are fun to keep and create an atmosphere of frenetic energy with their industrious search for food, their squabbling, egg-laying and dust bathing, and the way they vocalize all their activities with raucous exuberance. Many have beautiful plumage, and the Phoenicians and Greeks kept chickens as religious ornaments, living symbols of the gods Athena, Persephone, Eros and Hermes. What is more, chickens are productive and the flavour of the eggs and meat from a home-reared bird bears no relation to any mass-produced specimen.

keeping chickens

Chickens are a woodland bird and, assuming your vegetable and flower garden is rabbit-fenced, your chickens will thrive best running free, hunting for food in rough grass, eating weed and grass seeds, and scratching for insects. During the summer this is all they need, plus a little mixed grain and some scraps to keep them manageable.

Their housing is obviously of paramount importance. The main requirement for poultry is that they are protected from predators and the weather, and that they have adequate ventilation. They need to feel safe and comfortable. Like all stock, chickens are prone to stress and their performance will drop off if they are

unhappy. Lastly, though it is a secondary consideration to the welfare of the birds, the hen house should be easy for you to use.

Some people may have redundant farm buildings which could be converted into poultry housing but generally speaking these tend to be too close to the house and away from the area where the hens should be grazing. In any case, I like to see chickens with their own house.

There are plenty of companies making poultry housing that is ideally suited to the smallholder. I would recommend a solid, decent-sized, purpose-built freestanding shed with skids on the bottom so it can be dragged to a clean new site when necessary. It must be easy for you to get in and clean and so will need a door for your own access. I

choosing a breed

There are so many breeds of chicken available today, thanks to the nineteenth-century craze for exotic breeds and the endless experimentation by geneticists, that a novice is spoilt for choice. My advice is to go for a traditional tried-and-tested, old-fashioned dual-purpose breed. This will provide more than enough eggs for the average family and delicious table birds at two years. Light Sussex are my favourites; they are hardy, independent, great table birds and capable of producing around 200 eggs a year. Rhode Island Reds are another traditional dual-purpose breed, while French Marans are wonderful, slow-maturing table birds and good brown-egg layers. The blue or buff Orpingtons are reliably meaty birds but produce fewer eggs while the white, black and brown Leghorns, Barred Plymouth Rocks, Scots Greys and Wyandottes are all excellent, long-established dual-purpose chickens.

suggest having a hen house that is 1.5m square and 1.68m high at the front, sloping to 1.42m at the back. It should have a wooden roof covered with tarred felt. In addition you will need a ramp and hatch for the hens, and lighting. This is particularly important if you live in the north where the days are shorter and if you want an extended laying period. You will also need a 12-litre plastic drinker and an ad-lib galvanized feeder that can be attached to the inside of the door, plus a broody coop and integral run, and 40cm-deep external nesting boxes complete with a hinged lid. Be sure to position the hen house on a dry, free-draining site.

breeding

You have various options for starting a flock. These include hatching eggs under an incubator, rearing chicks or buying half-grown pullets or point of lays – birds that are ready to lay – in September. I would suggest buying point of lays. A cockerel and eight hens is a good starting point for a dual-purpose family-sized enterprise.

Make your purchase either privately, at an auction or through one of the many businesses specializing in poultry and poultry equipment. When you get your hens and cockerel home, shut them in the hen-house for four days so they can become acclimatized, making sure that they have plenty of food, fresh water, a little hay in each nesting box and small, clean wood shavings on the floor. On the morning of the fifth day, open their hatch, scatter a little feed down the ramp and let them find their way out. Feed scraps and a little wheat in the afternoon near the shed, so they get used to the idea of being in its vicinity when it comes to shutting them before dark.

Realistically, pure-bred dual-purpose pullets are unlikely to give many eggs before the spring, particularly if the home producer lives in the north. Sunlight influences a hen's productivity and as the hours of daylight diminish, fewer eggs are laid. I have childhood memories of the bottling activities of the autumn. We preserved the eggs in isinglass – a form of collagen made from the swim bladders of certain tropical fish and still used today as finings in the brewing industry – and stored them in big glazed earthenware crocks for the lean winter months (see page 183). My hens in southern Scotland tail off into November and start again in early February, with just one or two laying sporadically through that period. To ensure a flow of eggs during winter, create daylight artificially by using a timer to set an electric light to come on for a few hours before dawn and then again at dusk.

I feed my hens standard layers pellets from the ad-lib feeder in the hen-house during the summer, plus wheat and household scraps in the afternoon. I increase the wheat by feeding them twice a day during the winter period. In spring and summer, in addition to the layers pellets, my hens get a large percentage of their protein from insects and weed seeds. You also need to give the hens access to grit to help eggshell production. They like a dustbath to clean their feathers and help get rid of mites and will find their own if they are running around freely. As long as the hen-house is cleaned out scrupulously, your hens will be disease-free.

With egg production starting in the spring, the second phase of the dual-purpose poultry enterprise begins when one of the hens turns broody, squatting on the nest with tail feathers erect, refusing to move and clucking in outrage at being disturbed. Now it is time to prepare the broody coop by cutting a turf, turning it over, making a depression in it, covering it with broken straw and putting it inside. Move the broody and her eggs into the coop. Fresh water, grit and a dustbath made of dry soil, ash and sand should be made available in the run together with a daily feed of wheat.

Eggs take 21 days to hatch and for the first ten, shut the hen off the nest for twenty minutes while she feeds. For the next eleven days, keep her off for 30 minutes. While she is feeding, turn each egg to stop the foetus adhering to the side of the shell and check that the turf remains damp. Always feed her at the same time each day.

after hatching

When the chicks hatch, they should not be fed for at least 48 hours while they live off the membrane that is left in the egg. Then they need plenty of fresh water and chick-crumbs feed pellets for a month.

Divide the run with a slatted partition to keep the hen separate and move the divider every day to give the chicks some fresh ground.

How you look after the chicks from now on depends on the amount of time you are able to devote to them. My view is that the sooner they get out and learn to forage with the hen the better. They will scuttle about the place with her and she will hide them away at night in some long grass. As they become older, they will begin to feed with the rest of the hens and will be roosting with them in the hen-house by the autumn. There is obviously the risk of predators when you have young chicks running about like this; the alternative is to keep them in an enclosure, feeding them growers pellets for up to 14 weeks.

How many hens you allow to turn broody and rear a clutch depends on the number of table chickens you require. Of an average clutch of ten, roughly half will be young cockerels. To take a hypothetical example, three hens will supply fifteen pullets and fifteen cockerels in the spring and early summer. The cockerels will all be killed in the following autumn and winter. In January the flock will stand at 33 hens of which eight will be entering their most productive second year, to be culled as boiling fowls at the end of it. Seven pullets or a combination of pullets and second-year hens that have proved to be poor layers will be surplus to requirements and could be culled. When more hens than are required for breeding turn broody, a trick to stop them is to feed them in a small wire or slat-bottomed coop raised off the ground. This is so uncomfortable that within a few days they lose the desire to squat and within a fortnight will return to laying.

Young cockerels from the brood will be ready to eat at eighteen weeks. It is well worth putting a couple in the broody coop and fattening them for a fortnight on a thrice daily feed of a fattening ration. The same applies to the boilers that have passed through their second laying season.

When handling a chicken, pick it up by the body with the wings closed. If they can't flap their wings, they remain quite calm. Place the bird under your right arm and press her gently against your body so the wings are kept closed, and hold her feet together with your hand.

To kill a chicken, hold it as described, take the head in your left hand and in one fluid motion, jerk the right hand back and the left hand down, twisting the head to the left. The neck will snap instantaneously as the body is pulled rigid. Hang it up by the legs until cool and pluck (see page 128).

turkeys and guinea fowl

Another breed of fowl for the home-producer to consider is the guinea fowl. These are kept much like free-range chickens, to which they make a delicious alternative. Turkeys, however, are extremely delicate creatures, difficult to rear among other poultry and fatally susceptible to diseases which your other fowl may carry but be immune to. Unless turkeys are going to be the sole enterprise of your fowl yard, they seem hardly worth the trouble.

chicken for the table

Of all the differences that will bring home to you your altered lifestyle I suspect it will be chickens that provide the biggest shock. You will have been used to the bland but tender meat of a supermarket roasting bird or the more tasty but still tender free-range bird sold to you by your butcher. This is all about to change. You will now be keeping hens for eggs and killing them for the table when they have stopped laying. The problem with this is that such a bird will have a wonderful flavour but if you simply roast it, it will be as tough as old boots. Instead, you will have to slow-cook it, braise it, pot-roast it or poach it. An old cockerel can also be delicious if it is properly cooked.

What you cry, am I never to eat roast chicken again? And of course you are. In the spring when your chicks hatch you will find among them a proportion of cockerels; there is no point keeping these long term as they will simply kill each other. You have various options: either to kill them young and eat them roast or caponize (castrate) them and kill them at about 3.6–4 kg. To my mind a caponized cockerel is one of the most delicious things you can eat. It produces a layer of fat under the skin which melts during cooking, sef-lubricating the bird while it is roasting.

The practice of caponizing fell out of favour 40 or so years ago because farmers started using hormone pellets for this purpose, which raised (quite rightly) all types of anxieties. There were rumours of men in America growing breasts and women sprouting beards and so the use of hormones was made illegal in the UK. However capons have been around since Ancient Greece. In fact, the Athenian City Council passed a sumptuary law that forbad the eating of fattened hens as it was regarded as a waste of grain.

hindle wakes

(SERVES 8)

I love this medieval recipe which can only be made successfully with an old fowl. The name of the dish comes, I believe, from the lost Derbyshire town of Hindle which, due to absence of water, failed to survive the Industrial Revolution, and not, as some would have it, from Hen de la Wakes. Whatever the naming, it is scrumptious. The dish was designed for Wakes Week – a traditional summer holiday celebrated in Lancashire – as a cold dish to cut and come again. I have cooked it overnight in the bottom of an Aga using light ale instead of water and it was even better. I have used chicken blood like the original recipe and as we're being true to self-sufficiency I suggest sorrel instead of lemons unless you have retired to the sun or have got the orangery working to strength.

1 boiling fowl 1.8 kg–2.2 kg
600ml wine vinegar
2 tbsp brown sugar (for purity use honey)
salt and a handful of peppercorns

For the stuffing
450g large prunes, stoned and soaked but not cooked
225g fine white breadcrumbs
150ml chicken's blood mixed with a little vinegar to prevent curdling
50g blanched almonds, roughly chopped
1 tbsp fresh mixed herbs, chopped
50g suet, shredded
600ml beer
salt and pepper

For the sauce
1 tbsp cornflour
225ml chicken stock
150ml verjuice (see page 151) or rind and juice of 2 lemons
2 eggs, well beaten
salt and pepper

Mix all the stuffing ingredients in a bowl and stuff the fowl both under the breast and in the cavity and sew up. Place in a large saucepan of cold water and add the vinegar, brown sugar, salt and peppercorns. Bring to the boil and simmer for 4 hours. Allow to cool in the liquid. While the chicken is cooling make the sauce.

Mix the cornflour with the stock, bring to the boil and stir in the verjuice as you do this. Season and cook for 2–3 minutes. Remove the pan from the heat, allow to cool slightly and beat in the eggs. Cook a little longer but do not allow to boil. Allow the sauce to cool. Place the chicken on a dish and pour over the sauce.

braised hen

(SERVES 6–8)

This is a dish our cook Louise Leeds used to make when I was young. She was a remarkable woman and most of what I know is based on the foundations she laid for me. I suspect that, as my mother was an elegant woman who bought her clothes in Paris and Louise was the one to show me all the benefits of cooking, Louise was more my role model than my mama! She had a great deal of energy and a fine, enquiring mind.

1 boiling fowl
3–4 rashers bacon
200ml dry white wine
1.3 kg potatoes, peeled and diced
110g butter
20 small shallots
300ml chicken stock
125ml double cream
salt and pepper

For the marinade
125ml olive oil
2 tbsp finely chopped chives or spring onions
4 shallots, finely chopped
3 garlic cloves, crushed
salt and pepper

Mix all the marinade ingredients and leave the fowl in the mixture for 1 day, turning from time to time. Place the bacon rashers in the bottom of a heavy casserole, place the fowl on them and pour over the marinade. Season, add the white wine, cover and cook over a low heat for 3 hours.

Meanwhile, fry the potatoes in 2/3 of the butter. Fry the shallots in the remaining butter until coloured. After 2 1/2 hours add the potatoes and shallots to the casserole, heat the stock and pour it on. Finish cooking. Remove the fowl, carve it and place on a dish with the shallots and potatoes. Reduce the juices by boiling vigorously. Remove from the heat, stir in the cream, heat through and serve the sauce separately.

josie's chicken

(SERVES 6)

This is a traditional boiled fowl with rice but I have named it after my friend Josie Coleman, who always cooked it so beautifully for all the hungry mouths around her all-welcoming table, and who taught me so much.

1 boiling fowl, cleaned and trussed
2 carrots
1–2 onions, studded with a few cloves
1 bouquet garni
1 tbsp salt

For the rice
50g butter
1 small onion, chopped
225g rice
600ml chicken stock

For the sauce
25g butter
1¹/₂ tbsp flour
350ml chicken stock
grating of nutmeg
3–4 tbsp single cream
1 egg yolk
salt and pepper

Put the bird and its accompanying ingredients into a deep pan and cover with water. Bring to the boil, skim and cook slowly for 2 hours.

After 1¹/₂ hours prepare the rice. Melt 25g butter and fry the chopped onion until golden. Add the rice and shake over the heat to coat the grains with butter. Add the stock, cover and cook over a low heat for 20–25 minutes or until the liquid is all cooked away. Add a further 25g butter and stir into the rice with a fork.

Make the sauce while the rice is cooking. Make a roux with the butter and flour, add the stock a bit at a time and stir when it is heated until the sauce is smooth and thickened. Taste for seasoning, add a grating of nutmeg and cook gently for 10 minutes.

Mix the cream and egg yolk together, remove the sauce from the heat and stir in the cream mixture. Keep warm. Place the prepared rice on a platter. Carve the fowl and arrange the pieces on the rice. Pour over some of the sauce and serve the rest separately.

turkey goulash

SERVES 12, but will go further if the meat is taken off the bone

This is not a true goulash but a very good way of cooking turkey. The recipe was designed to be cooked slowly on a kitchen range. If you want to cook it more quickly, feel free, but for no less than 2 hours.

1 turkey, cut into serving pieces
500g fat bacon, rubbed with paprika and cut into flat strips
450ml chicken or turkey stock
4 tbsp soured cream
20 cherries, fresh or bottled, and stoned
2 red peppers, skinned and cut into strips
4 tbsp sweet white wine (Muscat or Tokay)
1 tbsp extra paprika

Preheat the oven to Gas Mark 2/150°C/ 300°F. Wrap each piece of turkey in the prepared bacon. Brown the pieces well on all sides in a frying pan, then transfer to a casserole dish. Add 400ml stock, cover and braise in the oven for 2 hours. Add the soured cream, cherries and pepper strips. Cook for a further 2 hours.

When the turkey is cooked, remove to a serving dish. Add the remaining stock, the wine and the paprika to the casserole dish. Bring to the boil and reduce to the desired consistency. Serve the sauce with the turkey. This dish is delicious accompanied by noodles.

ducks

There is no point in even considering keeping a paddle of ducks, unless you have a pond – at least two square metres – with good water circulation or a source of running water that could be dammed to create a pool for them. Ducks need water like hens need a dust bath, but what they do not want is an unhealthy, stagnant, muddy wallow. If you are able to provide the right environment, keeping them can be enormously rewarding and there is plenty of choice for the beginner who will probably want a dual-purpose breed – for laying and for the table.

housing your ducks

A drake and six young ducks make a good unit. They will require a 3m x 1.2m duck house, 105cm high at the front sloping to 95cm at the rear, with a wood and tarred felt roof, a hatch and ramp for the ducks, and a door for you. The duck house should be on runners so it can be moved to clean grass periodically as, over time, ducks reduce any ground to a muddy puddle. It should also have removable sides so that the inside can be cleaned. In addition you will need a broody coop with an integral 4-metre run covered in wire netting, plus a couple of troughs and water feeders.

As with chickens or any other poultry, when you get your ducks home, leave them shut in for four days with plenty of litter, food and fresh water. By the time they are let out, their duck house will be the only home they know. On the morning of the fifth day open the duck house, scatter some food down the ramp to draw them out, put the rest of the food on the ground and have a happy time cleaning out the house whilst they waddle off quacking contentedly to swim in their pool. They should be fed twice a day, first thing in the morning when they are let out and half an hour before they are shut in for the night. They need a ration of 150g of duck pellets per bird per day, or just under 40 kg per bird per month. You must also cut the flight feather on one wing short to stop them flying off.

breeding

The young ducks will start nesting around the end of winter. Housed duck tend to make a nest in the corner of their hut so I nail 40cm-square frames of 5 by 10cm timber to the back wall of the hut for them.

choosing a breed

My choice would be Silver Appleyards, named after the great pre-war poultry breeder, the striking-looking Blue Swedish, with their dark green heads and slate coloured bodies, or the white Aylesbury, the original farmyard bird. All are reasonable layers, providing about 100 plus eggs per year – and they are good table birds too.

Some may construct nests in the rushes beside their paddling pool. You also might like to position wooden nesting boxes raised on little stilts, with a ramp and lid for access to the eggs, at the edge of the pond. The ducks like them and they might encourage their wild cousins too.

Either let the duck hatch her eggs naturally and accept the risk of losses or move her into a broody coop where she will hatch the eggs in much the same way as a chicken. You can then let them run free after a month. Another alternative is to take the eggs and let a broody hen hatch them. This is useful with first-year layers since broody hens have a much more highly developed mothering instinct than ducks and make a marvellous job of rearing their young.

How many you rear depends on the number of eggs and young ducklings you require. Ducks have an advantage over hens in having a productive laying life of four years or longer in some cases. They are better breeders in their second, third and fourth years so this will influence your kill ratio, depending on whether you want more for the table and less for breeding stock, or the other way around. Whatever you do, you should remove all young stock before the drakes become sexually active.

duck with quinces and preserved lemons

DOMESTIC DUCK WILL SERVE 6–8

This is a dish I made up because I liked the combination of ingredients. I hope you like it too.

2 ducks, plucked and drawn, livers reserved and quartered
2 quinces, peeled
1 dessertspoon clear honey
25g unsalted butter
1 wineglass red wine
150ml duck stock
1 large preserved lemon
1 tbsp brandy
salt and pepper

Preheat the oven to Gas Mark 4/180°C/350°F. Peel and core the quinces and put the peelings inside the ducks. Rub each duck with salt and pepper and then with the honey.

In a frying pan melt the butter and fry the duck livers briefly. Reserve. Cut the quinces into quarters and toss them quickly in the melted butter. Put the ducks in a lidded casserole dish and add the quinces and livers.

De-glaze the frying pan with the wine and stock, and pour over the ducks. Cut the lemon into thin slices and arrange around the duck.

Cook covered in the preheated oven for 1¹/₂ hours. Uncover and cook for a further 15 minutes. Remove the ducks to a serving dish. Ignite the brandy and pour over the pan juices. Let it burn until it goes out.

Arrange the quinces and lemon slices around the duck in the serving dish and pour on the brandy and pan juices.

geese

Geese are noble birds of great domestic antiquity. All European domestic geese descend from the wild greylag, the only migratory bird which remained behind to breed when the others returned to the sub-Arctic in spring. Geese were among the first animals to be domesticated and were highly prized for their meat and feathers. When Britain's might lay in the longbow, geese provided flights for the hails of arrows that were fired by the country's archers, but even more valuable was goose 'grease'. In the days when all lubrication was provided by animal fat, goose fat was the softest and most malleable and therefore the most versatile. It was used to soften and water-proof leather, to lubricate axles and the moving parts of mills, it protected against rust and, when rubbed on copper or brass, kept verdigris at bay. A mildly medicated form of face cream was made from the sulphurous flowers of gorse beaten into goose grease and a sovereign cure for bronchitis was goose fat rubbed into the chest. And it has always been the finest cooking fat you can use.

keeping geese

A gander and and two geese is a good number to start with and you will find a 2.7 x 1.2-metre shed, similar to the duck house, perfectly adequate. Because of the size of geese, the shed should have a door whose bottom can be opened while the top remains closed rather than a hatch. For the same reason, the nesting frames should be double the size of those for ducks. Should you increase your gaggle, you can achieve extra nesting space simply by covering a nesting frame or old car tyre with a simple wooden shelter and positioning it near the hut.

Geese will do quite well on grass, with a few handfuls of grain through the winter. They lay early, in late winter or very early spring, so feed them up a bit beforehand. A goose will hatch and rear a dozen eggs without any bother as long as you are vigilant about predators such as rats and foxes. Alternatively, take the eggs from one goose and leave the other to sit or, take half a dozen and hatch them under a broody, leaving the goose to rear the rest. Rearing goslings like this is an alternative to buying young birds in the autumn.

preparing to kill

Whenever you decide to eat your geese it pays to fatten them on ground barley for the preceding three weeks.

Killing geese is slightly more complicated than killing smaller fowl, although the same principal of quick dislocation of the neck applies. It is a job that requires an assistant. Holding the geese by the legs and wing tips and, with its back towards you, lower the head to the ground and get the assistant to position a broom handle or poker across the back of the goose's neck, just behind the head. Put your feet on either end of the broom handle or poker and gently but firmly pull upwards. You will feel the neck dislocate.

michaelmas goose fairs

In England, goslings born in the early spring were traditionally killed at the great Michaelmas goose fairs at the end of September. Nottingham had a particularly famous goose fair, with flocks of geese walked many kilometres to the market over several days, their feet dipped in tar and sand to protect them for the journey. The other traditional feast day for geese was Easter, when geese would be only just over a year old and still young and tender. Nowadays in northern Europe, most young geese are killed for Christmas.

pigeons

Pigeon meat, particularly squab, or young pigeons, was a popular 'living larder' food in Britain from the time of their introduction with the Normans, until well into the nineteenth century. Every manor house had a substantial dovecote, some with beautiful architectural detail. The pigeons required no feeding, but simply foraged for food in the surrounding countryside. Eventually, as grain production increased, keeping a dovecote was considered excessively anti-social as your pigeons would eat your neighbour's grain, so dovecotes gradually became redundant.

Nowadays there are endless options for housing pigeons. Wallcotes are fixed to the outside of an existing building or you might consider converting the face of a building so the pigeons have access to the pigeon loft on the inside. Polecotes, where the pigeons are housed at the top of a sturdy pole, are yet another alternative. Whichever you choose, the most important feature is the door that allows access to the nesting area. The nesting areas must be 30cm square, stacked one above another, and each with a landing platform.

When you first get your pigeons, keep them shut in, well watered and fed for three weeks. Make sure they can see out of the pigeon loft. Then let them out and enjoy watching them fly around, soar over the trees, and strut and preen on the perches at the front of their dovecote.

The squabs are ready to eat at about 30 days or when the undersides of their wings are fully feathered. It is perfectly possible to have four or five broods a year.

choosing a breed

Of the main squab-breed pigeons, I recommend White or Silver Kings, Mondain, Carneau or Strassors. Half a dozen pairs will keep you well supplied, with each pair providing around ten squabs.

preparing a bird for the pot

You will need to hang your birds for 2–3 days (depending on the weather) in a cool, fly-free place such as a game larder. Hang it by its neck until you are ready to pluck it.

When faced with your first chicken plucking it can seem awfully daunting. I think the trick is not to rush it but to allow yourself enough time and go slowly and carefully. Although in theory all birds are plucked the same way, some are harder than others. I find the worst is a farmyard goose. Although Johnny and other kind friends sometimes give me my favourite pinkfoot geese and I pluck these with no difficulty, domestic geese are hard. If you have more than one to pluck it might be worth your while finding a friendly butcher or game keeper with a plucking machine. I always do the breasts by hand but your fingers (and mine are pretty strong and deft) get tired if you're plucking more than one goose.

Duck are pretty difficult too. The food writer Joanna Blythman ordered two organic geese one Christmas and the butcher who sent them made a right mess of plucking them. When she complained, he said organic ducks were harder to pluck than non-organic ones, which is total rubbish. Some sources advise plucking ducks wet as this help the feathers come out more smoothly, leaving fewer broken-off stubs. Don't soak the birds; just dip each quickly in a pail of cold water as you come to dress it. I don't wet-pluck as I don't like the sensation of clammy wet feathers whilst I'm working, but it is true that this process leaves fewer stubs. I just have to resort to my tweezers. Turkeys present other problems. I can remember in my teens helping to pluck

> 'When faced with your first chicken plucking it can seem awfully daunting. I think the trick is not to rush it but to allow yourself enough time and go slowly and carefully.'

turkeys. The friends I was visiting had a holiday job plucking turkeys to earn some money for Christmas and not wishing to be left on my own, I went too. It was a bit like a scene from a Breughel painting. Turkeys continue to flap when dead for longer than other birds and as they were being killed and sent straight through on a production line it was somewhat alarming. Since then I have learnt that turkey should also be hung for a day or two. I think it is the sheer size and appearance of a turkey that makes one quail from the task (forgive the pun!)

plucking a bird

Pluck the breast first, pulling carefully and against the grain. Pull the feathers upwards as you go. As your fingers get stronger you will find it a relaxing occupation.

When the bird is plucked you will probably need to singe off any fine feathers that are left and then remove them. Use tweezers for the stubs of any feathers that have broken off. For singeing use a candle, a small blowtorch or even your gas stove.

Next draw the bird's guts out through the anus, reserving the heart and liver. Cut off the feet and keep for the stockpot along with the neck. Discard the head, although a cockerel's wattles – the skin under the chin – are good eating. On her wedding day Catherine de Medici ate so many wattles (rumour says 110) stuffed with artichoke hearts that she got indigestion and was unable to consummate her marriage. As Henry II was said to be quite a hunk, the wattles must have been delicious. Finally, rinse the body cavity with water. Cook immediately or there is a salmonella risk.

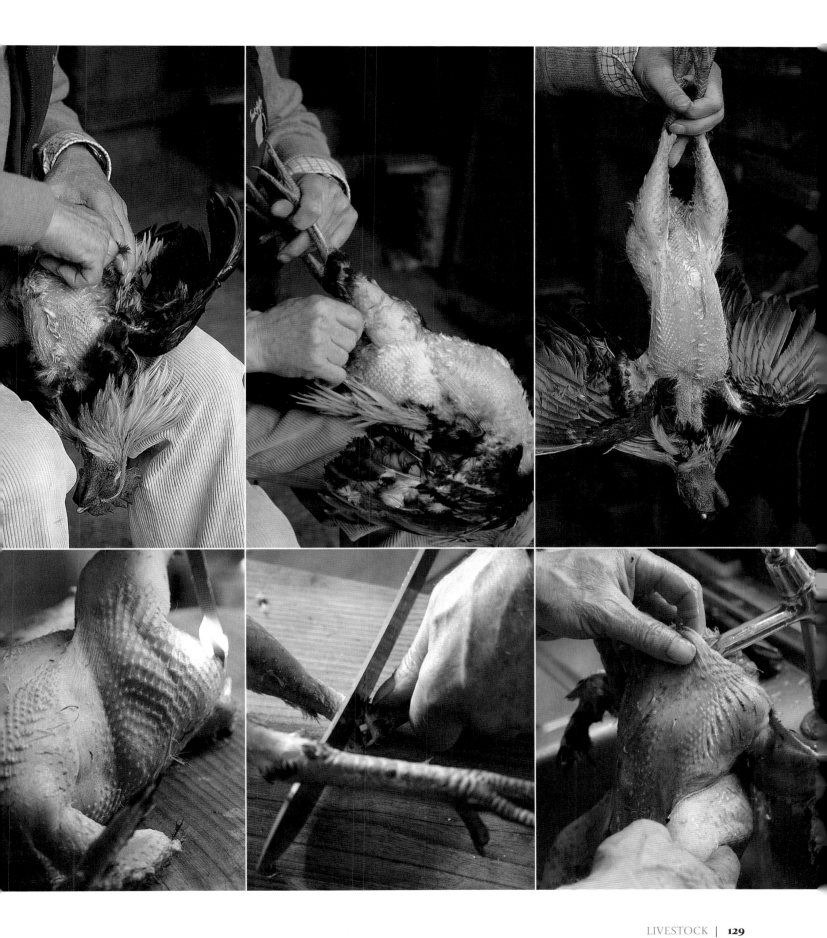

beekeeping

The great thing about starting out as a beekeeper, as I discovered years ago, is that there is no shortage of enthusiastic, experienced people willing to share their knowledge. Keeping bees is one of the most fascinating and rewarding forms of husbandry. Your bees will provide you with a much healthier alternative to sugar for all your sweetening, as well as a certain amount of wax. Until sugar cane started to come into Europe in the late sixteenth century, honey was the only means of sweetening food and, for most rural people, remained the only source of sugar for many centuries thereafter. Virtually every family, both rural and urban, kept bees in conical straw bee-skeps and the beeswax, for which there were hundreds of different uses, was of equal value to the honey.

the modern hive

A modern hive has a shallow wooden base to raise it off the ground, an alighting board for the bees to land on and above, a wooden box called the brood chamber with a little entry port. The brood chamber is filled with brood frames – sheets of wax commercially embossed by a stamping machine to replicate the pattern made by comb-making bees and set in wooden frames. They are known as 'foundation'. They hang vertically inside the brood box where the queen and her grubs live, with just enough space for the bees to move between them. On top of the brood chamber is a metal sheet with holes in it big enough for the worker bees to get through, but not the queen – this is called the 'queen-excluder-sheet'. A shallower

box, known as a 'super' is placed above the brood box and is similarly filled with sheets of foundation wax hanging inside wooden frames. Worker bees build up the patterning embossed in the wax to store the honey. Depending on the weather or

a revolution in beekeeping

By the middle of the nineteenth century, agricultural expansion had removed huge areas of natural habitat and the bee population dropped. The old, low-maintenance straw bee skeps that were used for centuries tended to be wasteful and many bee broods were lost when the honey and wax were extracted. Beekeeping needed to modernize as there was now less demand for wax and consumers wanted jars of clean, clear honey. In 1851, an American called Langstroth revolutionized beekeeping. He invented a hive with a lower chamber in which the queen lived with her brood, but which allowed the workers access to an upper chamber where they stored the honey. This enabled beekeepers to remove combs as they filled up, without disturbing the queen.

how frequently you require honey, there may be two or three of these supers above the brood box. On top of these is the roof, which has an exit hole which allows the workers out, but not in. This facilitates a more efficient through-put, with bees arriving at the bottom of the hive and leaving at the top, thus avoiding delivery jams and minimizing mid-air collisions.

getting started

To get started on beekeeping, you should contact your local beekeeper's group via your National Beekeepers' Association. They will put you in touch with someone who will be prepared to sell a nucleus stock of worker bees and their queen, as well as a brood box and a super. You should buy these early in the spring and should site them on a south-facing, level piece of clear ground, with a water source not far away. The other essentials you will need are a protective white suit, a bee veil and hat, sting-proof gloves and a smoker, all of which you can obtain from a specialist supplier.

handling the bees

Having established your hive, let the bees get to know you. Visit them as often as you can, wearing protective clothing, with your trousers over wellington boots and tied at the ankle – bees crawl about on the ground near the hive. Always handle a hive in the early evening when bees are sleepy, never during the day when they are busy and, in beekeepers' parlance, 'hot'.

On some of your early visits, get acquainted with the workings of the hive. Using the smoker, filled with dried leaves, straw or hay for fuel, puff a little smoke into the hive entrance. This will draw bees from the super down into the brood chamber. Lift off the super and lid all in one and place it on the ground. Pop a 'clearer-board' in place on the queen-excluder sheet, then reposition the super. As this is only an exercise for removing honey-filled frames, dismantle the super and lid again, remove the clearer-board and leave the hive as you found it.

To take off the honey, repeat the exercise with the smoker and put a clearer-board in position. The next evening remove the lid and lift off the super. Remove the clearer-board, replace the lid and take the super, filled with frames, home.

As summer progresses and the frames start to fill, you may need to add one or two more supers. If you do not do this, the bees will run out of space and might swarm, leaving you with only about a third of your bees and without a queen.

extracting the honey

To do this, you will have to borrow or buy a honey extractor, which works by centrifugal force. Lift out the honey-filled frames from the super. Each frame has two honey-filled sides. Cut off and carefully save the capping on one side using a long-bladed knife heated in boiling water. Hang the frame inside the extractor, which will hold four frames. When all four are in place secure the lid and rotate the handle vigorously. Once the honey is extracted from one side, take out the frames, remove and save the caps from the other side and replace the frames in the extractor. The honey will spin out and run down the walls, to be drawn off into a jug via a tap at the bottom, before being strained through muslin into jars. The empty frames must be taken back to the hive so the worker bees can start filling them again.

how much honey will I get?

In a decent summer one hive should provide you with about 40 kg of delicious honey. This is about half your bees' output; the remainder must be left for their winter food. If you live not far from heather moorland, taking the hives up in late summer will give you a few kilos of exquisite heather honey. This will be comb honey as it is too thick to extract. The little pieces of wax cappings that you will get will, in time, become a quantity that can be made into the finest furniture polish (see below) or beeswax candles (see page 147).

beeswax

Cappings cut from the frames will eventually accumulate into a sticky mixture of honey and wax. This can be cleaned by gently heating it, then pouring the honey off through muslin and putting the pure beeswax into a container. You can then use this to make beeswax polish.

beeswax polish

The simplest, best and most natural form of beeswax polish is made by putting equal quantities of beeswax shavings and pure turpentine in a jar, with the lid on to avoid evaporation, and placing it in hot sunshine until the two emulsify. Alternatively, gently warm the beeswax until it melts at about 48°C. Pour in the turpentine, stir well and allow to set.

rabbit and fish farming

rabbits

With so many wild rabbits about it seems unnecessary to keep rabbits commercially but I have to accept that they are an ideal food source for the home producer and have an entirely different flavour – which some people may prefer – to their wild cousins.

The Normans started commercial rabbit farming in Britain in the eleventh century, establishing vast warrens anywhere there was sandy soil, but particularly in the East Anglian Brecklands. The town of Brandon in Suffolk was built on the lucrative trade in rabbit furs and meat. The last commercial warren was at Lakenheath.

A couple of medium-breed does and a buck are a good number to start with and I recommend New Zealand Whites, Californians or All Greys. These are all hardy rabbits, easy to look after and will produce a 4.5 kg carcass at between eight and ten weeks. To keep this number of bunnies and breed from them you will need an area of about five square metres – a piece of rough ground with a good mix of weeds, grass and some shelter – fenced off with small-gauge rabbit wire dug in 15cm deep, to stop the rabbits from digging themselves out. You will also need a small handling pen in one corner, plus a metre-square wooden-floored hutch for them to sleep in and a couple of 2-metre-long arks or runs with a nesting box at one end. The arks can be inside the fenced area if there is

sufficient grass. They should have rabbit netting on the bottom and should be capable of being moved. You will also require galvanized water drinkers.

breeding

Buy your rabbits in the spring at six months old, leave them shut in the hutch for four days with plenty of water and green food or rabbit pellets to acclimatize. Let them out and watch them carefully as they will mate fairly soon. The gestation period is thirty days. After three weeks, move the does into the arks to kindle or give birth. Pregnant does need 125g of rabbit pellets for the last ten days of pregnancy but feed them ad lib during the winter. The buck now inhabits the hutch on his own. Move the arks as new grass is required.

A doe will comfortably rear between seven and ten kinder (babies). If there are more, the excess should be removed and killed. Three weeks after they have kindled, remove the arks so that they can all run about together. The young will be ready to eat at eight weeks. To kill, skin and joint a rabbit see pages 88–90.

The does will come in season again seventeen days after the young have been taken off them and the process then starts again. They will breed three and possibly four times a year. In many parts of the world winters are so mild that wild rabbits seem to breed all year round. At some stage you may need to consider expanding your enterprise or retaining some young does to breed from. They start breeding at sixteen weeks.

rabbit hotpot

(SERVES 4–6)

This is a good warming dish made with belly pork. Now that you have turned off your central heating you will need dishes like this to keep you warm. The dish is of French origin and calls for Dijon mustard but I prefer the strength of English mustard. The choice is yours.

450g skinned belly of pork, sliced, skin reserved
2 carrots, diced
2 onions, finely chopped
1 clove garlic, crushed
1 tbsp each parsley and thyme, chopped
1 bay leaf
2 jointed rabbits
150ml dry white wine or dry cider
150ml stock
1 tbsp white wine vinegar
4 egg yolks
300ml double cream
1 dessertspoon made mustard
salt and pepper

Arrange half the pork on the bottom of a large ovenproof dish. Add half the vegetables and the garlic and sprinkle with herbs. Season and add the bay leaf. Lay the rabbit joints on top of this and add the remaining pork and vegetables. Lay the pork skin on top. Pour on wine or cider, stock and vinegar. Cover and cook at Gas Mark 4/180°C/350°F for 2¹/₂–3 hours.

Remove and discard the pork skin. Remove the rabbit joints to a dish and strain the cooking liquid. Remove any excess fat and reduce the cooking liquid by one-third.

Beat the egg yolks with the cream and mustard and add to the sauce. Heat to thicken but do not boil. Pour the sauce over the rabbit joints.

fish

If you have running water on your holding – and it is surprising how little you need – you could create a mini fish farm. Fish farming goes back centuries; the Chinese had been at it for several thousand years before the Normans brought it to Britain as part of their culture of the living larder. The 'stew pond' was essential to every medieval castle, manor house and monastery, with the monastic houses specializing in carp husbandry. Carp are hardy, prolific and fertile and there was fierce competition among the monasteries in the breeding of bigger and better strains. Stew ponds remained in use until well into the nineteenth century, when railways made sea fish readily available.

making a fish pond

A pond is a lovely thing to have and creates a whole new bio-diversity. Apart from your fish, there will be dragonflies and clear wings, newts and frogs and, in the winter, mallard and teal may come there to feed.

You need to give some careful thought to the size of your pond and how you manage it. Cost is largely determined by the soil type in your area: sandy soil will require waterproofing by plastic sheeting whereas with clay you can probably avoid that expense. I made a pond a couple years ago that was about fifteen metres square, with a two-metre earth dam. It was rectangular in shape as this helps improve water circulation which, in turn, aids the growth of nutrient life. I then had a happy time planting willows (*Salix*), water iris (*Iris laevigata*), flowering rushes (*Butomus umbellatus*) and greater reed mace (*Typha latifolia*), as well as bog bean (*Menyanthes trifoliata*), bog myrtle (*Myrica gale*) – to keep the midges away – and Canadian pondweed (*Epodea canadensis*), which fish love. Brandy bottle (*Nuphar lutea*), whose flowers have a brandy-like scent and fringe lilies (*Thysanotus tuberosus*) were other favourites. This is a manageable size of pond for carp, rainbow, brown trout or sturgeon. If you intend to use the pond for a regular supply of fish, it would be as well to have a sluice built into the dam wall so the pond can be emptied periodically, enabling you to check your fish stocks and clear excess weed.

A pond this size could be stocked with about 60 juvenile 500g fish, which would put on 500g a year. If you feed them every day at the same place, they can easily be caught in a net at feeding time or you can have a bit of fun with a rod and line. Nicholas Cox, writing in 1679, recommended a bait made from bean flower, cat's flesh and honey for carp. Colin Willock, in his *New ABC of Fishing*, suggests worms or bread.

eels

There is every chance that you might get an unexpected bonus in the form of eels. They are delicious, highly underrated and plentiful. There are several ways of catching them. The first is to use a rod, stout line and a fine hook, baited with fish, meat or offal. Or you can trap them in a baited pot like a lobster pot, but with a very fine nylon mesh covering to stop them wriggling through. Another method is 'dabbing' – gathering together twenty or so earthworms and weaving them into a ball with strong woollen yarn attached to a piece of string. You should end up with a tangle of worms, string and woollen yarn. Tie this onto another piece of string fastened to a stick and 'dab'. Eels have inward-pointing teeth like a snake, which become tangled with the string and wool. This method of catching eels is very popular in the West Country of England. Another couple of techniques, which also take advantage of the angle of an eel's teeth, is to make a small bag out of a jute sack, fill it with fresh chicken guts, tie the neck firmly with strong string and chuck it out into a pond on the end of a piece of rope. The eels get caught when they bite into the sack. Or, make a big ball of cotton wool. Tie it to a stick and soak it in fish essence, obtainable from a tackle shop, then dab using this.

Like all fish, eels should be killed as soon as they are landed with a sharp blow to the head using a short weighted stick, known as a 'priest'.

stuffed trout

(SERVES 8)

I thought I would never do anything to brown trout but eat it plain until I worked for my dear boss Rebeka Hardy. Her husband Lawrence and their son Allen caught so many brown trout that one needed to ring the changes. Rainbow trout, which isn't so tasty, should usually be stuffed.

8 trout, each 175g
225g veal forcemeat, or the same weight of breadcrumbs mixed with herbs and
75g butter
115g butter
1 tbsp flour
150ml white wine
1 tbsp capers
1 tsp lemon juice
salt and pepper

Stuff the trout with the forcemeat or herbs and breadcrumbs and sew up or close with skewers. Place the fish in a buttered ovenproof dish, season and dab on 85g butter. Cover and cook at Gas Mark 4/180°C/350°F for 30 minutes, basting from time to time. Remove trout to a serving dish, reserving the cooking liquid. Melt the remaining butter and make a roux with the flour. Gradually stir in the strained cooking liquid and the white wine. Stir until it just comes to the boil and add the capers and lemon juice, then season. Simmer to cook the flour for 2–3 minutes and serve with the trout.

dogs and cats

dogs

I was brought up to believe that one should never have a dog unless it was going to be used, as a result of which I have owned many sheep dogs and terriers over the years and the occasional gun dog. Whatever breed you decide to have, remember that dog ownership is a big responsibility, particularly in Britain where, since November 2004, a series of nonsensical laws were passed through parliament, making it illegal for a dog to chase mice, hares, deer, foxes and squirrels, but not rats or rabbits. Anyone now wishing to own a dog should familiarize themselves with dog law and check what a dog might unwittingly do to criminalize its owner.

Before buying any dog you need to be aware of the downsides of each sex. Bitches can be a bore when they are on heat as they have to be shut up and they are messy around the house. They lose some of their working instinct if they are spayed. Dogs on the other hand are a nightmare if they take off whenever they scent a bitch on heat, though it is rather the luck of the draw. I have had some dogs that never left and others that could scent a bitch from ten kilometres away.

Once you have made a decision, the options are to buy a dog that has already been broken or an eight-week old puppy, and learn how to train it. Your local agricultural college should be able to advise on this. If you have chosen a Beardie (see opposite), he should learn obedience in his first year but will not begin to work until he is a year old –

'The old adage "familiarity breeds contempt" is no truer than when applied to dogs.'

although he will probably start rounding up the ducks and chickens at three months, which should be encouraged.

Remember that this is a working dog and a dog will only work for you if he believes you are a superior sort of dog and the leader of the pack. Beware of making him into too much of a pet. A dog should earn your affection and the old adage 'familiarity breeds contempt' is no truer than when applied to dogs.

caring for your dog

Beardies have a thick coat which needs to be trimmed several times a year, but even so, they will get pretty mucky. They should have a good straw-filled bed clear of the ground, in a dry, draught-free place or a purpose-built kennel with a run. My sheepdogs are fed 350g of a working sheepdog compound mix containing vitamins, minerals, flaked maize, dried meat extract and dried vegetables.

Dogs must be inoculated when they are puppies against the major canine diseases – distemper, provirus, leptospirosis, canine hepatitis and kennel cough. Without documentation to prove that they have had all the essential inoculations, no responsible boarding kennel will accept your dog should you wish to go away. A dog should be wormed every three months in addition to which all the usual signs of animal ill-health should be looked out for and veterinary advice sought if necessary. Look after your dog well and it will give you many years of loyal service.

cats

The traditional farmyard moggy was an extremely useful creature who lived in the farm buildings, well away from the farmhouse. This semi-wild cat was never fed once it was out of the kitten stage and was expected to live off the mice and rats it killed round the farm buildings. There are still cats doing sterling work in farm buildings across Britain, Europe, North America, Australia and New Zealand.

If you must have a cat, make sure it is spayed if it is a female or neutered if it is a Tom (Toms stink and get smellier as they become older), otherwise you will have kittens everywhere. If you provide a kitten with a warm box in an outbuilding and three meals with plenty of milk, it soon accepts its surroundings as home and won't come into the house unless encouraged to do so.

A non-pedigree kitten is easier to acquire than a common cold. Your local paper will be full of adverts for kittens being offered to good homes. Be sure to have the little creature inoculated against feline enteritis and cat flu.

unwanted visitors

ants

● The bruised leaves of sage, mint, pennyroyal or thyme will drive ants away if they have invaded a larder or dry foods cupboard, these plants grown by doorways will stop them entering a house.

● I hate destroying ant nests, but if you have to, boil up any of the above, make an opening and flood the nest with the liquid. Alternatively, mix a strong solution of alum or even of ordinary salt and pour into the nest.

● Paint a ring of eucalyptus oil or pure turpentine round the base of fruit trees to keep ants away.

badgers

In Britain badgers have gone from being one of our best-loved woodland animals to being a serious pest species. Increasing badger numbers have led to a shortage of their natural food sources – slugs, amphibians, baby rabbits and other small surface-dwellers, like hedgehogs, which have completely disappeared in some areas. Badgers here are now a liability to small livestock, particularly fowl and lambs, to say nothing of the thousands of flowerbeds that they dig up nightly in their search for bulbs.

● A determined badger will get through any fence, electrified or not and virtually nothing will deter them. Not long ago, when one broke into my chicken house, I tried putting heaps of dried powdered wormwood mixed with rue and cayenne pepper where a run passed under the bottom wire of a fence. The theory was that the poor old badger would get a face-full and would totter off sneezing. It worked for a night or two, but then they came in from another direction.

birds

● The only effective way of keeping birds from damaging seed beds, emerging plants and small fruit trees is to cover them with fine netting. I have not found any bird scare that works for any length of time.

cockroaches

I once had a job loading sheep carcasses into the cold-storage holds of ships in the Auckland docks and there were enormous cockroaches scuttling about in the freezers. I have never understood how they survived the sub-zero temperatures but it gives an indication of how difficult they are to get rid of. Even our ancestors, who had so much knowledge at their fingertips, relied on biological control. Until the beginning of the twentieth century, there was a weekly trade in caged live hedgehogs at London's Leadenhall Market. The hedgehogs were put down in cellars and dry-food stores and lived off the cockroaches there.

● There are a number of sugar-based herbal recipes for killing cockroaches – recipes using powdered dried black (*Tamus communis*) and white bryony (*Bryonia dioica*) and henbane (*Hyoscyamus niger*) are examples, but these are poisonous and likely to be eaten by the family pet.

● Fresh leaves of Christmas rose (*Helleborus niger*) or black horehound (*Ballota nigra*), scattered on the floor of a larder are very effective; their drastic purgative and narcotic properties usually have the desired effect.

● Mullein (*Verbascum*) leaves are another possibility. The powdery down covering the leaves is said to ball in their throats and choke them.

deer

These are becoming an urban pest, particularly in Britain and parts of North America. There are more deer in the USA now than there were when the Pilgrim Fathers arrived. Roe deer and muntjac regularly predate on gardens in the suburbs of London and other major UK cities. If you live in an urban area, the council has an obligation to deal with pest species, but this is not always fulfilled.

● To keep deer out, one option is deer fencing.

● Deer repellents are another option. A mixture of olives, cloves, oil and lemongrass, can be effective.

● Planting shrubs and flowers that are distasteful to deer is another possibility. Rosemary, sage, tulips, lupins, buddleia, daffodils and Siberian squill (*Scilla siberica*) are a few examples.

● Medieval flowerbeds and vegetable gardens had low box hedging planted around them which deer found visually confusing.

- If you live in a rural area and have the appropriate firearm certificate, you can sit up and wait for the deer with a rifle at dawn and dusk, when they come out to feed. If you do not have a firearm certificate, I am sure a neighbour will put you in touch with someone responsible who does.

fleas

The general standard of hygiene nowadays has reduced the risk of human fleas, but you can never be too careful.

- In medieval households, alder (*Alnus glutinosa*) leaves, which have a clammy texture, were spread among rushes on the floor in spring to catch fleas.

- Bunches of fleabane (*Pulicaria dysenterica*), hung up in the corner of a room or the smoke from burning dried leaves were also used to repel fleas, as were bunches of wormwood (*Artemesia vulgaris*), rue, pennyroyal (*Mentha pulegium*) and fennel – dry or fresh – as well as borax and oil of turpentine.

- To prevent dogs from getting fleas wash them in infusions of rue, wormwood or walnut leaves.

- Several hill shepherds I have known worm their sheepdogs by giving them a whole unpeeled clove of garlic. They claim that this, done often enough, also keeps their sheepdogs free of fleas and, more importantly, ticks.

flies

● Bruised elder (*Sambucus nigra*) leaves, strategically placed around the house in bowls will deter flies.

● A border of rue (*Ruta graveolens*) or basil planted under a kitchen window helps keep flies away from food.

foxes

Foxes are as destructive as badgers, are considered vermin and are becoming, like coyotes in some parts of America, an urban pest. Until recently, the fox population was controlled by foxhound packs, as they are in America, Australia, Ireland and large parts of Europe. Of the available options for control, this is recognized as the most humane. In Britain foxes may be shot at, snared and poisoned or driven from cover with no more than two dogs in England and more than two dogs in Scotland. This enables hunts to continue providing a historic service to farmers and the rural population, so if you are having trouble with foxes, contact your local hunt kennels.

In America coyotes and foxes are the principal pest to small livestock. Australia has its dingos, foxes and feral pigs, while in New Zealand, feral pigs are the worst offenders. All these are disposed of by whatever means is most suitable to the species and location.

mice

● There is nothing better than a good cat for mousing, but they tend to be selective. Some days they might feel in the mood for a mouse while on others, mice are completely ignored in favour of a small bird.

● A terrier is a useful deterrent, but uniquely to Britain, it is illegal for a dog to chase a mouse.

- Another alternative mouse deterrent is to use fresh leaves of dwarf elder (*Sambucus ebulus*) or dried wormwood (*Artemesia absinthium*) or rue (*Ruta graveolens*). Crumble the leaves until you have a powder, push as much into the mouse hole as possible and blow it in with a set of bellows or a tube made from a rolled-up newspaper. Be generous.

- I have achieved astonishing results using the same technique with cayenne pepper.

moles

Having been a hill farmer all my life, I have never regarded a mole as an agricultural pest in the way that an arable farmer would. In fact 'nature's drainage expert' was a welcome sight on damp moorland and a friend of mine used to buy live moles that he put down on damp areas in the hope that water would drain away into the mole runs. If a mole appears, I suggest trying to drive him away rather than killing him. There are a number of ways this can be achieved.

- Moles have an acute sense of smell so anything with a powerful smell, like oil of eucalyptus, poured into a run will see them off.

- They rely on their whiskers to pick up vibrations of worm movement so the vibration transmitted from a child's windmill stuck in the ground above a run can be enough to drive them away. When I was a child, an old man used to arrive on a motorcycle, lower the tyre pressure, ride onto the lawns, stick a pipe connected to his exhaust into a mole run and sit there revving the engine. It was highly effective.

moths

Nothing is more irritating and destructive than the common clothes moth, which gets into clothes cupboards and feasts on anything woollen.

- We always put little muslin bags filled with rosemary, sage, lavender and a pinch of orris root, in all the wardrobe drawers and hang bunches of thyme or rosemary clothes cupboards

- Leaves of wormwood (*Artemesia absinthium*) and southernwood (*Artemisia abrotanum*) are other good moth-repellants.

- Clothes that moths have just begun feeding on can be saved by putting them in the deep freeze for a few hours. This kills both the moths and their eggs.

rats

If you have livestock, rats are an inevitability. As I have always had dogs around the place, I have never risked using poison but have always relied on good ratting terriers to keep rats down.

- Rats live in dread of ferrets and a Jill (female), small enough to enter a rat hole, will either kill the rats underground or bolt them into the open to a terrier. A ratting ferret will need careful looking after and any scratches or nips must immediately be disinfected as a rat bite will nearly always turn infectious. Remember that a ratting ferret is no use for rabbiting as they kill underground, rather than bolting the rabbits out.

- An alternative to a ratting ferret, but not nearly as effective, is the live trap. This is an oblong cage with a hinged trapdoor, connected to a balance plate to which bait is fixed. When a rat mounts the plate to eat the bait – strong cheese or fish such as kippers – the trapdoor closes. The rat can then be humanely dispatched.

wasps

- The simplest way to get rid of wasps is to stop them coming into the house in the first place. Make a solution of wasp sugar, by boiling 1 kg of Barbados sugar in 600ml of brown ale. As soon as the mixture comes to the boil, add $1/2$ kg of black treacle. Simmer for five minutes and decant whilst still warm into a tin. Put dollops of it in dishes slightly away from open windows.

- Pure turpentine or oil of eucalyptus mixed with glycerine and poured into the nest will destroy it.

weasels and stoats

Both these beautiful little creatures are terrible egg thieves and gamekeepers wage permanent war on them. I find them utterly enchanting and a constant source of fascination. They are totally devoid of fear and think nothing of attacking animals many times their size. A family of stoats or weasels will clear a farmyard of rats quicker and more effectively than anything else, but they will extract a high payment in eggs, chicks and sometimes hens. A stoat will kill just for fun and can play havoc in a hen house.

- Keeping a dog around the place will deter weasels and stoats from breeding nearby.

- A cage trap as used for rats and baited with fish or fresh rabbit liver is the only real recourse against weasels and stoats.

the green you

making and creating

I don't know why it is that I always feel that other people can create things but that I can't. I imagine it's simpler living in remote tribes or communities where one is obliged to have a go or else you have to do without. I suppose it is fear of failure in an age where political correctness is trying to erase the word 'failure' from the language. It's OK to fail isn't it, but only if you've tried? What is so bizarre is that when one does try, one rarely falls short. Obviously some people do things better than others but if it gives you pleasure, then so what? As my grandmother used to say, 'patience and perseverance made a bishop of his reverence!' So don't say you can't make candles or soap or that you can't spin or weave until you've tried it. As for mending, well, if you're following greener principles and not throwing everything away, then you have no option but to make do and mend. After all, the only way to get rid of shopping malls and supermarkets with their food miles is for people not to shop in those places and the way to cure this mercenary mercantile world is to make your own things.

candle making

Lest you should think that candle making is just a hippy thing to do, you should know that the world's fifth largest yacht is owned by a candle maker and is called 'Paraffin'. As a teenager this yacht-owner made his first candle for his mother. It was spotted by a neighbour. The boy sold the candle to the neighbour and bought enough material to make two more candles. He gave one to his mother, sold the second one and never looked back.

Older candles have an interesting history. Primitive people rose with the sun and went to bed with it or used the light of the fire for simple activities (sex and dancing spring to mind!) Once the need for extra light arose – for example for cave painting – simple artificial light evolved. The most primitive form of light was a hollow stone filled with animal fat into which a wick was inserted. Examples of these early lights, some made out of quartz or lapiz and some from carved soapstone, have been found in many prehistoric digs.

The first form of advanced lighting was the rush light, which people probably developed when they learned skills such as sewing and weaving and needed light to work by for longer periods.

candles – the next step

From the rush light it was a short step to making candles with cotton or linen wicks. These however needed constant trimming as the tallow burnt away faster than the wick. Then someone discovered that if you braided your cotton wick, it bent over as the candle melted down and was consumed in the flame. All modern candles have braided wicks.

The finest candles are made from beeswax. These were the preserve of the church and the very rich. They smell beautiful, unlike tallow, and give a good clear light. The principle for making them is the same.

dipping candles

This is the traditional way of making candles and I find that dipped candles burn better than moulded ones. Melt your beeswax in a saucepan over a very low heat. Loop a length of wick around a piece of dowelling and support the dowelling across the back of two kitchen chairs. The wick will hang down, giving you two lengths to dip. Make sure each length is the same. Dip the wick in the wax for a minute, then remove it and leave it to dry for a few minutes, until the wax hardens. Repeat until the candles are the desired thickness. Leave them until completely hardened before using.

moulding candles

If you prefer, you can use candle moulds. Almost any shape container will do, but you may want to go down the bought-mould route. Such a mould has a depression in the base, which gives you the point of the finished candle.

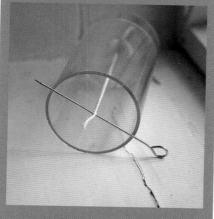

Thread your wick through the hole in the depression in the bottom of the mould and attach it on the outside of the base of the mould with a piece of mastic. Hold the wick taut with a skewer across the top of the mould.

Fill the mould with wax. As the wax dries it shrinks and you can pull the finished candle clear.

making a wick

Hammer a nail into a small board, measure off the length of candle you want, marking the board if you wish to ensure the right length. Attach three strands of cotton to the nail and plait it.

making a rush light

Take a rush and peel off the outside skin, leaving a strip of peel down one side to strengthen it. The pith provides a good wick which you then dip into melted tallow, that is to say, animal fat. When the tallow cools you have a rush light. A 40-cm light will burn for half an hour and two or three of them give enough light to read or sew by. They are smoky and smelly but faute de mieux. Mutton tallow makes the best rush lights, which suited the English, a nation whose economy was based on sheep.

'The finest candles are made from beeswax. These were the preserve of the church and the very rich.'

lye and soap making

As a child I used to visit the west of Ireland and I remember the strong smell of the cottagers making lye, an alkaline solution used for the washing of clothes and particularly for removing grease and heavy dirt from linen. Lye is made by straining water through wood ash or bracken ash and was one of the main uses for cut bracken.

lye

Drill holes in half a wooden barrel and place it on top of a galvanized bucket. Put a layer of gravel in the bottom of the barrel to strain the lye and cover with a cotton or linen cloth. Half-fill the barrel with wood ash from hardwood or the ash from burnt bracken. Pour on water and leave it to drain through to the bucket – it takes a surprisingly long time.

Now boil down the lye until the liquid is strong enough to float an egg (see box below). In Ireland you could buy blocks of bracken potash which I was told would keep for twenty years.

checking the strength of a saturated solution

If you are ever making a saturated solution of brine, in other words, one that is strong enough to float an egg, take a short stick and weight one end. Drop this into the brine and the stick will stand up straight. At the point where the stick emerges from the water, make a notch. You can then use the same stick to check the strength of your lye solution. When the lye is the correct strength, the notch will be level with the top of the liquid. This stick will save you from having to float an egg on your brine or in your lye.

special precautions

Take care with lye; it can give you a really nasty burn. You must handle it especially carefully if you are using it for washing fabric. Once the fat is added to make soap, it stops being caustic.

soap

Until the second half of the nineteenth century soap was a luxury because it was made with fat and fat was needed for the making of candles. Indeed, soap was quite heavily taxed to deter people from using too much of it. Instead, sharp sand and fuller's earth were used for washing such clothes as were washed.

When you consider that Elizabeth I was thought eccentric by her contemporaries of the sixteenth century because she bathed once a month, you can see that there wasn't much demand for soap. It wasn't until the 1860s that commercial soap became readily available.

making soap

For this it is necessary to ensure that your lye is the correct concentration. Pour the lye into an old pan. For every 500ml of lye add 900g of melted clean beef or mutton dripping, or lard or vegetable oil. Believe me, the animal fat makes better soap. When you have asked yourself why cosmetic companies buy the fat that drips off doner kebabs you will know that I am correct. Boil this solution together for about three hours. As the mixture starts to cool, stir in 450g salt. This will fall to the bottom of the pan but acts to harden the soap. Once the salt has settled, pour the liquid soap into wooden moulds lined with a damp cloth, leaving the salt behind in the pan.

scenting and colouring

At this stage, but before you pour the soap into the moulds, you can mix in herbs for scenting – lavender flowers, rosemary and lemon balm are all good. If you have fresh herbs, shred them, otherwise use a distillation of the oil or an aromatherapy oil. If you like you can also add vegetable colouring. The juice of beetroot, carrots and spinach were traditionally used. Don't add anything in alcohol as this will ruin the soap. Leave the soap to set. It will keep well in a cool airy place.

Soap can also be made with caustic soda and there are some herbs that are alkaline enough to replace the lye. In South Africa soap was made with ostrich fat and a member of the buckthorn family called seepbos (soap bush).

bath oils and fragrances

to make a herb bag

One of the easiest ways of transforming a bath into an aromatherapy experience is with a herb bag. Different dried herbs have a different effect. Peppermint, sage, chamomile flowers and rosemary soothe a fevered brow. Others, such as nettle leaves, elder bark, valerian root and comfrey relieve muscle tension. Oatmeal or bran can be added to the bag to soften the water.

Make a 12 x 8cm bag out of cheesecloth and fill it with dried herbs of your choice. You can close the bag with either a drawstring round the top or simply by tying it round the opening with a piece of string. Ensure that the string is long enough so that when it is attached to the hot tap, it dangles in the water flow. In that way, the scent of the herbs is released as the water fills the bath.

The use of flower petals, aromatic herbs and bark as scents and fragrances to sweeten bath water is as old as civilization. The knowledge of how to prepare them moved westward from China about five thousand years ago and the first documentation of their use is from Babylon, in 2000 BC. These skills were acquired and improved upon by the Egyptians and Greeks and reached perfection with the Romans, who loved strong, sweet-smelling scents.

flower-scented bath oil

Take two handfuls of flower petals and bruise gently between your hands to release the scent. Place in a wide-necked container such as a 500ml kilner jar, and cover with 350ml sunflower oil. Seal and place in sunlight for at least three weeks, shaking the jar daily. In the absence of sunlight, an airing cupboard will do. Strain through muslin, making sure to squeeze out all the oil. Repeat, adding another two handfuls of petals. The more often you add petals and the longer you leave it, the more intense the scent will become. When you are ready to use it, mix three parts of glycerine to one part of scented oil to your bath water.

herb and fruit-scented bath oil

The leaves of rosemary, lavender, chamomile, sage, fennel, yarrow, peppermint, eau-de-cologne mint, elder, nettle, lovage, marigold, raspberry and blackcurrant are other wonderful additions to your bath oil. The variety and possible permutations are endless. Follow the instructions as for the flower-scented bath oil, but crush the leaves with a rolling pin or put them through a mincer. For lemon or orange bath oil, remove the zest of the fruit using a sharp knife, making sure you do not include any of the pith. Twist the peel to release the oils as you put it in the kilner jar with the oil, then follow the instructions as before.

sweet waters

Sweet waters are a very ancient method of capturing the scent of flowers and herbs. In their simplest form sweet waters are basically the petals or leaves of flowers, herbs and spices infused and allowed to cool in boiling water. The scent only lasts a week or two, but whilst it does, sweet waters make a refreshing hand or face wash and can be added to the bath. Fill a litre jar with rose petals or any other strong-scented fresh or dried flower, herb or spice. You could try lavender, rosemary, lovage, a handful of crushed cloves – the options to experiment are limitless. Cover with boiling water, strain when cool and add a couple tablespoons of surgical spirit, which helps to hold the scent.

scented verjuice

Verjuice is similar to wine vinegar and in the Middle Ages, scented verjuice became popular. This precursor to eau-de-cologne is wonderfully refreshing on a hot day. I remember elderly ladies dabbing themselves with it through the summer when I was a child. Add 500ml of the best white wine vinegar to the same amount of water and heat until nearly boiling. Remove from the heat and add a couple of handfuls of dried crushed herbs or flowers – lavender, violets, rosemary, lemon balm flowers – or the zest of lemons or oranges. Leave overnight and strain through muslin. Add more herbs or flowers and repeat the process if you want a stronger scent. Witch hazel or chemical alcohol, which in some countries requires a prescription to purchase, may be used instead of vinegar.

organic cleaning materials

Sir Humphrey Davy invented sodium hydroxide in 1807 and borax was discovered in Death Valley, Alaska, during the 1880 gold rush. Both of these discoveries revolutionized kitchen cleaning. Until then washing-up was more about hot water, elbow grease and abrasive materials like sand, ash, chalk and salt. Soap and the use of leaves and roots of the soapwort plant were reserved for cleaning the body and textiles.

Pewter plates and cast-iron pots and pans were scrubbed with the plant, horsetail, (*Equisetum*) or scoured with fine sand, either 'Calais' sand or 'Silver' sand from Galloway in Ireland. With the arrival of stoneware, china, porcelain and copper, the acidic properties of vinegar – nature's marvel – verjuice (see page 151) and rhubarb were much appreciated for breaking down grease and giving a shine. China and porcelain dishes, for example, were cleaned by rubbing off detritus with a wet cloth and rinsing them in water to which a little white wine vinegar had been added. Nowadays lemon juice makes a pleasant alternative.

traditional cleaning techniques

● For copper pots and pans, wash, dry, then rub with lemon, vinegar or rhubarb leaves. Allow to stand for an hour then polish with a clean cloth.

● For stainless steel or aluminium, rub with rhubarb leaves, with the cut ends of rhubarb stalks or with half a lemon to remove stains. For persistent marks, keep dipping the lemon in salt.

● For wooden chopping boards, rub vigorously with a cut lemon to remove the smell left by chopping garlic, onions, fish or meat.

● Silverware should be washed after use in very hot water, dried with a soft cloth and wrapped in any non-woollen cloth (wool absorbs damp in the atmosphere).

● To clean tarnished silver, rub with wet salt or a paste of distilled water and powdered chalk.

● Only the blades of bone-handled cutlery should ever be washed otherwise the shank will rust through. Stand them upright in a jug full of boiling water, dry then wipe the blades over with olive oil.

● If your cutlery has old-fashioned stainless-steel blades and they become dull, rub them over with half a lemon dipped in salt.

● Before commercial oven cleaners appeared on the market, people cleaned their ovens much more frequently using a paste of salt and water or salt and vinegar if the oven was very greasy.

● Lemon juice or white vinegar will remove most stain and water marks from baths, basins and the lavatory. Rub vinegar on with a cloth or use a cut lemon directly on the surface. Leave for an hour for the acidic action to work, then wash off.

● For persistent stains on sanitaryware, rub with a cut lemon dipped in salt or mix some pure turpentine spirit with linseed oil and rub on. Leave for a couple of hours and wash off with soapy water.

● For those awkward places around taps that build up with dirt, use a short, stiff 5mm paintbrush to apply lemon juice or vinegar, then scrub with a toothbrush – bristle is more absorbent than nylon.

● What with your home-made bath oils (see pages 150–151), sweet waters (see page 151) and the vinegar, lemon juice and

turpentine, your bathroom should smell beautiful and a hundred times better than if it had been cleaned with commercial detergents. In extremis, don't forget lighting a match in the lavatory pan to get rid of any unsavoury odours.

● To clean wooden floors, sweep away loose dirt and dust, then scatter fine sand and brush off in the direction of the grain.

● When I was at school, the kitchen staff kept all the tea leaves, which the cleaners spread across the floors before sweeping them up.

● For washing floors, white wood ash mixed with warm water was used and then rinsed off.

● Take rugs and carpets out frequently and beat them on the reverse side, then turn them and brush.

● Scatter tea leaves on rugs and carpets then brush off to lift dust and grit. Hard snow would do the same job.

● Clean wallpaper with a loaf of stale bread, moistened on the cut surface or with a lump of flour and water mixed into a thick mass.

● Glass surfaces can be cleaned with an onion cut in half, then washed down with a solution of white wine or cider vinegar, then dried.

● Fresh fruit and red-wine stains may be lifted by the quick application of salt. If some of the stain remains after the salt has been brushed off, dampen with boiling water and repeat. Milk is also a good vehicle for drawing out stains.

● Grease and oil on fabric should be scraped off with a knife, then covered with a paste of Fuller's earth or fine wood ash and allowed to dry. If the marks are still visible, dampen with a mixture of water and vinegar and add ash or dry Fuller's earth.

● Oil and grease on fabric can be shifted by placing brown paper above and below the stain and ironing with a hot iron.

the best silver polisher

My grandparents had a butler called Mr Wild who was the best silver polisher I have ever come across. He polished everything with his forefinger, with his middle finger crossed over the top of it to keep it rigid. He believed that there was an interaction between the heat generated by rubbing and natural human oils in the skin that created the brilliant shine that he achieved. He also kept a tin full of cigar ash that he collected from the ashtrays. This he used with water to make a paste for removing discolorations and for working into ornate pieces with a brush made from badger hair. If a number of spoons became discoloured after boiled eggs had been eaten, he soaked them in sour milk.

spinning

Wool is as varied as the sheep it comes from. It can be coarse, soft, kempy (with hair-like white fibres in it), crimped, wavy or straight, and long- or short-stapled. Kempyness is more usually found in hill breeds where the sheep turn their backs to the prevailing wind and bad weather. Pliny, the Roman writer of the first century A.D., thought that animals became pregnant by turning their backsides to the north wind. Heavens knows how Pliny the Younger got here, but I digress.

preparing a fleece

First unroll your fleece. There are likely to be 'daggings' – areas covered by dung – near the tail which should be discarded along with the weak short wool on the belly and underneck and the coarse fibres at the end of the legs. The very edges of the fleece may have poor-quality wool as well. Discard too any 'twice cuts' – places where the shears have cut twice into the same bit of wool. The fleece over the hind legs is called 'britch'; this may be darker and not good for dying.

There is some argument as to whether to wash the fleece before spinning or not. Since grease is necessary for spinning, some people spin straight from an unwashed fleece. This leads to a very oily thread which, though wonderfully waterproof, can't be dyed, tends to stretch and has an unromantic smell. Others wash the whole fleece in a mild detergent, rinse it, dry it and then oil it before spinning. On the one hand, dirt spun into the thread is harder to wash out afterwards while on the other, washing can risk felting. One neighbour of mine used to keep sheep

simply for felted wool and simply slung the whole lot in the washing machine.

The middle way, and possibly the best, is a cold-water soak. Put 500g of fleece at a time into plain cold water, preferably rainwater. No cleansing agent other than the suint (a body secretion) in the fleece is required. Leave the fleece for at least eight hours and do not change the water even if it looks dirty. Then remove the wool, throw out the dirty water and put the fleece into more clean cold water. Do not pour water onto the fleece as it may

felt. Repeat this process two to three times until the water is clear.

Remove the fleece from the water, place in a cloth bag and spin it dry. An old spin drier is great for this. Otherwise squeeze out the surplus water and hang to dry in a net. Drying can be finished in an airing cupboard or other warm spot. Now the wool will be clean and handleable, and will have enough lanolin in it for spinning. If it is too dry, oil it with a little neat's-foot oil made into an emulsion with an equal quantity of cold water.

combing and carding

The next stage is to card or comb your wool to separate and arrange your woollen fibres and to remove any foreign matter. Carding involves transferring the wool from one carder to another. For a hand-spinning beginner, combing is enough. For this you will need a metal dog comb. Take a bunch, or staple, of wool, and working away from the end that was attached to the sheep, tease the wool until you have a bunch of free, parallel fibres which should slide easily past each other. Any fibres left on the comb can be used to stuff soft toys. Combed staple is also known as drafted thread.

Elongate a little of the combed staple and twist it together in your fingers. As you do this, note how the fibres will no longer slide past each other but become stronger. This is what spinning will achieve; it will draw out the fibres to a suitable thinness then will twist them together evenly to convert them into yarn.

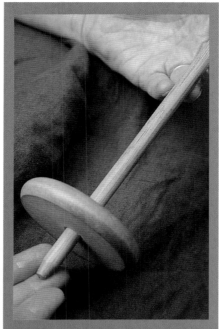

spinning on a drop spindle

Now you need a drop spindle. This is a straight smooth stick about 30cm long with a point at one end and a notch or hook no more than 1cm deep at the other. A pottery disc or whorl with a central hole is threaded onto the stick and is attached rigidly about 5cm from the bottom. You can practise using a garden cane and a potato until you feel confident.

the 'leader'

You start by making a 'leader'. Take a length of yarn, double it exactly, make a snitch knot round the spindle tip and pull tight. Put one hand over the spindle top and twist it clockwise. The two ends of the yarn will readily twist together to make the 'leader'.

starting to spin

At last you are ready to start spinning. Put the spindle on your lap or between your knees. Take a combed staple and partially draw out the fibres from one side. They must always overlap and remain parallel. Lay the drawn-out fibres round the last 5–8cm of the leader.

With your left hand, hold the left-hand end of the combed staple and the leader, and with the right hand, spin the spindle clockwise, allowing it to hang by the leader yarn until the leader twists into the combed staple. If you are left-handed, reverse the hands but still turn the spindle clockwise. Take care not to untwist the thread.

Continue turning the spindle clockwise and joining a new piece of combed staple to the yarn whenever necessary.

winding on

When you have spun about 45cm of yarn you must start winding on. This stops the wool from coming unspun. Ensure the yarn has a slight tendency to kink, ignoring any irregularities at this stage. Never release the left-hand hold on the spun yarn. Slip the original snitch knot from the top of the spindle to the bottom notch. Gather the thread in a figure of eight between thumb and little finger to maintain the tension of the spun thread while you turn the spindle in a clockwise direction. If the thread is underspun, put in more twist using the spindle. A good angle of spin is 45 degrees.

To start spinning again, carry the yarn under the whorl around the bottom of the spindle and up to the tip. Put in your snitch knot under the notch, and pull it tight.

You must leave 10–15cm of spun yarn beyond the loop to start spinning again. Continue as before.

All this may sound rather terrifying but it is all about practice. Failing that, you can always go on a spinning course. I am always overawed when I see the ease with which my dear friend and mentor April O'Leary spins her wool.

making 2-ply yarn

When your spindle is full, you can carefully lift off your cone of yarn and then, when you have two cones, you can make 2-ply thread. This is done in the same way as before but you will be spinning widdleshins, or counter-clockwise. Place the two cones on knitting needles – insert the needles in a shoe box or something similar so the cones of wool are standing upright – then you are ready to spin again. When your 2-ply wool is complete, wind it from the spindle into a hank. Tie the hank in four places to avoid tangling.

Now wash the hank at 40°F/60°C using well-deserved soap flakes. Immerse the wool in the soapy water and leave for eight hours until cold. Rinse several times in cool water. Squeeze or spin dry then hang with the hank slightly weighted with small meat hook or coat hanger (to avoid wrinkles) to complete the drying.

testing the strength of wool

Test for fibre weakness by holding a staple (length of wool) taut between the fingers and tweaking it. Practise on a length of britch as it is good wool but not the finest. If you find that it is very weak don't spin it but use it for stuffing toys.

how much wool from a sheep?

It is calculated that you can spin 28–58 hanks of 500 metres from a long-wool breed such as Border Leicester or Romney or Wensleydale, 28–40 hanks of 500 metres from the mountain and hill breeds such as Swaledale and Herdwick, 54–58 hanks from green hill breeds such as the Shetland sheep (see page 110), and 58 hanks from the short-wool breeds such as the Sussex, Texal or Charolais. Merino sheep produce the finest fibre of all and a single sheep has been known to produce 60–70 hanks. Nowadays, however, this fineness of fibre is quite rare.

Swaledales and Herdwicks have larger medullas – the hollow, rounded cells found in the core of the wool – and so their wool is used for Arctic clothing.

the spinning wheel

Only when you have spun using a drop spindle will you appreciate what a huge breakthrough the spinning wheel must have been in the lives of spinners everywhere. The wheel provides a more continuous method of spinning than a drop spindle; there is no need to stop and store the wool so your output will be much greater. However a spinning wheel is an expensive investment so it is necessary to have learnt the basic principals with a drop spindle first. There are a variety of types of spinning wheel and I will not attempt to talk you through them. Once you have found the one you prefer, I suggest you have a couple of lessons to get you started.

carders

Once you are quite proficient at spinning, if you have not done so before, you should invest in a pair of carders to replace your dog comb. These are boards inset on a bed of leather or tough cloth. They have fine wire teeth attached to the boards and handles.

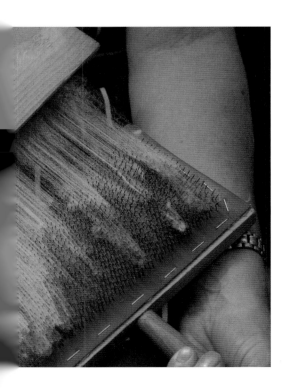

checking the gauge of wool

Once you have spun your yarn you can knit with it (see page 162) or weave it (see page 158). If you are knitting, note that hand-spun yarns do not necessarily correspond to commercial yarns and this can cause difficulty when you are following a pattern. The way to test this is to take a ruler and wind some of your wool round it so that the threads are closely touching, then count the threads per centimetre and compare with the thread count detailed on the pattern. Adjust accordingly.

the twist of the wool

During the spinning process, twist is inserted into the fibres to give them their strength and to produce a thread. The twist can be either an 'S' or a 'Z' twist.
In an 'S' twist, the twist follows the same direction as the letter 'S', in other words, it looks like this: \. In 'Z' twist it follows the letter 'Z', like this: /.

'Z' twist is produced by turning the spinning wheel or spindle in a clockwise direction. This is the normal twist of a singles thread.

In order to ply two threads together to make a 2-ply thread, they are twisted in the opposite direction. Two 'Z' twist threads are therefore plied together in an 'S' direction. To do this, the spindle or wheel is turned in an anti–clockwise direction.

weaving

When I was at primary school we all learnt to weave on little mini-looms. We made a small strip of cloth that we took home to our adoring and long-suffering parents who kissed us fondly, ostensibly used the woven strip as a bookmark for a week, and then quietly lost it! This did, however, have the advantage over the child-crafted concoctions made with egg boxes by later generations. As far as I know, these were of no use at all whereas I and my generation do at least know the basics of weaving – what weft and warp refer to and how a loom works.

Weaving is a fascinating craft. Get yourself a loom and discover how quickly you become addicted. It has been around for 27,000 years and pre-dates agriculture. Early woven cloth was made into bags for carrying, into nets for catching small game such as foxes and hares, and presumably for clothing as well.

getting started

Basic weaving is surprisingly easy. You take two rounded lengths of wood or rollers – it is of course necessary to have the wood on the rollers smooth and splinter-free – a bit wider than you want your piece of cloth to be. Mount each on a firm support so that they can be easily rolled whilst giving you access to the area you will be working on in the middle.

Secure the warp thread – the thread that runs lengthwise through the cloth – to the roller nearest to you, wrapping its end at least twice around the roller. Decide how long you want the finished cloth to be then run a warp thread of this length up to the farther roller, winding the surplus around the roller. As you work, you will be able to turn the top roller to release more warp thread and the bottom roller to roll up the completed cloth.

wefts and warps

The principle of weaving is that you run your weft thread over and under your warp threads consecutively. In order to make this easier, you thread the warp threads through a metal reed or comb which has holes on two different levels, in other words, one thread goes through the lower hole and the other goes though the lower one. Then, by raising or lowering your reed or comb, you separate the warp threads and can simply slide your shuttle (holding the weft thread) through the correct warp threads. After completing each row, you will be able to press the comb down onto the weft thread to keep the woven cloth tight.

vikings and bedouins

The Vikings made a cloth called 'walmar' which served as both sails and tents for their expeditions. It was woven from oiled wool and so was waterproof. The heavy hangings of the Middle Ages not only kept out the draughts in the baronial halls but were durable and easily rolled up for transport.

I have a beautifully and closely woven Bedouin salt bag made from camel hair in brightly dyed herbal colours. I often think of the woman who would have made it on her hand-loom, which would have had to be collapsed and stored on a beast of burden when her nomad group moved around.

It is important that you don't pull the weft thread too tight at the end of each row or this will drag the cloth skewwhiff. If you wish to weave with different coloured threads keep several thread-loaded shuttles handy. When you have woven enough of one colour, leave 5–7cm of loose thread and cut off the weft. Move onto the next colour with a new shuttle. The loose thread can be sewn into the cloth when you have finished. When your cloth is woven about three-quarters of the way up the warp threads, release the top roller and wind the woven cloth onto the bottom roller. Secure the top roller, check the tension and continue.

finishing the cloth

When you have finished weaving your piece of woollen cloth it will be hairy, so for comfort and elegance you will need to raise and cut the nap. The Clothworkers' Company – one of the livery companies in London – has a teasel in its coat of arms. The teasel is a type of thistle with short strong spikes, which was used historically to raise the nap of woven woollen cloth. When Johnny and I visited a commercial mill in Halifax, Yorkshire, I was delighted that they still used teasels fixed into a large metal machine.

You can, if you wish, grow your own teasels. Like all thistles, they are good for attracting butterflies. To raise the nap of

your woven fabric, gently rub the cloth with a teasel against the grain so that the hairy bits stand up. You then gently cut them back with a large pair of sharp shears laid flat on the cloth.

more complex weaving

The simple 'over one thread and under the next' technique soon changed to 'over one and under two or three or four or five', thus creating different weaves. The thickness of the cloth is dictated by the thickness of the wool, in other words, how many threads you have spun together to make your yarn or what beast it comes from. A skein always contains the same length of wool, but its weight will vary according to the thickness of the wool.

choosing a loom

Looms come in all sizes but a good size to start with is one that will allow you to weave a piece about 2 metres long by about 125cm wide. That is after you have practised on a little mini-loom of course. Proper weavers, of course, have wooden looms with foot pedals to raise and lower the warp, and beautiful bits of crafted wood they are, too.

the warmth of wool

Today we tend to take any sort of cloth for granted but I remember, when Johnny and I were filming with the BBC on the Isle of Mull, how warm we were in our woollen clothes and how frozen the BBC crew were in their synthetic-fibre garments. Wool gets warmer when it gets wet, plastic doesn't.

using a pattern

If you are new to weaving, I recommend that you use a pattern. This will tell you how long your warp threads are to be, how many you will need and how are they spaced.

felting

Felting is about 8000 years old, although I like the thought of felt made from woolly-mammoth hair. Britain doesn't have a tradition of felting cloth. Our climate is too wet, so it is much more popular in other parts of Europe. In Russia, during the winter, the army marched on felted boots, which were very warm and durable in freezing snow but they wore them with rubber overshoes in the slush of spring.

Felting comes about when the scales on the outside of wool are forced to cohere to each other. All wools will felt but merino is the best. Most of us have felted wool by accident when we have washed a woollen garment in water that is too hot. This is how you do it deliberately.

the technique

Equip yourself with carded wool, a bamboo mat for rolling (a bamboo window blind makes a good choice), a broom handle or section of doweling as wide as the blind, towels, detergent, a sink or large bowl, vinegar and both hot and cold water, and a supply of linen cloths as large as the blind.

Lay a towel on a spacious work surface then lay your blind on top. Place a linen cloth on top of the blind. Gently pull off 75cm of carded wool and lay it on the linen, then lay another piece of carded wool beside it, continuing until you have the width of cloth you want. Make sure the wool fibres are all lying in the same direction. Repeat laying a second layer of carded wool over the first and at right angles to it. Start you felting career with just two layers.

Sprinkle on hand-hot water mixed with detergent until the wool is wet all over. Push the water into the wool using another linen cloth until the wool is saturated. Add more water if needed and massage the water well into the wool, using your fingertips and paying particular attention to the edges.

Lay the broom handle along the bottom of the blind and roll the whole thing up. When it is fully rolled, push down hard and roll the thing back and forth about 50 times, keeping it tightly rolled all the while. This is hard work.

Unroll the blind and turn the piece of felt around 90 degrees. Repeat this process until the cloth has been rolled twice in each direction.

Unroll and remove the linen cloth, then put the felt directly onto the blind. Sprinkle liberally with very hot water and more detergent. Roll up again and roll 20 times in each direction.

Fill the sink with boiling water, put the felt in, leave until the water is cool enough for your hands, then remove the felt and

squeeze out the excess liquid. Throw the felt hard onto the table several times. Alternatively, you can pound the felt in the sink with a potato masher or some such instrument, or even run it through the washing machine.

rinsing

Rinse the felt in cold water to which you have added a little vinegar to counteract any excess soap, then leave to dry. You can then cut the cloth for whatever you need, using pinking shears to seal the edges.

special effects

Start by making handbags, hats or other such artefacts and build up to cloaks. Felt boots are moulded onto a last and allowed to dry. You can use as many colours as you like and can even sandwich different fabrics between layers of felt. To do this, lay the fabric over a first layer of felt, place some carded wool on top making sure there are gaps in it for the fabric to show through, then proceed to felt the top layer of wool as before.

dyeing

There is nothing more attractive than natural materials dyed using natural dyes and a whole range of colour sources are there for the asking, growing wild in our woods and hedgerows. There are endless permutations of shades and an infinite variety of possible blends. Dye was enormously important to our ancestors, with colour providing the distinction between the greys and duns of poverty and the colourful fabrics of wealth.

the dyeing process

Initially, wool was dyed by simply boiling it up with the relevant plant extract. This tended to wash out every time it rained and eventually – quite how has been lost in the mists of antiquity – various ammonia-based fixing agents were discovered to hold the dye. These are known as mordants and were made from urine, pigeon dung, cider or wine vinegar, potash and, by the Middle Ages, alum, a form of sulphate derived from shale.

Alum had been in use for centuries in the Middle East, was being manufactured in Italy by the fifteenth century and in Britain by the early seventeenth century. It remained the principal fixing agent until it was replaced by modern chemicals. It can still be found today and is the one recommended for a home producer.

home dyeing

You will need two 18-litre stainless-steel or aluminium dye vessels and a gas ring operated from a calor-gas canister set up in a shed.

To make the vegetable dye, pulverize the berries or chop up the vegetables. The quantity required obviously determines the depth of colour obtained and it is only by experimentation that you will discover the colours you want, but the minimum would be a kilogram for a 500g skein of wool. Let the berries or vegetables steep in cold water overnight. The following day, bring to the boil and simmer for an hour. Meanwhile, make the mordant.

For this, mix together 114g alum and 28g cream of tartar with a little water to form a paste. Bring 18 litres of water to the boil and add the alum and cream of tartar.

Add the dye and immerse a 200g skein of wool. Simmer for one hour. Allow to cool, remove the wool and press between two boards to remove excess liquid.

colour from nature

Blues – Blackberries make the most lovely navy blue and a range of blue variations are made from elder leaves.

Purple – The purple in tweed and tartan traditionally came from bilberries and sloes.

Yellow – Bee propolis (a resinous substance collected by bees from buds for use in building their hives) and the bark of apple, pear, elder, rowan, cherry, alder or ash trees were all used to produce yellows. The leaves and shoots of gorse and privet were also used, as were bracken roots for dyeing leather, particularly chamois, yellow. Lombardy poplar, lily-of-the-valley and bog myrtle were used to make yellow dye.

Greens – These came from elder leaves, the tips of heather leaves, buckthorn and privet berries, and ferns and alder catkins.

Pink – The freshly cut wood of alder saplings produced pink.

Reds – A red came from dogwood, magenta from lichen and khaki from cow dung and nettles.

Browns – All sorts of substances produced browns, among them soot, walnut roots, leaves and the husks of shells, which were also used for dyeing hair. Sloe and blackthorn bark, oak bark, juniper berries and dog dung were also used. Until relatively recently, hound dung was one of a hunt servant's perks and barrels of the stuff went to Bradford every week for dyeing fustian and corduroy.

knitting

Such a simple idea, and so many ingenious variations, knitting is now back in fashion. A group of fashionable young women were recently asked to leave the Savoy Hotel in London during teatime because of the noise of their knitting needles.

We don't really know when knitting began. Catherine of Aragon knitted hose for Henry VIII and it had been around long before then.

When I was a child everyone knitted. My grandmother, a woman of spectacular elegance who bought her clothes in Paris despite the fact that she lived in Singapore, used to knit the most exquisite baby clothes and the finest shawls. My great-aunt Jessica, who was born on a sailing ship passing through Hells Gates outside Aden – a fact recorded on her birth certificate in latitude and longitude – knitted dashing shooting stockings for great Uncle Bertie's shapely legs. My nanny from Eye in Suffolk knitted bulky sweaters for her farming brothers.

I suppose it was all a legacy of two world wars, when everyone sent knitted socks or sweaters in khaki wool to relatives at the

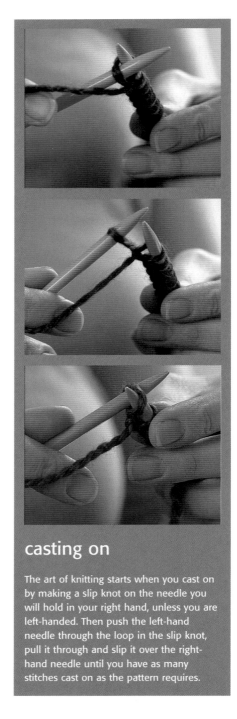

front. Knitting went out of fashion until the early 1980s when smart young women started knitting fancy wool jackets because they couldn't afford the haute couture ones.

My knitting career ended at the age of fifteen, when I endeavoured to knit a pair of bedsocks. I managed to knit just the one and on such small needles that it would barely have fitted a premature baby. I didn't do failure well so that was that, but I know the principles of knitting which I'm happy to pass on. After that, it's over to you.

Buy a good knitting techniques book, attend a knitting course or get a DVD but better still, find a friend who knits and get them to show you. It is impossible to explain but so easy to show.

the story of the guernsey sweater

Each fishing community had its own pattern for the Guernsey or Gansey sweater. The patterns were based on motifs related to the sea such as nets, ropes, ladders, herringbones and so on. If the body of a fisherman was washed up, it could be recognized from his sweater and returned home for burial.

casting on

The art of knitting starts when you cast on by making a slip knot on the needle you will hold in your right hand, unless you are left-handed. Then push the left-hand needle through the loop in the slip knot, pull it through and slip it over the right-hand needle until you have as many stitches cast on as the pattern requires.

'I managed to knit just the one bedsock and on such small needles that it would barely have fitted a premature baby.'

plain and purl

You are now ready to knit your first row, which you do by repeating the casting-on process but putting the new stitches onto the left-hand needle. This gives you plain stitch.

For a purl stitch, you put the needle through the back of the stitch instead.

yarn and needles

You can knit wool, silk or cotton and can knit using two needles, four needles or circular needles. Knitting yarn basically comes in five weights – 2-ply, which is very fine, 4-ply, which is still fine, double knit, which is the middle range, Aran, which is traditionally used for jumpers, and chunky, which knits up quickly. There is now also an extra-thick wool, which knits up really fast.

Wool can either be untreated, in which case it retains its lanolin and is very waterproof, or washed.

Needles start at the finest, 2.25mm and go up to 25mm They are made of aluminium, wood or plastic.

Check your pattern to make sure that you buy the correct size of needle; larger needles mean larger, more open stitches and a looser knit.

Boleros, capes and other similar seamless garments are made on circular needles of varying sizes and circumferences. Socks, mittens and so forth are knitted on needles with points at both ends so that you can more easily turn a heel. These needles are sold in packs of four.

crochet

I am afraid that for most of my life I was not much interested in crochet. At primary school we were taught that strange craft in which you hammered four nails into a cotton reel and, with the aid of a crochet hook and different coloured wools, made metres of coloured woollen worms. The woollen worms served no useful purpose but were great fun to make and, as I can now see, encouraged dexterity. This was my first brush with crochet.

At boarding school I greatly coveted my friend Carrots' multi-coloured crocheted bed covering known as Aunt Letts' Blanket. It taught me the meaning of the Tenth Commandment. I had no desire to replicate the blanket, only somehow to obtain it. I never succeeded and ALB now keeps Carrots' children snug.

I have never much liked babies and couldn't see the point of crocheting beautiful shawls for them to puke all over when a bit of old blanket you could throw in the wash would do just as well. Nor was I drawn to crochet when I moved to Scotland and was exposed to the beautiful crocheted Shetland shawls. This is surprising because I am deft with my hands and enjoy that type of work.

However, dear reader, don't despair. Somewhere in my fifties I learnt that something similar to crochet is used to make nets for rabbiting and ferreting and also for Haaf-netting – that wonderful type of fishing where you stand in a river up to your neck and wait for the fish to swim into your net, which is suspended on a sort of cedar-wood cross of Lorraine. As a result I have become quite keen on crocheting.

'I have never much liked babies and couldn't see the point of crocheting beautiful shawls for them to puke all over...'

yarn and needle

You will need a ball of wool or thread and a crochet hook. Hook sizes range from 2.25mm to 19mm. Practise with fairly thin wool or even string. Crocheting is all about maintaining tension and for this you must find a comfortable way to achieve an easy flow between needle and hand. As you get more skilled, you can use different-sized needles and heavier or lighter yarns.

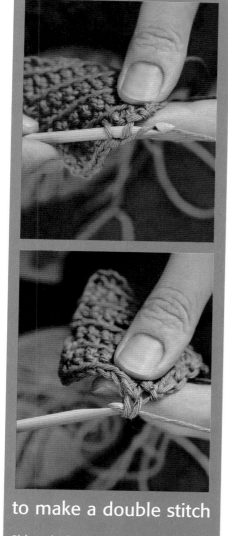

to make a double stitch

Pick up the first chain stitch on your hook, then loop the yarn over the hook and pull it through.

Loop the yarn over the hook again, and pull it through both stitches.

getting started

Before you start, promise me that you will persevere until you have successfully crocheted ten rows. The point of this request is that, to begin with, crocheting is maddeningly frustrating and you will be tempted to throw the whole lot away and give up just as you are on the verge of succeeding. Ten rows are all it takes and you are off.

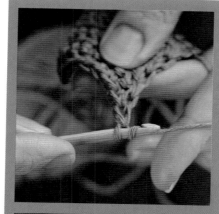

turning a row

When you have enough stitches for the width you want according to your pattern, you need to turn the row. To do this, make an extra chain stitch at the end of the row before turning to prevent bunching.

To increase the length of your rows, for example to make a piece widen out, work two stitches through one stitch of the previous row. To decrease, miss a stitch and work into the next one.

Make a loose slip knot and insert the hook through the loop. Assuming you are right-handed, hold the needle in your right hand about halfway along the shaft, as you would a spoon or a pencil, whichever you find most comfortable. Take the unused thread in your left hand, loop it over the index and middle fingers of the left hand, under the ring finger and over the little finger.

Use the hook to catch the yarn held in the left hand and to pull it through the loop on the needle, then tighten the yarn by pulling the loose end downwards. Repeat until you have a chain of stitches.

finishing off

To finish your work, cut the yarn leaving a tail, then use the hook to draw the stitch through the final loop. Finally, use a darning needle to weave the tail into the work. If you are crocheting a large item or one with sections worked in different colours, you need to join the sections when they are finished. To do this, use the same type of yarn as you have been crocheting with. Use a slipstitch and don't pull on the yarn or you will bunch up your crochet.

This may sound gobbledegook as you read it, but all will become clear as you follow it through your promised ten rows! When you look at the beautiful, gossamer-fine, state-of-the art crocheted shawls that are made in places like the Shetland Islands you may think they are impossible to make but the old adage 'practice makes perfect' was never truer than in crocheting.

incorporating new yarn

When you need more yarn, either to start a new ball or to add a different colour, wait until you are at the beginning of a row then work a stitch with the old yarn and complete the same stitch with the new yarn, laying a longish length of the new yarn along the top of the row and working over it.

quilting

I have always maintained that if the world were peopled solely by women, apart from the obvious problem of reproduction, we would still live in caves, but what comfortable, decorative caves they would be. Nothing, I feel, illustrates women's natural instinct for creating comfort than the art of quilting.

the layers of a quilt

Quilts were originally made for use and warmth as well as for their decorative qualities. They can be as simple or as complicated as you want but basically they are made up of three layers: the top layer which is the decorative layer, the middle layer, which is usually a worn blanket or large piece of felt, and a backing layer of some neutral or toning colour, often sheeting. If the quilt is mainly or purely for decoration then the middle layer should be of thin cloth.

It is the top layer that all the fuss is about. This is made up of different shaped pieces of cloth – squares, octagons, diamonds, indeed any shape you wish provided they are capable of having edges that align. Every household has a store of worn-out clothes, unused or stained table linen, or old curtains or sheets and any of these can supply the fabric you need to make your top layer. The trick when deciding which to use is to work out colours and patterns that work well together. Old jeans, for example, are good for providing neutral blocks of colour to break up areas of patterned fabric.

making the shapes

When you have decided on the shape of the individual pieces of quilt you must cut out templates of stiffish card in that shape. This is where you involve children, elderly relatives, harmless drunks, indeed everyone you know. Once you have your templates, you cut up your material, lay a piece over each template, turn the edges over the edges of the template, tack lightly to the template, and trim the edges. When you have assembled your fabric-covered templates you then lay them out on a work surface or even on a bed and arrange them to your satisfaction. Once you are content with the layout, tack the fabric-covered templates together at the edges to make manageable groups. Then sew each tacked group to its neighbouring group, according to your planned arrangement until you have completed your whole top layer. Turn this over, cut the tacking threads holding the fabric to each template and remove the templates.

Lay the backing layer flat on your work surface or bed, place the middle layer on top and, finally, the decorative layer, then tack round the edges to hold the three layers together. Then sew through all three layers along the edges of the fabric shapes. This can be done by hand and reinforced by machine stitching unless the quilt is for display only, in which case it should be solely hand-stitched.

Have ready some plain binding in a colour that will enhance your pattern and sew this carefully all round the edge of your quilt. If the quilt is to be used you can tack this and then oversew on a machine. In America quilts are often made on upright hanging frames and if you really take to quilting you may think of making one, but all my quilting experience has been with work laid on a flat surface.

quilt aftercare

When you store your quilt don't put it in a plastic bag but instead use a large pillowcase or a bag made from sheeting, depending on the size of your quilt. Fold the quilt with tissue paper to prevent permanent creases which will rub and cause damage, and re-fold them along different folds every three months.

If the weather is damp or humid hang your quilt out to air from time to time, avoiding bright sunlight which will fade it. Don't store it where it may attract rodents or moths. When washing, don't put it in the machine but wash by hand, unless you are sure none of the materials will shrink or run. Lay it flat on the ground to dry.

quilting in America

In America there are museums full of quilts that pioneer women made in the little spare time they had to brighten and decorate their sparse cabins. Quilting in America is now a folk art and memorial quilts are very popular there. I remember, when AIDS first hit America badly, seeing photographs of wonderful huge memorial quilts being made for the victims. Curiously, quilting is much bigger in America than in England, although the finest English examples are to be found in Lincolnshire and East Anglia, the parts of the country that provided so many of the original settler families.

mending

'Make do and mend', read the wartime posters. 'A stitch in time saves nine', my mother used to tell me. 'We will mend it, stick it with glue', sang the Clangers, the small, pink mouselike creatures of the 1970s BBC television series. Today in the United Kingdom, no child learns to mend in school unless they go to a Rudolf Steiner school. In our throwaway society we don't mend. Instead we are clothed by the sweatshops of the Far East in cheap synthetic clothing that has no real life span and when it tears or wears out, we go out and buy something else.

Mending is to my mind the practice for sewing without wasting expensive cloth. Once you have perfected the techniques of mending, sewing is a doddle. My eldest sister and, indeed, my sister-in law both earn good money with their curtain-making businesses and my sister-in law hand-covers lampshades too – a good home industry and one in much demand.

sewing on a button

Let's consider the different types of mending. First there's sewing on buttons. Buttons on manufactured garments are usually poorly sewn so they come off easily. 'Easy peasy!' you cry, 'What does one need to learn about sewing on a button?' Well, remember the thread. Don't sew back your button with white thread if all the others are sewn on with blue, green or black. It will stand out like a neon light. Button thread is a special tough thread designed for sewing buttons on thick cloth, men's jackets and ladies' coats. When sewing buttons on this type of garment you must remember to leave

higgledly piggledy buttons

Johnny and I were both given buttons by the Saltersgate Hunt at their Hunt Dinner after we filmed with them during the second series of *Clarissa and the Countryman*. Johnny was hunting the next day and was eager to have the buttons on his hunt coat for the occasion, so I got up early and painstakingly sewed them on. The Melton cloth of these hunt coats is very thick indeed and I had to use a glass for a palm – a block of wood set into a leather strap that's held in the palm – to push the needle through as I had no thimble. Looking at his coat six months down the line I was horrified to discover the buttons were all higgledy piggledy, with the embossed crests on them at a variety of angles. It isn't enough to sew buttons on strongly; they must also all be facing the same way.

a long stem, or shank, of thread which you wind round with more thread to strengthen it. If you don't do this, the wearer will not be able to do up their buttons. You will also need a thimble or you will puncture yourself.

Thread your needle, make a small knot in the long end of the thread, push the needle through from the reverse side of the garment and pull the thread through. Don't ever have your thread too long or it will tangle and knot. Put the needle through one eye of the button, back through another eye and through the material, leaving the thread slightly loose. Continue this process several times. When the button is secure, wind the thread round the shank several times and finish off securely.

mending a ripped hem

Where the material is actually ripped, open up the hem, insert a new strip of material under the rip, re-fold the hem and sew the two sides together.

No-sew method
You can buy iron-on adhesive tape to take up your hems but frankly I find it more trouble than it's worth.

patching

When a piece of cloth is very badly ripped or a hole has formed and the edges of the tear can't be joined together, you may need to insert a patch. If you have a matching piece of cloth you can use that or you can chose a contrasting colour and make a feature of it. If the hole is in an appropriate place, you could cover it with a pocket. I remember a young man in my youth who had ripped his good new jeans on the inside of the upper thigh. He had sewn a patch over it on which was embroidered with the words 'Custer had it coming.' I found it very distracting.

Cut out your patch so that it is slightly larger than the tear in the garment, then trim the edges of the tear carefully. Lay the patch on the reverse side of the cloth with the right side facing through the tear and tack carefully round it and the edge of the tear. Then hemstitch round it with small stitches. If you are making a feature of your patch, choose a vivid, contrasting thread and make your stitches larger.

Trim the edges of the patch on the inside. Sew a second line of stitches to strengthen.

sewing a hem

If a shirt or dress is too long or if fashions change, you will need to take up the hem. You could, of course, like one very grand and stylish lady of my acquaintance, simply cut off the excess with pinking shears but you need a lot of style to carry that off without looking a slut – and what if hemlines drop again?

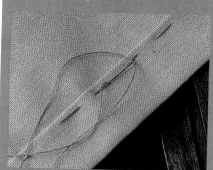

Using a tape measure, pin up the hem to the length you want, fold a narrow edge over, pin it, then tack it with long running stitches – – – – thus, which will be easy to pull out. You can now try the garment on and ensure it is even all round, either by asking someone to help you or by looking in a mirror. Once you are sure it is even, you will be able to hemstitch it. Yes, you can do this on a machine but hand-sewn stitches are stronger and neater – though not when I do them!

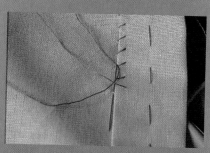

Hemstitch is a small, even, diagonal stitch / / / / thus, which joins the edge of the hem to the material of the garment. If the material is thick enough, you can hemstitch without going right through the cloth. Otherwise, make sure your stitches are small so that they don't show on the right side and don't pull them too tight or they will pucker the cloth. If you are right-handed, sew from left to right. Make sure the thread matches the cloth. When all is done, pull out the tacking thread.

Fallen hems need to be sewn up by the same method. Doing this is a good example of a stitch in time saving nine. Once a hem starts to unravel, pinning it up won't last long.

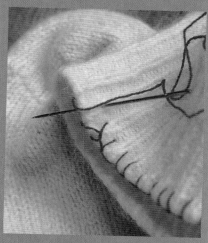

Blanket stitch is a strong stitch designed for hems that are under pressure, such as side seams which have undone. The technique is to make one stitch then loop the thread through itself before making the next stitch. Visually, blanket stitch looks like a line of capital T's all joined together TTTTT thus. It is stronger than hemstitch.

Contrast patching

Contrast patching can be made from leather. Leather patches are placed over the hole on the right side of the garment and are then carefully sewn around the edge through the leather and the cloth.

You can also edge the frayed edges on cuffs and lapels in leather or cloth which can look very smart.

The practice of sewing leather or suede patches over the holes in the elbows of men's tweed jackets has become so fashionable in country clothes that tailors are now asked to sew them on new jackets, which I think looks quite ridiculous. Johnny has a favourite tweed jacket that is so beautifully patched, edged and mended that it is an artwork in its own right.

'The practice of sewing leather or suede patches over the holes in the elbows of men's tweed jackets has become so fashionable in country clothes that tailors are now asked to sew them on new jackets...'

Embroidery cover-up

An alternative to a patch if the mend is going to show is to embroider a motif over the top of it. I have an old and much-loved olive-coloured waistcoat with many pockets. It is of an irreplaceable type. I wear it every day at home instead of carrying a handbag around with me. I once caught the back of the waistcoat on a nail, which left a jagged tear. The edges of the tear weren't going to meet, so I embroidered the word's 'NO BAN' on the L-shaped tear. It makes me a lot of new friends. The enemies I have already! It's the same principle as those embroidered T-shirts that people pay a lot of money for.

If you are embroidering any motif it is advisable to trace it on in pencil or Biro first and then sew, following the line. Use silk or cotton embroidery thread. Either use satin stitch, a simple embroidery stitch where the stitches are placed so close to each other that they appear to be joined together, or cross-stitch.

invisible mending

This is really darning (see below) but done with such care as to replicate the angle of the grain of the cloth and its texture so that you cannot see the finished result. It is best left to a professional.

where to learn to sew

I learnt sewing in school, taught by a gentle ageing Belgium nun called Mother Receiver. She must have bypassed any time in Purgatory that might have been pending for the pain she suffered watching our cackhanded stitches. I was a poor, little rich girl. I didn't mend things as we had servants to do that and they, being Spanish, sewed beautifully. I embroidered and I did tapestry, but that was it.

The Women's Institutes in Britain and the Junior Leagues in America will teach you how to sew and mend and I bet there are women mending all over Iraq and Afghanistan. War and poverty teach you to make do and mend, though I'm not suggesting you move to a war zone to learn the skill.

'I was a poor, little rich girl. I didn't mend things as we had servants to do that...'

darning

Now that you are buying or making woollen cloth instead of the synthetic stuff, you will need to rediscover the art of darning. I love darning and even won prizes for it. When I was small I would make holes in my father's shooting stockings especially so I could darn them.

You will need a large-eyed darning needle and matching thread. If you haven't any, go mad and darn using some totally flamboyant colour and flaunt the finished darn. Then you need a darning mushroom. If you don't have one, use a small saucer or anything you can stretch the hole and its surrounding edges tightly over. Thread your needle and start by running a line of stitches round the hole to stabilize the edges of the hole. Then, following the grain of the material as best you can, take the needle across the hole and through the material on the other side.

Reverse direction and repeat, working your way up the hole until all of it is filled with thread drawn across. Sever the thread then, starting at the top of the darn, repeat, working at 90 degrees to the first lot of stitching and weaving over and under the first threads. Continue until the hole is filled. It may then be necessary to weave in a few more stitches if there are any gaps. Remove the darning mushroom and, hey presto! a perfect darn.

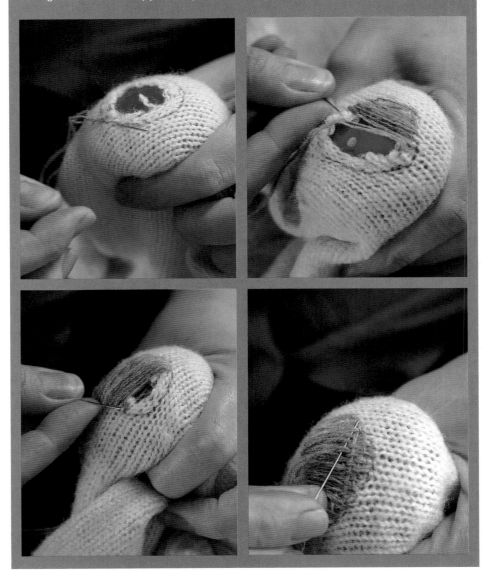

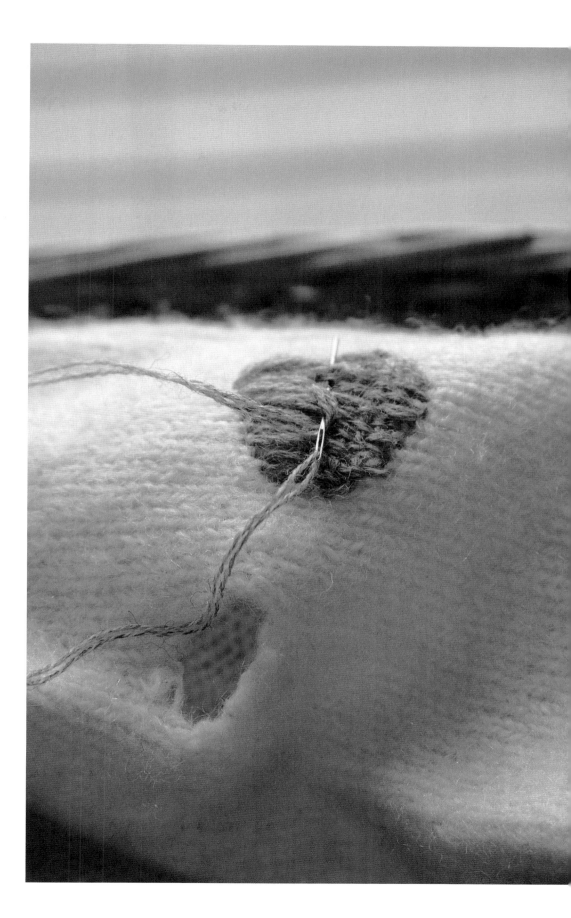

sewing in history

Saint Madeleine Sophie Barrat, founder of the Sisters of the Sacred Heart, wrote a short book of advice, some of which was read out to us at the start of the school year. She was writing before the French Revolution for the children of the well-to-do and was an advanced educator who wanted women to be taught the sciences. She also wrote of the importance of sewing and – one point I remember – of the dangers of carrying open scissors in your pocket.

There are displays of mending in local museums – children's work with exquisite tiny stitches practising hem and buttonhole stitch, invisible mending and darning.

At the turn of the twentieth century, young ladies were sent to Holland and Belgium to learn the sewing techniques they would need in their married lives, but nothing like this happens any more.

My friend Arianne, President of the Scottish Embroiderers' Guild, tells me that during the Second World War, when things were in short supply, she used to wear the legs of her mother's old stockings – the feet had worn out – sewn onto the feet of her father's woollen shooting stockings that had shrunk in the wash.

herbal remedies

There are literally thousands of different flowers and herbs. A hundred years ago, the countryside was a riot of wild plants, most of which were used either because they were edible (see page 78) or for their medicinal properties. The need for agricultural expansion, particularly after the Second World War, destroyed huge areas of rough pasture where these plants had previously thrived. Now that it is cheaper for the government to feed the nation on imported food and farming subsidies are directed towards landscape enhancement, the countryside has once more become a herbalist's paradise.

the early history of herbalism

The first documentation in the western world concerning the medicinal properties of certain plants were the writings of the Greek physician, Hippocrates, in 400 BC. The next notable work, *Materia Medica*, was by his fellow-countryman, Dioscrides, in 100 A.D. The Roman, Galen, followed with a series of books on herbal cures written in the second century A.D. and these remained in use for the next fifteen hundred years. The Romans brought their extensive knowledge of herbs and their cures to Britain and we have them to thank for the introduction of many of the herbs that grow wild in this country today, thyme, rosemary, parsley, fennel, sage and borage, to name only a few.

The great Norman religious houses brought an immensely sophisticated standard of herbal healing with them to England and every monastery had an extensive herb garth or garden. The

infusions from country lore

● For a head cold – leaves of agrimony, fennel and sage, and the flowers of chamomile, linden (lime) and verbascum.

● For a feverish chill or a cough – elderflower, peppermint and yarrow.

● For catarrh – borage, hyssop, coltsfoot and comfrey leaves.

● For flu and rheumatism – elderflowers mixed with honey.

● For constipation – dandelion and basil.

● For varicose veins – daisies.

● For colds and flu – eucalyptus leaves.

other country remedies

● For teenage spots and acne – the sulphurous properties of gorse and broom flowers were capitalized on by being beaten into a paste with goose fat.

● For headaches and sleeplessness – a handful of lavender leaves, crushed and rubbed into the temples or sprinkled over hot water and inhaled under a towel.

● For insect bites and stings – fresh dock leaves and parsley juice.

● For a tick bite – bracken juice, once you had got the wretched creature off.

● To repel midges – eucalyptus leaves and bog myrtle.

● For pulled or stiff muscles – horseradish in a poultice.

● For chilblains – horseradish mixed with lard.

Augustinian monks at the twelfth-century Hospice of Soutra in southern Scotland developed a form of anaesthetic for amputations from black henbane, opium and hemlock. Juniper berries and the fungus, ergot, were use to induce childbirth. St. John's Wort, nature's answer to vallium, was used to treat melancholy. The little yellow-flowered tormentil was used to remove internal parasites and a diffusion of bracken fern cured bronchitis. Nineteenth-century colonists in America, Australia and New Zealand were slightly nonplussed to find the aborigines there using it for the same purpose.

Over the last hundred years, modern medicine has suppressed much of the knowledge of natural cures that was detailed in the sixteenth-century works of Turner and Gerard and in Culpeper's more famous herbal of a hundred years later. The recent interest in holistic medicine is to be applauded.

the power of nettles

Old Joe, our gardener was a great believer in nettles, rubbing his hands with the leaves to ease rheumatism. He also used nettle leaves as a dressing for septic cuts, for the nettle beer he made in the spring as a post-winter tonic, and for the grey-green lotion he made from the boiled leaves, which he rubbed into his thinning hair, convinced that the astringent properties would activate the hair follicles and promote growth.

joe's sleeplessness

Like so many country people, Joe was a martyr to rheumatism – the 'screws' – and on the nights he was unable to sleep, he would drink an infusion of valerian leaves and would lie on a pillow filled with hop flowers. In the morning he would be heavy-eyed and bad-tempered until the effects wore off.

using your produce

Apart from the real feeling of achievement a well-stocked
larder and store cupboard bring to the gatherer, there is the
added joy of exquisite tastes not often found in this modern
world of nasty supermarket foods. Refrigerators and freezers
may have brought new economies to distant lands but their
downside is obscene wastage of food and starving nations.
Do you really believe buying third-world vegetables feeds
those nations? Surely the money that is earned goes to
provide cars and palaces for the politicians whereas the
general populace would have prospered better eating the
food they grow themselves rather than exporting it to us.
Preserving your own produce not only makes you self-
sufficient but adds a whole range of different flavours to
your diet, whatever that diet may be. I have recently been
doing some vegan cooking for a friend (don't faint, dear
reader) and it is amazing what a spoonful of pickled cabbage
or a slice of preserved lemon will do to enliven that dullest of
diets. When food is preserved by one of the means suggested
here, it ripens and develops wonderful flavours that our
increasingly bland world has forgotten. And just think how
much electricity you save if you don't throw everything in
the freezer?

milk

In this sanitized, pasteurized, sickly age we have forgotten the joy of whole milk straight from the cow. Cooking with this wonderful milk, especially if it comes from Guernsey or Jersey cows, is like hearing the heavenly choirs singing the Alleluliah Chorus! Your sauces don't curdle and your rice puddings are a feast for the gods.

I have never believed the argument for skimmed milk. In my view, the increase in osteoporosis and depression that we see today is directly linked to the rise in the consumption of skimmed and semi-skimmed milk and now, after all these years, the pundits are beginning to agree with me. According to the Royal Society of Chemistry and Dr Harold Macgee, the body needs the fat in the milk to absorb the calcium, hence the increase in osteoporosis in these days of low-fat milk. And the rise in depression is because the only substance that naturally stimulates the body's serotonin levels is animal fat. That's why you reach for a cream bun when you're feeling low.

'In my view, the increase in osteoporosis and depression is directly linked to the rise in the consumption of skimmed and semi-skimmed milk...'

selling your excess

You may want to sell your excess milk and if you pasteurize it, it is quite legal to do so. In Britain unpasteurized milk can be sold under license, the milking parlour must be checked by the Dairy Hygiene people and obviously your cow's inoculations must be in order. After that you can obtain a licence to sell milk at your farm gate but only to the end-consumer, not into restaurants or cafés. This is to ensure traceability in the event of any brucellosis outbreak. Unless you are truly dedicated to selling unpasturized milk it will cause you many headaches but those who prevail truly bring joy to mankind and cooks alike.

milk from other animals

Of course, milk from cows is not the only milk. My mother was so allergic as a child that she was fed on mare's milk, which she always reckoned accounted for her great love for horses. Then there is camel's milk, which is very rich in fat and makes great butter. Goat's milk and ewe's milk are more used in cheese production, the milk being less strong and less sweet than cow's milk. Sheep and goats will only milk for nine months in the year, unlike a cow who, once she has had her first calf, will continue to produce milk all year round. In recent years there has been a growth in the making of artisan cheeses from the milk of these beasts. I know of a goat farmer who makes over 200 blocks of goat cheese a day from his flock of 200 goats, each of which gives about three and a half litres a day. He sells all he produces to a specialist cheese shop and delicatessen market, feeling, as I do, that supermarkets are the road to ruin for an artisan producer.

Vegans scream that drinking milk and eating butter and cheese is wrong as it deprives the calf of sustenance. As usual with such bigots, ignorance prevails. A dairy cow produces so much milk that the calf could not possibly consume it all so it is taken off its mother and fed separately. If it were not, the cow would not let down its milk to the machine and would suffer and even die.

cream

In the summer, when the cows are at pasture, you get a lot more cream than during winter feeding when they are on

hay and sugar beet. Fred, an 84 year-old farmer with six Guernsey cows that he now just keeps for pleasure, has a wonderful cream separator made by Alpha Laval about 120 years ago. It has 22 blades and at the turn of a handle can separate just over a litre of milk in five minutes. If you do not have such a machine, you must separate the cream by pouring the milk into a large shallow glazed earthenware dish and leaving it to stand in a cool larder. The cream will then rise to the surface. It takes twelve hours for single cream and 24 for double. Then you must scoop the cream off with a specially designed flat ladle with holes. Cream separates naturally from unpasteurized milk as the fat globules are too large to remain suspended in the emulsion. Industrially produced cream is separated by centrifugal force. This pasteurizes it instantly and so the cream does not have time to ripen and the taste is quite inferior. You will know once you have tried the real thing.

Some historians allege that clotted cream came to the West Country of England via Phoenician tin traders. They would have been used to the Middle Eastern kaymac, a very similar cream made with water-buffalo milk. It is nice to think of Joseph of Arimathea and Jesus sitting down to a Cornish cream tea!

To make clotted cream you put the whole milk in shallow pans to allow the cream to rise. It takes twelve hours in summer and 24 in winter. You then heat the whole to 82°C/180°F and keep it at that temperature for half an hour. Allow the cream to cool overnight, then skim it off in layers and cut it with a knife.

cream in different countries

In Britain, single cream is 20 per cent fat and double is 48 per cent fat, but this varies from country to country and in some countries they do not have the distinctions that we have here.

butter

Butter is a universal of any dairy culture. I remember at school being quite turned against the ancient Greeks when I discovered that they ate olive oil and kept the butter as an ointment. In the West Country of England they used to make a very rich butter with clotted cream. Thomas Hardy describes the dairymaids plunging their linked hands and forearms into the cream until the butter was formed. No wonder dairymaids were so sought after; they had lovely soft skin and great upper-body development!

Fred and I used to make butter together in a wonderful old butter churn, the likes of which I have never seen since. It was a chest about 60cm square, made of thick elm planks and inside, turned by a handle, were four latticed paddles, side by side and two by two. Butter is made from ripened cream so Fred and I kept the cream in an earthenware crock standing in a cool place for three days before we used it.

It is the lactic-acid bacteria present in milk that cause the fat globules to cohere and make butter. Commercial butter made from pasteurized milk needs the addition of milk acids for the process to occur. Butter made from fresh cream is sweeter and keeps for less time.

yoghurt

In this day and age we have got used to yoghurt but when I was young it was a rarity that was only eaten by eccentric ladies wearing sandals and floral wrap dresses, and smelling vilely of stale lentils. In the 1960s I was introduced to commercially produced yoghurt for the first time. With its chemical flavouring and strangely vivid colouring, it put me off yoghurt for years. Then, like so many others people, I went to Greece on holiday and discovered what yoghurt really should taste like.

making butter

You can churn butter in a jam jar, shaking it to and fro until the butter sets, or you can use a glass jar with paddles on the top turned by hand. When the butter sets, drain off the buttermilk. This contains the lactic acid and can give a sour taste to unsalted butter. Then you need to squeeze the excess buttermilk from the butter. I am the proud possessor of an antique butter table with hand-turned rollers, designed for squeezing butter, but more usually the squeezing is done with wooden butter pats. Divide the butter into 250g lumps. Put a lump between the pats and keep patting it into a block, pressing as you go to extrude the excess liquid. It is quite a knack. The French wash their butter to remove any remaining buttermilk.

At this stage you can add salt to help preserve the butter longer. This is purely a matter of taste; the Welsh, for instance, like their butter quite salty but I, being a hedonist, like almost none. You can then wrap your butter in paper, or put it in a crock, or even stamp it with a pretty pattern.

The buttermilk that remains is great for baking and is very healthy to drink.

Real yoghurt is wonderful – a marvellous gift from Asia Minor to the world. It is great for cooking and is the alleged reason for so many centenarians fathering children in Bulgaria. Yoghurt is digestible by people with lacto intolerance as the heating and fermentation involved in its preparation cause the bacteria in the milk to convert most of the lactose to lactic acid.

To make the yoghurt you will need to keep back a little live yoghurt from your last batch as a starter. Heat your milk to 180°F/82°C. You must use a thermometer as overheating will kill the bacteria and underheating will not start the process. Middle-Eastern nomads put the milk out in the sun. Pour the heated milk into clean containers and allow the milk to cool to between 106°F–109°F/41°C–43°C. Take some of the cooled milk and stir in half a teaspoon of starter for each 500ml of prepared milk. Distribute this evenly between the containers and stir well. Place all the containers in a tin or baking tray to hold them steady, cover with a linen cloth and wrap in a blanket. The temperature must not drop below 60°F/15°C so you may need to use the airing cupboard or stand the containers on top of the kitchen range. The yoghurt will set in eight hours. Be careful not to jolt it during this time or the yoghurt-making enzymes will stop working. Store in a covered container once it is set.

which milk to use for yoghurt?

All milk can become yoghurt but if you are using cow's milk, it is better to use semi-skimmed as it will keep better. Goat and sheep's milk give a more stable product, especially for cooking and just in case you need to know, yak and camel milk are so rich in fat that it is better to use them skimmed for making yoghurt.

buttermilk scones

(MAKES APPROXIMATELY 10)

These little griddle scones are found all over Ireland and are very good. You can also substitute buttermilk for the milk when making any conventional sweet or savoury scones.

450g plain flour
1 tsp bicarbonate of soda
1 tsp cream of tartar
1 tsp salt
85g butter
300ml buttermilk

Sift together the flour, bicarbonate of soda, cream of tartar and salt. Rub in the butter and mix to a soft dough with the buttermilk. Roll out to 1.25cm thick and shape into small flat rounds. Cook on a hot griddle for about 2 minutes until golden brown or bake at Gas Mark 7/220°C/425°F for 10 minutes. Eat when they are cool.

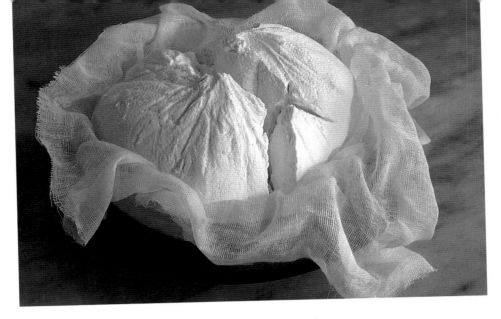

cheese

In your new greener life you can make cheese from any of your ruminants, though probably not from the yaks or camels. Cheese-making is as varied as there are countries with ruminants to supply milk and manuals (mostly unhelpful) for the aspirant cheese-maker.

Making cheese

The first stage of cheese-making is to let your milk ripen, allowing the lactic-acid-producing bacteria to sour it. Keep the milk fairly warm during this time then raise the temperature to blood-heat. Now you must set the curd with the help of rennet. This process involves the casein fraction of the protein in the milk coagulating and shrinking, forcing out the whey and trapping the fat globules.

With the milk at blood-heat, add the rennet and the curd will separate from the whey fairly speedily. You must then cut the curd with wire harps into smaller flakes or grains which you then lift from the whey. One exception is curd cheese or the very soft French-type cheeses in which the curd is simply lifted from the whey with a perforated ladle and hung in a cloth or other perforated mould to drain. Once the curds are removed, they are salted and, in the case of hard cheeses, the salted curds are added to the cheese. Hard cheeses such as Cheddar are then piled into moulds and a weight applied to drive out still more whey. You can still find hand cheese presses for sale. The pressure applied to a full-sized Cheddar may be as great as a tonne and a half. The pressed cheese is then wrapped in a bandage and heat applied with an iron to seal the cheese and stop mould getting in.

For semi-soft cheese, the salt is rubbed on the outside, while for soft cheese, the cheese may be immersed in brine for hours or even days.

Once the cheese is formed and removed from its mould, it must be matured. Hard cheeses are kept in cool, dry conditions but for soft cheeses a moist environment helps ripening and aids the growth of surface organisms.

rennet

Rennet is usually obtained from the lining of the fourth stomach of a ruminant calf. It can be dried and re-used many times. Nowadays one buys it commercially in liquid or powder form. There is also vegetarian rennet, obtained from the infloresence of various plants. The most successful vegetarian rennet comes from my old friend the cardoon, although in Britain lady's bedstraw (*Galium verum*) was most commonly used. Vegetarian rennet is harder to use and is more commonly confined to the making of goat's and ewe's milk cheeses.

whey

This is what is left after the curds have been removed. It is also what Cleopatra and Mary Queen of Scots are said to have bathed in as it is supposed to give wonderful skin tones. Italian ricotta is a whey cheese – the name simply means re-cooked. To make whey cheese the whey is heated to a high temperature then allowed to cool slightly and some sour whey or other coagulant is added. The resulting curds are then lightly pressed and eaten 'fresh', in other words, unsalted, or they can be more heavily pressed and salted, and used in cooking. In Italy fresh ricotta is eaten as a pudding with sugar or honey.

eggs

Primitive people have always regarded eggs as a symbol of fertility and magic. The Romans, for example, kept sacred chickens for divination purposes and the egg crop was the preserve of the priest in charge! Christians are supposed to abstain from eating eggs during Lent. This has religious significance but more probably it was to allow the first eggs of the spring to hatch. Yeastre, goddess of fertility, had as her symbols the hare and the egg; these were speedily adopted by the early Christian church as the Easter egg and the Easter bunny. The taint of the old religion accounts for a number of superstitious links between eggs and witchcraft – for instance children are sometimes told to bash the bottom of their empty eggshell to stop witches using them as boats or, the white of an egg dropped into water on New Year's Eve by a young virgin is supposed to show, in the patterns formed, her marriage prospects. In Brazil young children are given dew collected during a full moon in an eggshell to help their speech development.

Your worry as a new henwife however is what to do with your egg glut whilst the hens are laying. First you need to test your eggs for freshness. The simplest way to do this is to put the egg into a deep bowl of water; a really fresh egg will sink virtually flat but as it ages the pointed end will sink and the egg eventually will stand upright. If an egg floats on the top then save if for throwing at a politician.

We are told that eggs keep fresh at room temperature for about twelve days, and three weeks in a refrigerator or at 7–8°C. However the reality is that kept in a cool, slightly damp cellar, they will keep for up to three months and I have incubated pheasant eggs kept in such conditions after four weeks.

cooking with your egg glut

Pasta is a great way of using up eggs and freezes well, either cut into strips or as sheets for dishes such as lasagne. Eggs cooked into made dishes will also freeze but do check that the recipe is suitable for freezing. Other ways of storing eggs are to make mayonnaise or curd with the yolks, and meringues, which keep well in airtight containers, with the whites.

Another good use for whole eggs is to convert them into pancakes, which freeze perfectly, or keep in an airtight container for about two weeks. Not all methods are advisable – the islanders of northern Scotland and Ireland stored their eggs, probably seabirds' eggs, between layers of peat ash in underground chambers known as souterraines. Sir Lindsay Scott, who I am convinced must be related to Johnny, visited the islands in the 1690s and reported that the eggs were kept for six to eight months, after which they became very appetizing and satisfactorily loosening, especially those that were on the turn! I must remember to get some in for Johnny's next visit.

Top centre: Burford brown chicken egg; Top right: Old Cotswold legbar chicken egg; Bottom right: duck egg; Bottom left: quail's eggs; Top left: goose egg

pancakes

MAKES 8–12

Pancakes are hypnotically pleasant to make, but always remember the first one is for the dog as it never seems to work! Pancakes are not fried in fat; the pan is rubbed with fat merely to stop them sticking. Use a 15cm cast-iron pan or a special omelette pan. Some people prefer to use half milk and half water for a lighter batter, extra butter or oil for a richer crêpe, and cream for some recipes. This is however the best batter for freezing. Instead of stacking the pancakes between paper before freezing you can freeze them individually and then stack them afterwards.

A rather charming recipe I came across from the days of harder winters suggests briskly beating 3 tablespoons of snow into the batter just before cooking. As I found this recipe after I stopped skiing, I haven't tried it yet.

110g plain flour
salt, a pinch
1 medium egg
300ml milk
1 tbsp oil or melted unsalted butter, for frying

Sieve the flour and salt into a bowl, make a well and drop in the egg. Add a little milk and stir gradually, drawing the mixture in from the sides. When it has become a thick cream, stir in the oil or butter and beat well, then stir in the rest of the milk. Strain the mixture into a jug for easier pouring and to ensure there are no lumps. Heat your pan and grease with a smidgen of butter or oil. I use two pans the same size and turn the pancake from one to the other as tossing wastes a lot of time and pancakes unless you are incredibly adept. Grease your pan between each pancake and if you aren't using two pans, use a palette knife to turn them.

an excess of eggs?

Apart from cooking delicious dishes using your eggs, there are several ways of keeping your glut.

● Preserving – Eggs to be preserved whole in the shell should be clean and dry, but do not wash them as the shell is porous and this practice can cause disease. Instead, wipe them with a damp cloth and then a dry one. You can then rub them with buttered paper or liquid paraffin so that all air is excluded and they will keep for six months or longer.

● Storing in isinglass – When I was a child we used to store eggs in isinglass (see page 119), which can be bought from a good pharmacist. The eggs are layered point downwards in an earthenware crock or glass jar. You pour over the cool liquid, ensuring the top layer of eggs is completely submerged, and then cover to keep out bugs and dirt and prevent evaporation. Eggs stored like this will keep from six months to a year, but they should be used for baking or made dishes as they have a slight taste if boiled or poached and the shells will crack if boiled. After six months the whites go a little thin so they are not really suitable for whipping.

● Freezing eggs is another successful way of preserving your glut. Remove them from the shell and freeze them separately or, if you are freezing larger numbers, fork them together, adding a teaspoon of salt or sugar per 5 eggs. Make sure you label them carefully as to whether sweet or savoury and how many eggs are in each package. Eggs treated in this way are good for scrambling or baking and you can even fry or poach them straight from the freezer.

Yolks and whites can be frozen separately too – add sugar or salt to yolks and, as usual, don't forget to label them.

bread

In these days of Chorley Method baking when dough is steamed and glutens are stretched, it is difficult to remember how delicious properly baked bread is. I can remember driving down from London with a school friend and stopping in Uckfield to buy a loaf of white bread from the baker for her mother. The smell of the warm bread was so wonderful that we stopped in a lay-by six kilometres further on and ate the lot just as it was, and then had to go back for more.

The great thing about breadmaking is that it gets rid of anger and lowers your stress levels. This is thanks to the kneading, which distributes the yeast evenly through the flour and helps to develop the gluten. Kneading is an almost hypnotic practice that requires intense energy. I once shared a house with a woman who would get up at three in the morning when she couldn't sleep and make bread to relieve the tension caused by her nasty divorce.

bread in history

Historically, bread was, quite literally, the staff of life. Shortage of flour for its making invariably led to rioting in the streets. The Romans conquered North Africa and Egypt because the area was the bread basket of Italy, providing huge amounts of grain. 'Bread and circuses' was the motto for government and they used both as a way of subduing the mob just as social services today ensure the poor have a television. In the Middle Ages your wages from the great household you worked for were partly paid in loaves of bread. I never cease to be amazed at how much of it people ate then.

what flour can I use?

Bread can be made from all sorts of flour, some of which you may be growing yourself.

First and foremost, wheat has been a staple provider of flour for centuries. It is a good source of fibre, protein and vitamins B and E.

Barley flour (known as bere in Scotland) gives a dense, heavy loaf and has a mealy flavour. It is good when mixed with other flours. Barley is low in gluten which means that it may be tolerated by celiacs. Bere cornmeal or maize flour are not to be confused with the thickening agent cornflour.

Cornmeal must be mixed with wheat flour for making leavened bread but is used for flat breads and tortillas, mostly in the southern states of America, and in Mexico, Italy and Africa.

Oatflour is most easily obtained by grinding porridge oats. It is used to make oatcakes. An enzyme in oats is good for lowering cholesterol and healing wounds and adhesions. Oatflour can be added to wheat flour for flavour and nutrition.

Rye flour is the staple of much of Eastern Europe. It gives a dense, chewy dark loaf that can be eaten by celiacs. It is often mixed with sourdough for flavour.

Buckwheat is obtained from a plant of the rhubarb family and is native to Asiatic Russia. It is generally used to make blinis and pancakes and has a distinctive flavour.

Millet flour, or spelt, is the earliest known grain, high in protein, vitamins and minerals, but so low in gluten it is almost invariably mixed with wheat or rye so that it makes a risen loaf. In its natural state, it is very suitable for celiacs.

white versus brown

White flour has a lot less fibre – only about 75 per cent – and most of the bran and wheatgerm have been removed. If you buy bolted white flour – referred to as farmhouse flour – much more of the kernel is left. This type of flour is usually from stone-grinding mills.

Brown flour retains about 85 per cent of its kernel but some of the bran has been removed, hence the theory that brown bread is better for you. Sadly, that is only true of proper bread. I won't tell you what they do to the commercial stuff.

Wholemeal or wholewheat flour contains 100 per cent of the kernel, and is sold in either coarser or finer varieties. The bran will hinder the development of the gluten and hence the rising of the bread, which is why a wholemeal loaf tends to be heavy. Hard, or strong, flours will rise better as they are made from hard wheats which have a higher proportion of protein to starch.

getting the bread to rise

To make leavened bread, you need to add yeast. It was the Egyptians who first made yeasted bread and it is generally believed to have happened by accident when some yeast spores floated across from a brewing plant. Beer is really bread without flour, or so a lot of my drinking friends try to tell me.

Yeast is a living organism and needs gentle warmth, sugar or flour to stimulate its growth. It is the carbon dioxide it produces whilst growing that causes the dough to rise. It is most important to get the temperature right: too cold and it inhibits the yeast's growth and too hot and it dies. The ideal temperature is 38°C/98.6°F or, as it is usually referred to, blood heat.

Bread rises in the warmth but some advocate a slower, cooler rise for a better-tasting loaf. I don't know if my nerves could take it! Cover your dough whilst it is rising or you will get an impenetrable crust. If dough rises too long it will collapse in on itself whilst cooking.

You have a choice of fresh or dried yeast. Fresh is better but is not always available. Using too much yeast causes the bread to become stale more quickly.

greasing the tins

When greasing my loaf tins, I use unsalted butter as I find there is less sticking, but vegetable oil or lard will do.

be consistent

Once you have made dough successfully, remember its consistency. That is the consistency you should always aim for and you may find that you need to add more or less liquid than a recipe dictates to achieve it.

basic white loaf

MAKES A 900g LOAF

15g fresh yeast
680g unbleached white flour
15g salt
430ml water
unsalted butter for greasing
flour for dusting

Crumble the fresh yeast into a bowl and add 4 tablespoons lukewarm water. Cream to a smooth liquid. Sift the flour into a larger bowl, add the salt, make a well in the centre and pour in the yeast, then pour in the remaining lukewarm water. With your hands, draw the flour into the liquid and mix thoroughly to form a smooth, thick batter in the well, with flour still unmixed around the outside. Sprinkle this with a little flour to prevent a skin forming. Leave the mixture to stand, covered for half an hour during which time it will become frothy and aerated.

Now mix the remaining flour into the batter. Form the dough into a ball, adding a little more water if it is too dry or a little more flour if it is too sticky. Knead the dough on a lightly floured surface. Stretch it away from you, form it back into a ball then give it a turn and continue for about 10 minutes. Fascinatingly, the dough will change texture, becoming elastic and glossy.

When you have finished kneading, form the dough into a smooth ball. Put it into a lightly greased bowl to prevent sticking and cover with a clean tea towel. Leave to stand for anything up to two hours, depending how warm the place is where you have left it. It will double in size. Place on a lightly floured surface. If properly risen the dough will not spring back when you stick a finger in it.

Punch the dough with your knuckles to flatten it. This is known as knocking back. Gently knead the dough to shape it

into an oval. As if practising a karate chop, make a good crease lengthways along the dough with the edge of your hand, then fold over and roll into an oval ballotine. Slash the top of the dough diagonally two or three times, cover with a damp tea towel and leave to rise again to double its size. Meanwhile, lightly grease a baking sheet, transfer the risen dough to the sheet and bake in a preheated oven at Gas Mark 7/220°C/425°F for about 15 minutes. Reduce the heat to Gas Mark 5/190°C/375°F for a further 20-25 minutes.

If you are using a loaf tin, lightly grease a 900g loaf tin, put the risen dough in the tin and bake in the same way.

Remove the loaf from the oven and from the tin, if used. Tap the underneath of the loaf and if it doesn't sound hollow, return it to the oven for a further 5 minutes. Cool on a wire rack.

granary loaf

This is a good nutty brown loaf that isn't too heavy.

MAKES A 900g LOAF

680g granary flour
1/2 tsp salt
400ml water
1 tbsp vegetable oil
unsalted butter for greasing

Make as for the basic white loaf. When you add the last of the water, also add the oil. Leave the dough to rise until it has doubled in size. Meanwhile, lightly grease a 900g loaf tin. Knock the dough back and gently shape it to fit the tin. Place the dough in the tin, seam side down, and leave to stand for about 1 hour, until it has doubled. Cook in a preheated oven Gas Mark 8/230°C/450°F for 15 minutes. Lower the oven to Gas Mark 6/200°C/400°F for another 25–30 minutes until the loaf sounds hollow when tapped underneath. Cool on a wire rack.

cottage loaf

There is something very cosy about a cottage loaf, especially eaten by a winter's fire with lashings of butter and jam. I suppose it is the shape that makes it so cosy. The Germans would call it gemütlich.

MAKES A 900g LOAF

15g fresh yeast
680g unbleached white flour
15g salt
430ml water
unsalted butter for greasing
flour for dusting
1 egg, beaten
unsalted butter for greasing

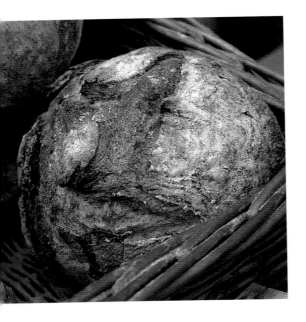

Lightly grease a baking sheet. Proceed as for the basic white loaf. When you reach the knock-back stage, knock back the dough and take off one-third. Form both pieces of dough into balls. Set them well apart on the baking sheet and cover with a tea towel. Leave to rise for about 40 minutes; they will not quite have doubled. Gently flatten each ball and put the smaller one on top. Push your thumb and first two fingers into the middle of the loaf and leave it rest for another 10 minutes, no longer. Glaze with the beaten egg.

Slash round the edges of both layers with a very sharp knife. Bake for 15 minutes at Gas Mark 8/230°C/450°F then reduce the heat to Gas Mark 6/200°C/400°F for 25–30 minutes until the loaf sounds hollow when tapped underneath. Cool on a wire rack.

baps

In Scotland we eat baps at breakfast. When I was in charge of the catering at the Museum of Flight in East Lothian, we were voted as having the best bacon butties, but actually they were baps.

MAKES 12

15g fresh yeast
430ml lukewarm milk and water mixed
55g diced lard
680g unbleached white flour
1/2 tsp salt
1 tsp caster sugar
milk for glazing
flour for dusting
unsalted butter for greasing

Crumble the yeast and mix to a paste with 2 tbsp of the milk and water mixture. Rub the lard into the flour to a fine crumb. Make a well, add the salt and sugar, and pour in all the liquids. Mix to a soft dough. It should not stick to you or to the bowl. Knead for 10 minutes on a floured surface until silky, put into a lightly greased bowl and cover with a damp towel. Leave to rise until about double the size. Meanwhile,

lightly grease 2 baking sheets. Knock back the dough and knead briefly, then divide into 12 portions.

Pat each into an oval about 1cm thick. Put on the baking sheets, glaze with milk and sift on a fine dusting of flour. Leave to stand for 30 minutes until doubled in size. Flour again and press your thumb into the middle of each bap so that it stays flat. Bake in a preheated oven at Gas Mark 7/220°C/425°F for 15 minutes. Transfer to a wire rack and eat when they can be handled.

swedish rye bread

My dear friend the Swedish food photographer Carin Simon introduced me to the joy of this delicious bread.

MAKES A 450g LOAF

170g white flour
370g stoneground rye flour
1^1/$_2$ tsp salt
25g unsalted butter
15g fresh yeast
140ml lukewarm milk
140ml buttermilk
1 tbsp treacle or molasses;

Put the flours and salt in a large bowl and mix in the butter with your fingers to fine crumb. Cream the yeast with the milk and pour into the flour. Add the buttermilk and treacle and mix together. Work the mixture until you have a soft, sticky dough. Turn onto a floured board and knead for 10 minutes. Return to the bowl, cover with a damp tea towel and leave to rise for 2 hours or until the dough has doubled. Meanwhile, lightly grease a baking sheet. Knock the dough back, turn it onto a board and shape into a loaf. Place on the baking sheet and slash the dough straight down the middle lengthways with a knife. Cover and leave to rise until it has doubled again. Bake in a preheated oven at Gas Mark 6/200°C/400°F for 40–45 minutes until it sounds hollow when tapped underneath. Cool on a wire rack. Do not cut this bread warm.

spelt bread

You will either love it or hate it, but if you're a celiac it's safe.

MAKES A 900g LOAF

15g fresh yeast
570ml water
1/2 tsp salt
1 tbsp vegetable oil
680g spelt flour
unsalted butter for greasing

Lightly grease a 900g loaf tin. Mix the yeast with half the water. Mix together the remaining water, the salt and the oil. Pour the yeast liquid into the flour and mix roughly. Add the remaining liquid and mix thoroughly by hand for 5 minutes. The dough will cease being sticky as you work it. Pour the mixture into the tin and smooth the top with a damp pastry brush. Cover with a tea towel and leave to rise for 35–40 minutes, or until the dough reaches almost to the top of the tin. Bake for 45–50 minutes in a preheated oven at Gas Mark 6/200°C/400°F, until the loaf sounds hollow when tapped underneath. Cool on a wire rack.

corn dabs

Flour was scarce in the early American Colonies. The main crop was maize or Indian Corn as it was known, but if a woman had followed her man halfway round the world in appalling conditions, she wasn't going to let a little thing like the lack of flour deter her. I love corn bread. It's a thing you scarcely ever find unless you make it yourself and it's delicious with fat pork and collard greens or clam stew.

This recipe has no leavening agent and should be made in bun tins or the sort of shallow loaf tin you use for tea breads. Muffin tins will do. If you are in America and visiting a historic house you can buy corn stick pans. If you aren't grinding your own maize yet, you can buy cornmeal in Italian delicatessens.

I copied this recipe into my own book from an American Heritage book but cannot this far on remember which historic house it came from. It works very well but you must guard against scorching.

MAKES ABOUT 6

140g yellow cornmeal
pinch of salt
170ml boiling water
58ml sour cream
1 tbsp bacon fat, plus extra for greasing
1 medium egg, beaten

Add the salt to the cornmeal, then pour on the boiling water and let it stand for a few minutes. Stir in the cream. Mix well and leave for a further 10 minutes. Meanwhile, brush your tins with melted bacon fat and put them into a preheated oven, Gas Mark 7/220°C/425°F, to heat up. Stir the bacon fat and the egg into the corn mixture. Spoon the mixture into the pans and bake for about 15 minutes or until an inserted knife comes out clean. The pans should be very hot when you put the mixture in. The recipe works on the same principle as Yorkshire pudding. Serve warm.

sourdough bread

This is the most ancient way of making leavened bread and is probably the same as the method used by the ancient Egyptians. It involves using a 'starter' made of unbleached plain flour and water, which you can then use with any other flour – though wholemeal or rye flour are more commonly used – to make your sourdough bread. To make a starter takes three days but with any luck you will only make it once and you can then keep it and leave it to your grandchildren. It is also used for making friendship cakes – so called because you give a piece of the starter to a couple of friends before adding all the fruit and other goodies that make the cake.

When you make your starter, remember that it picks up fresh yeast from the air, so when you leave it to stand, cover it with a damp cloth and re-dampen it daily – no nonsense with clingfilm or foil. The famous Poulin bakers of Paris, who only make sourdough bread, bake their bread in a cloth-lined basket.

Sourdough bread has amazing keeping qualities. In that lovely book *A Wild Nettle Soup*, the family who live in the French mountains were snowed in all winter and baked their sourdough bread in October to last them until the snows melted. They stored it in a wooden chest where it went hard, not bad. You know when it tells you in soup recipes to place some bread in the bottom of the soup bowl and pour on the soup, and you wonder why it doesn't work with modern bread. Well, those recipes really call for hard sourdough bread which people sometimes had to chip with an axe.

Yukon miners used to carry a piece of sourdough starter under their shirts to prevent it being stolen and to stop it from freezing. Now there's a gourmet flavour for you.

To make the starter
Take 240g unbleached plain flour and 230ml lukewarm water. Mix these together into a thick batter, cover with a damp tea towel and leave at room temperature in your kitchen for three days, re-dampening the towel each day. After this, the batter should smell sour but not bad and should be slightly grey and bubbly. If it smells bad it has failed, in which case throw it out and start again.

On the fourth day, pour the starter into a larger non-metal bowl and add 140ml lukewarm water and 230g of the same flour. Mix thoroughly with your hand, cover with a damp tea towel and leave for 24–36 hours, depending how strong you like your bread. The starter is now ready to use and will be spongy and slightly bubbly.

To make the sourdough bread
Stir the starter well and add 55ml lukewarm water and up to 230g flour to make a soft but not sticky dough. Knead for 10 minutes and return to the bowl. Cover with a damp tea towel and leave to stand for 8–12 hours until it has doubled in size. Meanwhile, lightly grease a baking sheet. Knock back the dough and cut off a 225g piece to keep as your future starter. Make the rest into a ball and stand on the baking sheet. Cover with a damp tea towel and leave to stand for a further 8 hours or until it has doubled in size. Slash the top 4 times with a very sharp knife; the loaf may collapse if the dough is dragged. Bake for 20 minutes in a preheated oven at Gas Mark 7/220°C/425°F. Reduce the heat to Gas Mark 5/190°C/375°F for a further 40–55 minutes, until the loaf sounds hollow when tapped underneath. Turn onto a wire rack and do not eat until completely cool.

Your saved starter will keep for 3 days in a plastic bag in the fridge or 2 days at room temperature under a damp cloth. To re-use start the process as at the fourth day above.

soda bread

This is probably the easiest bread to make. The recipe was given to me by my friend Marianne whose mother's family came from Drina in Northern Ireland. Isabel of the weeds (see page 24) tells me that she used to make her soda bread in an old terracotta flowerpot, but you had to put a tin lid in the bottom to stop the dough coming through the hole.

Fried soda bread cooked in hot bacon fat is the best. My maternal grandmother came from Gory in County Wexford and there they make soda bread farls (triangles) on top of the stove in a frying pan with a

---

upsizing a cake recipe

Mary Berry once gave me a great tip for working out how to upsize a cake recipe. Fill the tin you usually bake the cake in with water up to the level that the cake mixture usually occupies. Pour the water into the bigger tin and repeat until the bigger tin is filled to the same level. The number of times you have to do this gives you the multiplier for the larger cake recipe.

---

metal lid. To make them, form your dough into a 2.5cm-thick disk and cut it into 4 triangles. Cook in a frying pan in hot bacon fat over a medium heat, turning every 5 minutes.

MAKES A 345g LOAF

230g stoneground white or wholemeal flour
115g self-raising flour
1 tsp salt
1 tsp bicarbonate of soda
30g unsalted butter, cut into small dice
sour milk or buttermilk, as required
flour for dusting

Put the flours, salt and the bicarbonate of soda into a mixing bowl, rub in the butter and add enough sour milk or buttermilk to make a stiff dough. Knead until the dough is smooth, shape into a flat loaf and put on a baking sheet. Sprinkle with flour and cut a deep cross into the loaf. Bake in a preheated oven, with a large cake tin over the top at Gas Mark 6/200°C/400°F for 20–25 minutes until the loaf sounds hollow when tapped underneath. Wrap it in a tea towel to cool or the crust will be very thick.

home baking

Well, you now have a good cross-section of breads to try your skills on so let us move on to home baking. I learnt to make cakes one frenetic weekend when I was in my thirties and about to start my first domestic job. My new boss said, 'We always like to have a cake knocking about

---

the place.' I froze. Though I had made bread and puddings, I had never baked a cake. I fled to my friend, the author and poet Christine Coleman, and we spent an intense weekend baking, since when I have never looked back.

One thing you need to remember about cakes is that you can make them in any old container but for an easy life, buy springform tins. These have springs on the side and detachable bases. Remember, take care to line and grease your cake tins before use. Otherwise, the pain of breaking a cake when you take it out of the tin is indescribable.

singing hinnies

I love the name of these little Northumbrian teacakes. When they are cooked you cut them into wedges, butter them, stick them back together again and eat them warm by a roaring fire after a day's hunting – or should I now say hound exercising – on the cold Northumbrian hills.

MAKES 6–8

450g self-raising flour
1 tsp salt
100g lard
100g caster sugar
170g currants
2 medium eggs, beaten
140ml milk
unsalted butter for greasing

Grease and preheat a griddle. Sift the flour and salt together, then rub in the lard. Mix in the sugar and currants. Make a well in the flour and add the eggs and the milk. Mix thoroughly into a soft, elastic dough. Roll out to 1.5cm thick and cut into 2 rounds. Cook on the griddle for about 10 minutes until golden brown, turning them over halfway through.

boiled fruit cake

This is a very easy cake believed to hail from Gloucestershire.

MAKES A 150mm CAKE

3oz caster sugar
50g unsalted butter
50g golden syrup
3 medium eggs
75g dried fruit
50g plain flour
1/4 tsp bicarbonate of soda
1 tsp mixed spice
unsalted butter for greasing

Grease a 150mm cake tin. Boil the sugar, butter and syrup in a pan and set aside to cool. Beat in the eggs and add all the other ingredients. Spoon into the cake tin and bake at Gas Mark 4/180°C/350°F for 1¹/₂–2 hours. Turn out and cool on a wire rack.

devon black cake

This is a wonderful cake that should be stored for a year, then covered in marzipan and royal icing. The Cornish version has no black treacle. Black Cakes, like Scottish Black Buns, are made to be eaten at New Year rather than Christmas. This very rich cake is great to wrap and take in your pocket when you are out shooting or walking.

The idea of beating the eggs over hot water is not to cook them but to warm them through slightly and stop them curdling when they are added to the butter and sugar. If you are nervous about this, beat them into the mixture instead, adding a little flour before each egg.

MAKES A 230mm CAKE

350g unsalted butter
350g caster sugar
12 medium eggs
225g plain flour, sieved

3/4 tsp baking powder
1/2 tsp bicarbonate of soda
1 tsp mixed spice
1 tsp grated nutmeg
2 tsp ground cinnamon
225g rice flour
900g currants
100g chopped raisins
350g chopped sultanas
225g chopped candied orange peel
225g chopped candied lemon peel
225g blanched, chopped almonds
2 tbsp brandy
170g black treacle
unsalted butter for greasing

Double line and grease a 230mm cake tin. Cream the butter and sugar well together. Beat the eggs into a large bowl over hot water until they are creamy then whisk into the butter and sugar mixture. Fold in the sieved flour, baking powder, bicarbonate of soda, the spices and the rice flour. Finally add the fruit, the brandy and the black treacle

Pour the mixture into the tin. Bake at Gas Mark 4/180°C/350°F for 3 hours. Leave to cool slightly in the tin for 30 minutes then turn out and cool completely on a wire rack.

marlborough cake

Marlborough in Wiltshire was once a great coaching stop. This Georgian recipe was offered to stagecoach passengers with a mug of beer whilst their horses were being changed. The caraway seeds would have provided a good palliative against the nausea caused by travelling.

MAKES A 230mm CAKE

4 medium eggs
170g plain flour
225g caster sugar
30g caraway seeds
icing sugar for dusting
unsalted butter for greasing

Grease and flour a 230mm cake tin. Whisk your eggs over a pan of warm water until creamy and thick enough for the whisk to leave a trail. Remove from the heat and sift in half the flour and the caster sugar. Add the caraway seeds with a metal spoon, then fold in the remaining flour. Bake in a preheated oven at Gas Mark 7/220°C/425°F for 10 minutes. Turn out and cool on a wire rack. Sift icing sugar over the top when cool.

crumpets

It always seems to amaze people if you make your own crumpets, but it isn't hard and they are much nicer than the bought ones.

MAKES 18–20

15g fresh yeast
500ml warm water
550g plain flour
1 tsp salt
unsalted butter for greasing

Preheat a griddle – otherwise use the hot plate of your oven. Grease and preheat the crumpet rings. Dissolve the yeast in a little of the warm water. Sift the flour and salt together, then stir in the remaining water. Add the yeast liquid, cover with a cloth and keep in a warm place until the dough is well risen. Thin to a batter consistency with a little warm water and leave for 5 minutes. It is a good idea to try cooking one crumpet first; if the batter is too thick the holes will not form, in which case add a little more water and console yourself by eating the imperfect one with butter.

Place the crumpet rings on the hot plate and fill them half-full with batter. When the mixture is dry on top and slightly browned on the underside, turn the rings over to cook the other side. Remove the crumpets from the rings and serve with butter.

preserving in salt

Quite when salt was first used to preserve food has been lost in the mists of time. What is certain however, is that for thousands of years, until the invention of refrigeration in the late nineteenth century, salt was essential to the winter survival of people living in temperate latitudes. Salting and pickling of meat and fish was still commonplace in rural areas well into the 1980s in Britain and still is across large parts of Europe and rural north America, with many farm workers making their own bacon and hams and pickling mutton and beef.

salting

Salt works as a preservative by draining moisture from fresh meat or fish through osmosis. Without water, access is denied to bacterium and so decay is prevented. The removal of superfluous water also means that the flavour is better as it is more concentrated.

Traditionally, cattle and beef were slaughtered in October, when they were fat from summer grazing and before the grass ran out, with pigs slaughtered a month later. This is the best time to salt: the cooler the weather, the less bacteria and the lower the risk of contamination from flies.

dry-salting

This method involves rubbing a joint of meat with a mixture of salt and sugar over a period of several weeks. The juices are drawn out of the meat and allowed to drain away. At home, I have an old stone larder next to the cellars, with deep, slate curing shelves. These have channels that direct fluids to holes above a drain. A simple alternative is a grid made of several wooden rods, sterilized by boiling, and placed across an old earthenware sink or shallow wooden box.

bacon flitch (belly pork)

I am lucky to have eaten bacon like this for much of my farming life. It is delicious and bears no resemblance to that insipid muck they sell in the supermarket. A ham can be cured in the same way, although it must be pressed with heavy weights balanced on a board to hasten the de-moisturizing process. A leg of mutton or venison may also be cured this way to make mutton and venison hams. Simply add dried juniper berries to the mixture. Many hill shepherds, who could not keep a pig, made mutton ham and ate it fried it for breakfast like bacon.

FOR A 5 kg BACON FLITCH

1 kg sea salt
225g Barbados sugar
1 bay leaf

Mix all the ingredients together. Divide half the mixture into 3 batches. Rub one batch well into every crevice of the flitch. Layer the second batch across the bottom of the sink or box. Lay the flitch on top, cover with the third batch of mixture and cover with a muslin cloth.

After 3 days, repeat using half the remaining mixture. Leave for a week and repeat. If you find that you have run short of the salting mixture, simply make up some more.

Leave the flitch, well covered in the mixture, for 3 weeks. If your flitch happens to be smaller than this, leave it for 2 days per 0.45 kg.

After 3 weeks wipe off with a dry cloth, then put it in a muslin bag and hang it in a dry place. It will last like this for ages, getting harder as time goes on. If it becomes too hard, you may have to soak it overnight before frying it.

pickled meat

This is a recipe I have adapted from Jane Grigson, which we often make for Christmas. It is absolutely delicious and, if kept in cool place, will easily last through Christmas and into the New Year.

FOR A 3 kg JOINT OF SILVERSIDE

90g Barbados sugar
120g sea salt
30g freshly ground black pepper
30g crushed juniper berries
20g crushed allspice
suet, to cover

Rub the joint all over with the sugar and leave in a deep pot for 2 days. Mix together all the other ingredients except the suet and rub well into the joint every day for the next 10 days. Keep the pot covered. The mixture will soon turn to liquid. Do not discard but continue to rub it into the joint.

Preheat the oven to Gas Mark 1/140°C/ 275°F. Remove the joint from the pickling mixture and wipe clean. Stand it in a deep pot with 250–280ml water. Cover the top of the meat with suet. Fix the lid of the pot on with greaseproof paper so that it is tightly sealed and no moisture can escape. Bake in the preheated oven for 45 minutes per 500g. Allow to cool in the liquid. Drain, place on a dish and cover with a wooden board with a weight on top. Leave for 24 hours after which it is ready to eat.

fish fillets

Fillets of salmon, bass or sea trout are very good cured using a similar method to the pickled meat. They will keep for about 5 days.

FOR A 1 kg FILLET OF FISH

500g sea salt
500g demerara sugar
1 tsp ground black pepper
zest of a lemon
50g chopped dill

Mix all the ingredients together. Divide the mixture into 2 batches. Lay half of the first batch in the bottom of a glass or porcelain dish and put the fillet on top. Smother with the remainder of the first batch. Put a weighted board on top. Leave for 36 hours then drain off the liquid and remove the fillet. Put half the remaining batch of mixture in the dish, replace the fillet in the dish, turning it over and cover with the rest of the mixture. Leave for another 36 hours.

salted cod

Smother cod fillets in salt in a wooden box or similar receptacle that will allow the fluid to drain away. Leave for a fortnight, then hang up somewhere cool and dry, shaking off any excess salt. When you require some cod to eat, hack off a piece and soak in water for 48 hours, changing the water at least twice.

meat in brine

Some of the great recipes of English cuisine, which you rarely see nowadays, involve boiled salt meats, for example boiled salt beef and carrots or boiled salt mutton and caper sauce. A properly made and well looked-after brine tub is a wonderful way of preserving a variety of meats through the winter.

FOR A 4 kg JOINT SUCH AS BRISKET OF BEEF, HAM OR A LEG OF MUTTON

1 kg sea salt
200g Barbados sugar
2 tsp black pepper
2 tsp juniper berries
2 tsp mustard seed
2 tsp coriander
2 tsp cloves
2 large bay leaves, crumbled

Mix together all the ingredients. Rub a handful of the mixture into your joint and leave to drain for 24 hours to draw out the moisture.

The following day, bring the rest of the mixture to a boil in 4½ litres water. Simmer for 30 minutes. Pour into a glazed crock or other non-metallic container – your brine tub – large enough to submerge the joint. When the mixture is cool but not cold, put the meat in. Keep the joint below the surface of the brine with a board weighted down with a stone. Cover to exclude the light.

As a rule of thumb, small joints should be kept in the brine for 2 days per 500g, larger joints for 3 days. The longer the better. Turn the joints every 4 or 5 days.

Remove the joint from the brine and hang it up somewhere cool and dark in a muslin bag. It will keep for a long time in a cool, dry place but is best eaten within 6 months. Generally, brisket of beef and leg of mutton are eaten fairly soon or are smoked (see page 196). York hams were traditionally buried in oak sawdust after they had been brined.

The brine will stay good for several months and can be used over and over again. If it happens to turn viscous, boil it up again, this time using half the recipe quantity. Sterilize the crock and return the brine to it.

using a drying box

Dried meat delicacies are the speciality of countries with arid climates. They are produced by air curing, where moisture is drawn out by the sun. This process is simple to replicate – and well worth the time and expense – if you build or buy a drying box or dehydrator. Virtually any meat or fish can be dried in this way as long as it is taken off the bone and salted for a couple of hours first. The options for the marinades are endless.

biltong

A delicious type of biltong or 'jerky' can easily be made in a drying box. Use any lean red meat – venison is delicious, while the best South African biltong is made from antelope. Cut the meat along the grain into 1cm-thick strips 20cm long. Smother in sea salt and leave for 2 hours. Brush off the salt and lay in a marinade of your choice for 24 hours. Hang up to drain and when dry, roll in bruised peppercorns. Transfer to a drying box for 4 days.

sausages

One of life's never-ending adventures is making sausages. There is an enormous range of cured salamis – saucissons de montagne, morcillas, chorizos, to name but a few. They are preserved by a combination of a fermenting agent, drying, smoking and storing. The permutations for experimenting are endless.

The acidophilus guarantees the necessary fermentation and I recommend its use if you live in a temperate climate. In the arid country areas of places such as France, Spain and Italy, they can rely on the bacteria forming naturally.

MAKES A 1.5 kg SAUCISSON DE MONTAGNE TYPE

1.3 kg fatty boneless pork
250g pork back fat
6 cloves garlic
120ml red wine
45g bruised peppercorns
45g sea salt
45g cayenne pepper
45g caraway seeds
sausage casing
1/2 tsp acidophilus (optional)

Coarsely mince the pork. Cut the back fat into 6mm chunks and mix with the pork. Add all the remaining ingredients. Stuff the casings with the mixture and hang in the drying box for 2 days. If you live in a dry, arid environment, hang outside for 2 days. Then smoke (see page 196) using beechwood sawdust for a further 3 days. Tie with string and hang somewhere dry, airy and with a constant cool temperature for 6 weeks. The sausages will now be ready to eat, but will continue to mature the longer that you leave them.

making a drying box

Make or buy a tightly sealed wooden cupboard, with a hinged door. The cupboard should be 80cm high by 60cm wide and 75cm deep. Drill holes at 5cm intervals along the bottom and top of the sides of the cupboard.

Fix two hanging rails 15cm apart near the roof, and a removable 60cm by 75cm perforated board 45cm from the bottom. Rest the board on battens fixed to the walls. Connect a light fitting to the middle of the bottom with an 80-watt bulb pointing upwards. Keep the box in a dry dark place. When the light is switched on, warm dry air rising from the bulb circulates round the box, drying whatever is hanging up inside.

fish

You can cure any easily skinned fish such as salmon, pike, perch or cod.

FOR 1.5 kg FISH

2 litres water
340g sea salt
juice and zest of 1 lemon
handful chopped fresh dill
lemon juice for seasoning
ground black pepper or chilli powder for seasoning

Skin the fish and fillet it. Mix together all the ingredients except the seasoning. Soak the fillets in this brine for 8 hours. Remove from the brine and drain for 12 hours. Season with the lemon juice and pepper or with chilli powder if you prefer. Cut into 2.5cm strips, then hang in the drying box for 3 days.

smoking

Smoking as a form of preserving became popular where there was not enough salt for either a prolonged dry-salt or to make a large quantity of brine. The anti-oxidants in the smoke preserve the flesh and the fact that they add a delicious flavour to fish and meat is an unintentional bonus.

Chimneys in many old houses had a recess in which hams were hung for smoking, which people have often mistaken for priest holes. The two crucial factors for smoking are the sawdust – beech and oak are best but any will do as long as it is hardwood – and that the temperature does not rise above 25°C.

A smoker does not need to be elaborate or complicated to do the job. All that is required is an enclosed chamber, in which a small sawdust fire can be lit, and an outlet for the smoke. At one time I used to use an old 90-litre beer barrel.

kippers

Can you imagine anything nicer than a home-smoked kipper? Buy really fresh herrings. Gut them, cutting right up through the ribcage so they can be flattened out. Wipe clean and place in a brine solution made by mixing 330g sea salt per litre of water. The quantity required will depend on the number of fish you are preparing. Weigh the fish down with a board and a stone, to stop them floating to the surface. Leave for 30 minutes, or longer if you like them salty. Hang them up to drain. Then suspend them in the smoker by their mouths and smoke for 12–16 hours.

salmon

For a bigger fish, like a salmon – the ultimate one-upmanship is to smoke your own catch. Follow the instructions for smoking kippers but immerse in the brine for 3 hours, or longer if you like your fish salty. Hang the fish up to drain then smoke for 3 days. If you want, you can make the following, more adventurous brine. It only suits salmon though.

1 litre strong beer
30g crushed juniper berries
30g black pepper
225g sea salt
225g Barbados sugar

Mix all the ingredients together, bring to the boil and simmer for 10 minutes. When cool, use to cover the salmon fillets for 12 hours, then smoke for 3 days. A rule of thumb of thumb for judging when the fish are ready is to weigh them just before they go into the smoker, then weigh them at 12 hour intervals. When they weigh just less than 75 per cent of their original weight, they are done.

beef

You need a well-hung, fat-free fillet of beef for this. Prick the beef all over with a thin needle to facilitate the penetration of the brine. Place in a brine solution made by mixing 330g sea salt per litre of water for 3 hours. Drain for 12 hours, then smoke for 5 days.

chicken

Prick the chicken with a thin needle down either side of the breast bone. Soak in a brine solution made by mixing 330g sea salt per litre of water for 3 hours. Hang to drain in a cool, dry place for 12 hours, then smoke for 24 hours.

You can use the same instructions to smoke pheasants, but soak for 2 hours and smoke for 18 hours.

goose and duck

You should only smoke the breasts. Cut the breasts from the carcass by slicing legthwise down either side of the breast bone and round the wish bone. Soak the breasts in a brine solution made by mixing 330g sea salt per litre of water for 3 hours, then smoke for 36 hours.

to make a smoker

Build or buy a hut, 2 metres high and with an area of 1.5 square metres, made of untreated wood and with a hinged door. Drill a couple of smoke holes on the three plain sides just below the roof. Place two breeze blocks end to end on either side and put a 1-metre-square perforated metal plate on top. A metre above this, hang a rack with hooks to hold the food to be smoked.

Place a gas ring under the metal plate and a bucketful of sawdust on top. Light the gas ring and let the sawdust smoulder away with the door of the smoker closed.

potting

Today we think of potted meat or potted shrimps as a delicacy but originally potting was developed as a means of preserving fish or meat. It is first recorded as a means of taking food to sea for long sea voyages. The food to be preserved was immersed under a layer of oil, clarified butter or lard in an earthenware pot whose top was sealed with a parchment cover tied tight with tarred twine. This excluded the bacteria, rather as canning or vacuum packing does today. Salmon was even exported 'potted' in red wine. Writing in 1609, Sir Hugh Platt, the Naval Secretary, recommends parboiling chickens, coating them in lard or clarified butter and laying them in stone pots filled to the brim with the same fat flavoured with some cloves and salt. These, he says, will keep for a good month.

The trick with potting is to cook your food with butter or lard, then mash it up and put more of the same fat as a seal on top. It is particularly pertinent if you keep ducks and geese, both of which exude large quantities of fat when cooked. The resulting confit is a great delicacy, as are rillettes, potted meat, still sold universally in Scotland, and of course potted shrimps.

glass or china?

So great was the clamour for potted goods that by the late eighteenth century the demand transformed the output of the pottery towns of Stoke-on-Trent and Colebrookdale. When cheaper glass jars became available, the demand for the china pots declined.

confit of goose

Confit is the most useful commodity to have in the larder. It is an essential ingredient for mutton stews, cassoulets, and so on, but also makes a delicious quick meal. Simply dig out the number of pieces required and warm in the oven. Use some of the fat to re-seal the jar and the rest to sauté some potatoes. Confit will last for several months.

The same recipe may be used for duck by halving the ingredients and the cooking time. The legs, wings and thighs of a roast duck or goose – pieces that are so often left – also make excellent confit material.

FOR A 4.5 kg GOOSE

110g sea salt
30g freshly ground black pepper
1 tsp grated nutmeg
2 bay leaves, crumbled
2 sprigs thyme, leaves removed

Preheat the oven to Gas Mark 3/170°C/325°F. Mix together all the ingredients. Joint the goose into 8 pieces – thighs, drumsticks, wings and breasts halved. Place on a baking sheet and cook in the preheated oven until the fat runs freely and the pieces are browning. Lower the heat to Gas Mark 1/2/130°C/250°F. Add more goose fat, if you have some, or lard, until the pieces are completely covered. Cook for 5 1/2 hours.

Remove the duck pieces and pour some of the fat into the bottom of a sterile terrine or large kilner jar. Add the pieces of goose in layers, ensuring that they do not touch the sides of the container. Cover each layer with fat. Seal and store in a cool dark place.

rillettes

Basically, this is a coarse meat paste preserved in fat in a sterile container. Cook pieces of rabbit, pork, duck and goose in the same way as you would for the duck confit (see above), adjusting the cooking time according to the weight of meat. When the meat is browned and running with fat, remove the meat from the baking sheet. Break it up with a fork and pot it and cover with fat as above. Rillettes will last for a couple of months in a cold dark place but must be eaten quickly once the seal has been broken.

potted shrimps

This recipe may be adapted to virtually any fish. It will keep for a fortnight or so in cool, dark place.

MAKES ABOUT 1 kg

350g unsalted butter
15g ground allspice
15g freshly ground black pepper
15g sea salt
15g freshly ground nutmeg
cayenne pepper, a good pinch
1 kg cooked Morecombe Bay shrimps

Preheat the oven to Gas Mark 7/220°C/425°F and sterilize jars of a convenient size. Melt the butter in a saucepan and mix with all the remaining ingredients except the shrimps. Place the shrimps in an ovenproof dish. Pour three-quarters of the melted butter over the shrimps and bake for 1 hour. Tip into sterilized jars and use the remaining butter to seal.

pickling, fermenting and ketchups

pickling

Pickling became popular in England in the sixteenth century when it largely replaced the salting of vegetables among the better-off. As pickling had been practised in China and Japan for centuries before, I like to think that, given the century and its improving trade routes with the Far East, someone may have brought back the idea but I'm afraid I have no proof.

Capers – the unopened flower buds of the Mediterranean shrub *Caperis spinosa* – became hugely popular in the eighteenth century but people who couldn't afford them made substitutes with pickled nasturtium and gorse buds, and very good they can be. Elder and hop shoots are also good pickled as are the unopened crosiers of the bracken plant, picked before any green appears. If you have a walnut tree, pick the fruits in their casings while they are still green and soft. They seldom ripen in Britain anyway. Prick them all over with a needle and leave in a brine solution (450g salt to 4½ litres of water) for 3–4 days, then rinse them off and leave them to dry on trays for a few days. When they turn black, pickle them in malt or wine vinegar.

Shallots are best for pickled onions and the Elizabethan society hostess Dame Eleanor Fettiplace pickled crab apples. Johnny made me some and they were very good but took a long time to mature. I suppose the most famous pickles are cucumbers or gherkins, for which you will need ridge cucumbers. Cleopatra apparently regarded them as a great beauty aid, which just shows how fashions change. History doesn't relate whether she ate them or added them to her ass's-milk baths. As W.C. Fields once said, 'Remember girls, you are born beautiful and if you ain't too bad but a good pickle cellar will still entice a man!'

Jars for pickling must be glass or stoneware as the vinegar reacts negatively with metal and the pickle will spoil. You can use any old jars really, as long as they don't leak. The trick lies in keeping the pickled object below the level of the vinegar so that the air can't get at it.

To sterilize your jars and seals, wash and rinse them in hot water then fill with boiling water and leave to stand for ten minutes. Then empty them and dry them in a cool oven.

sweetish pickle

If you are using this recipe to pickle fruit, add more sugar and use cinnamon, fresh ginger and allspice instead of the bay leaf, peppercorns and cloves.

MAKES 1¹/₂ LITRES

1 bay leaf
10 black peppercorns
6 allspice
6 cloves
1.7 litres vinegar
340g brown sugar
1¹/₂ tsp salt
1.3 kg prepared vegetables

Crush the spices slightly. Put them, together with the vinegar, sugar and salt into a pickling pan and bring to the boil. Add your vegetables and simmer for 5–10 minutes uncovered. Transfer to the pickling jars and pour over the hot vinegar to cover. Leave for 6 months before eating. The longer you leave them the better they will be. They keep for several years if you let them.

sour pickle

Make as for sweetish pickle but omit the sugar and add 7 small fresh or 10 small dried chillies instead. You can also add blades of mace, coriander seeds and fresh ginger according to taste.

ketchups

The name of these vinegar-based sauces may have originated in the Far East but, like kedgeree, they owe little else to the original. The eastern 'ketsiap' is a type of fish sauce.

In the nineteenth century, Britain became a haven of different sauces for the growing luxury food trade. The most favoured of these was perhaps mushroom ketchup.

Because the tomato is a relation of the deadly nightshade, the American settlers believed that it was only safe if cooked for several hours – hence the development of tomato ketchup. The original tomato ketchup was sharp but an American businessman called Davidson, recognizing his nation's passion for sugar, added lots. Now you wouldn't eat a hamburger without tomato ketchup. Curiously, British food snobs hate it whilst top French chefs adore it. Reading an English translation of an early Joel Reblochon book I was amused to find the translator writing, 'the chef only ever uses fresh tomato concasse'. The French original clearly had the chef using ketchup!

mushroom ketchup

You can use any mushrooms you like but the original mushroom ketchup called for horse mushrooms (Agaricus arvensis**), the large, flat, black-gilled wild mushrooms that can grow to the size of a dinner plate. The mushrooms are called by that name as it was believed the spores had to pass through the digestive system of the horse.**

1.3 kg horse mushrooms, sliced
2 tbsp salt
2 shallots, peeled and chopped
1 garlic bulb, cloves separated and crushed
850ml white wine vinegar
55ml port
3 anchovy fillets, preserved in oil
2 bay leaves, lightly crushed
6 cloves
10 white peppercorns
10 allspice
¹/₂ tsp freshly grated horseradish

Sterilize glass bottles or jars without metal lids. Cover the mushrooms with salt and leave in a cool place overnight. Remove from the bowl then throw everything into a pan, bring to the boil and simmer for 30 minutes. Leave to cool then bring back to the boil and cook for a further 30 minutes. Mix well in a blender, return to a clean pan and boil to reduce by one-third. Strain into the bottles or jars and seal. Keep for 1 month before using.

tomato ketchup

You will need really ripe tomatoes for this so let them go soft on the vine.

4.5 kg tomatoes
1 tsp white pepper
1 tsp ground nutmeg
1 tsp ground cinnamon
1 tsp allspice
2 tsp paprika
2 tsp salt
6 cloves garlic, chopped
225g sugar, according to taste
190ml white wine or cider vinegar

Sterilize glass jars without metal lids. Put all the ingredients into a pan, bring to the boil and simmer gently to reduce by one-third uncovered, for 2–4 hours. The slower you reduce it the better. Pass everything through a food mill and if it is too thin, simmer strongly to reduce further. Bottle in jars, seal and store for 10–12 months without opening, but shake the jars every 3 months.

walnut ketchup

MAKES ABOUT 1¹/₂ LITRES

2.5 kg green outer shells of walnuts
675g salt
50g bruised ginger root
50g whole allspice, lightly crushed
30g freshly ground black pepper
30g cloves

Sterilize glass bottles without metal lids.
Layer the walnuts in a tub with salt
sprinkled between each layer. Leave
uncovered or covered with a cloth to
stand for 6 days, stirring and mashing
occasionally until all the shells are soft
and pulpy. As liquid appears, drain it
away and reserve. The mixture should
produce several litres of liquid, with the
amount varying from year to year. (You
can put the rest of the walnuts on the
compost heap.) Simmer the liquid in a
cast-iron pan until the scum ceases to
rise then add the ginger, allspice, pepper
and cloves. Bring to a boil and simmer for
30 minutes. Strain and bottle, sealing
with a cork and wax. Leave for 6 months.

pickled lemons

**My favourite thing to pickle is lemons.
The best and easiest recipe comes from
my great heroine Claudia Roden.
Hopefully some of you reading this have
a lemon tree in your garden or even
your conservatory.**

6 thick-skinned lemons
6 tbsp sea salt
fresh lemon juice, to cover
4 tbsp olive oil (optional)

Wash the lemons if waxed, otherwise leave
unwashed. Cut the lemons into quarters,
but not right through so that the pieces are
still attached at the stem end. Stuff each
lemon with plenty of salt. Put them in a
sterilized glass jar, pressing them down so
that they are squashed together. Seal the
jar. Leave for 3–4 days. The skins will
soften and the juice will be drawn out of
the fruit. Press the lemons down as far as
they will go in the jar, placing a stone
inside to hold them down. Add fresh
lemon juice to cover them entirely, close
the jar and keep in a cool larder for at least
2 months, the longer the better. Wash well
to remove the salt before using. You can
also add olive oil at the end to keep the air
out if you like.

myths and cabbages

The cabbage is a curious plant. We all love
to hate it but it has survived since early
Egyptian times. The ancient Greeks believed
it sprang from the sweat of Zeus's armpit.
One can see why. The smell of the Inner
London Sessions when I was a barrister was
actually like boiled cabbage but was
indistinguishable from the sweat of the
prisoners in the cells below! I am not sure
whether cabbage has survived because it
is an excellent anti-scorbutic or because of
the myth that it diminishes the after-effects
of alcohol.

fermenting

Fermentation uses micro-organisms to
ferment food rather than turn it into
poisonous substances. It is a means of
processing that is well suited to cold,
damp climates with long unproductive
winters. It is still used in Scandinavia
where the surströmming, or sour herring,
of the Swedes and the rotted shark of the
Icelanders are still national delicacies. The
Finns too have a type of fermented small
fish which I actually quite enjoyed but I
desperately needed to call for the Epsom
salts the next day.

Russian borscht is another example of
fermentation. The reason it tastes
different and better than ordinary
beetroot soup is that the beetroot are
packed in barrels and left on the roof of a
shed to freeze. This causes fermentation
without the tedium of distilling, rather
like making applejack – a juice very like
Calvados – where the apples receive the
same treatment.

Two staple foods are fine examples of the
fermentation process. The first is kimchi,
the Korean pickled cabbage which is
placed in pots and buried in the ground
to ferment. Koreans are still given time
off work at the appropriate time to make
their kimchi and would not eat a meal
without it.

tofu

I know you can buy tofu in all its guises in Chinese supermarkets but you have just harvested a crop of soya beans, so why not make your own? The development of tofu, according to my late friend Yan Kit So, parallels the spread of Bhuddism in China and Japan with its vegetarian precepts. The similarity between cheese-making and tofu is quite noticeable. Once the curds are made they can be eaten soft, pressed, smoked, flavoured and fermented, just like cheese.

Take your dried beans and grind them quite finely. Add water to cover and bring them to the boil, stirring well so that they form a milk. This is of course soya milk, much used for dairy-allergic people and added to the tea and coffee of vegans.

You must now set the curds in the same way as cheese, but using either calcium sulphate or a substance called nagari, obtainable from Chinese and Japanese food shops, in place of rennet. Nagari is, as far as I can tell, sea salt with some added dry seaweed and I have no doubt that you could use sea salt just as efficaciously.

Once the curds are set you can eat them soft as a sort of pudding with honey or as a savoury with a little chilli and soy sauce. Or you can lightly salt them, wrap them in cheesecloth and press them. Before pressing you can add flavourings according to taste.

The other, and much more familiar example, is sauerkraut. For centuries, this has been the staple peasant food of central Europe, Germany and Russia and the making of sauerkraut is a serious matter. Once the potato harvest was over the peasant communities pulled together to make their stores. Originally sauerkraut was made in large pits in the ground lined with boards, but as barrels became more available, these were used instead. The cabbage was chopped and packed in layers in the pits or barrels with salt, then it was kept warm for a few days either in the kitchen or in some cases in the sitting room where a fire was lit specially. It was then transferred to a cool cellar for a month or two before broaching. Caraway or dill seeds were added and sometimes gherkins. The liquid remaining in the barrels when the sauerkraut was taken out was used as a flavouring. The smell must have been awesome. Maybe it is my Danish great-grandmother's genes, but I do love sauerkraut and in the dark days following Christmas I sometimes have an overwhelming compulsion to eat it.

sauerkraut

2 heads of cabbage
salt, 1 tbsp per 500g cabbage
2 tbsp caraway or dill seeds

Core and finely shred the cabbage. Sprinkle a layer of salt on the bottom of a large non-metallic container. Layer the cabbage with more salt and the caraway or dill seeds. Place a plate or board over the top and weigh it down with a non-metallic object. Cover and leave in a warm, dark place for 2 weeks, to ferment. Then either move the container to a cellar or re-pack in sterilized jars and store. Don't eat it for several months. It will keep at least a year.

drying fruit and vegetables

drying fruit

As a child I was fascinated by the differences between sultanas made from the white grapes of Smyrna in Turkey, Malaga raisins made from Muscat grapes, and currants, which are also actually dried grapes and have nothing to do with red, white and black currants. The smell of dried apricots takes me to warm sunny days with the fresh fruit ripening against a south-facing wall and dried prunes remind me not of the sanatorium but of boxes of sugar plums at Christmas. Also reminiscent of Christmas are dried dates in long sticky boxes.

If you live in a sun-drenched climate anywhere in the world, in most years you will have the advantage of being able to dry fruits in the sun. You can dry any fruits in this way. Lay them out flat on wooden wattles and leave them in the sun, turning them once or twice. You will, of course, have to fight off wasps, bees, birds and other predators. In North Africa they wash their figs in seawater before drying them, which seems to help.

If you don't live somewhere with enough sun, then you can always dry your fruit in the oven or kitchen range. Fifteen hours on a rack in the bottom oven of a four-door range or in a cooling bread oven will do the trick. If you only have a two-oven range, close the oven lids and lay the fruit on racks on top.

If you have an old-fashioned oven, you can try drying your fruit in it at Gas Mark 1/2/130°C/250°F. If you have a modern one and make meringues in it,

dry your fruit at the same setting, but do experiment first with a small quantity. I am lucky to live in a stone-built seventeenth-century cottage and I find that things just dry naturally hanging about the kitchen.

climate change?

I imagine the British habit of turning their fruits and vegetables into jams, chutneys and fruit leathers is dictated by the climate, though the ever-optimistic Scots surprised me by producing a six-hundred-year-old recipe for drying haddock on the rocks in the sun. Can't you see it now? 'Willy haste and bring in the fush? It's raining again!'

dried fruit tricks and tips

● Cut the peel of oranges and grapefruits into strips with the pith removed and dry them for adding to puddings and stews. Lemons will dry whole and can be added to stews or stick one in the cavity of a boiling fowl before poaching.

● If you live where your figs ripen, dry them, flatten them, then mix them with toasted sesame, anise, fennel and cumin seeds. Form them into balls, wrap them in fig leaves, then store them in stone jars. The Romans were very fond of eating figs this way. They go brilliantly with ham.

● Apples can also be peeled and cored and threaded on strings to hang by an open fire, as can mushrooms. The smells

will permeate the house all winter and make it wonderfully cosy. There is a particular type of apple called the Norfolk Biffin which was traditionally grown for drying.

● If you have a plum tree and want to dry your plums, let the fruit fall from the tree rather than pick it so that they are completely ripe for drying.

drying vegetables

Drying vegetables is much the same as drying fruit. I know the Poles dry green beans in the pod, but don't rush for them. Tomatoes should be dried in the oven, as can capsicums or chillies. The latter two can also be dried on their own on a rack or hung in a bunch to dry.

Sun-dried tomatoes for soups and stews take about fifteen hours. Sun-blushed or semi-dried tomatoes, which are good for

making fruit 'leather'

Another good way of drying fruit is as fruit leather. I love the name of the South African *plat perskie*, or flat peach, which is really just a fruit leather.

Any fruit can be made into a leather. Cut the fruit into pieces, put in a saucepan with a little honey or sugar and simmer gently for 5 minutes to make a purée. Put a silicon mat or sheet of greaseproof paper on a baking sheet and pour on your purée. Cook at Gas Mark 1/2/130°C/250°F for about 6–8 hours. The leather should be tacky but not sticky. Remove from the paper, roll the leather up and store in a cool place.

salads and risottos, take less time and should be watched to make sure they don't get over-dry. Once dried, sun-blushed tomatoes should be stored in jars of oil. When the tomatoes are eaten, the oil, gently infused with the tomato flavour, is a great addition to dressings.

Dried strips of parsnip, carrot or beetroot make good suckies for children as they are full of sugar. A Swedish friend of mine remembers them as sweet substitutes during the war. Sweet potatoes cooked as a fruit leather also keep well and can be reconstituted or added to soups and stews.

Legumes and pulses should be dried carefully, either in the sun or the oven. If they are not properly dried they will start to sprout.

mincemeat

So called because the original contained minced beef, mincemeat nowadays is a mixture of spices, dried fruits and suet, all chopped together. The basic recipe is as follows, but I have seen raspberries, prunes, dried apricots and russet apples added.

MAKES 800g

100g currants, finely chopped
100g sultanas, finely chopped
100g raisins, finely chopped
100g chopped suet
100g mixed peel, finely chopped
100g tart apples, finely chopped
100g demerara sugar
1/2 tsp mixed spice
grated rind and juice of 1 orange
grated rind and juice of 1 lemon
70ml rum
70ml brandy

Mix together all the ingredients except the liquids. Add the rum and and juices and mix well. Leave 2–3 days before potting in sterilized jars.

bottling

When I was a child, my mother's family farmed in the Hunter Valley in New South Wales. Back then, it was a long way from anywhere with bull dust roads. My aunt spent a lot of time bottling the produce of her vegetable garden. The sun is both friend and enemy out there and growing any food meant fighting the elements as well as the bugs and other predators, so she was particularly proud when admiring the bottled fruits of her labours.

bottling in brine or syrup

Use perfect, unbruised specimens. Wash vegetables in a solution of permanganate of potash (follow the instructions on the bottle) to kill any organisms, rinse in cold water then dry. Wash and dry fruit and if you are using stone fruit, cut in half and remove the stone. In the case of fruit, make up a syrup of 450g sugar to 1 litre water. (Some fruits of very high acidity can be bottled with no sugar at all.) For vegetables make a brine of 50g salt to 1 litre water. Put the fruit or vegetables in the jar then pour over enough salted water or syrup to cover.

Cover the jars loosely. In other words, don't screw the lids down, just place them on top. Put some wooden slats or a thick layer of paper or cloth in a large fish kettle to stop the jars cracking. Stand the jars on top and add cold water up to the necks of the jars.

Bring the water gently to the boil and simmer until the fruit or vegetables are cooked – between 10 and 30 minutes for fruit, an hour for vegetables.

If you are bottling ready-cooked food put it into the jars hot and proceed in the same way.

Screw the jars down as soon as they are cool enough to handle. They will take up to 24 hours to cool completely and can then be stored indefinitely. In the case of vegetables it is recommended that you bring them back to the boil for a few minutes before finally sealing and storing but I don't really find it necessary.

bottling in oil, honey or alcohol

Fruit and vegetables can also be stored by immersing them in oil or honey. These practices were beloved by the ancient Egyptians and Romans. There are two methods for immersing in oil, the first of which is suitable for mushrooms, artichoke hearts, and so on, in other words, for harder vegetables. First simmer the vegetables in brine for about 10 minutes then put them into sterilized jars (don't touch them with your hands at this stage). Pour on good virgin olive oil and leave to cool before sealing.

The other method for vegetables such as red peppers, aubergines, courgettes and so forth is to char-grill them a little first, and in the case of red peppers, peel them after char-grilling. I'm sure you know the method where you keep turning your pepper under a flame until it is black all over, then put it straight into a plastic bag, after which the skin simply washes off. They can then be put in a sterilized jar with the oil.

Sun-dried vegetables are, of course, partly cooked already, so they can go straight into the oil. In the case of completely dry vegetables it is a good idea to steam them a little to rehydrate them before putting them in the oil.

If you wish to bottle in honey, choose perfect specimens of fruit – nectarines, apricots, peaches and dates are all delicious. Wash and dry them, then put them in sterilized jars and cover with liquid honey.

learning from the past

The first known recipe for bottling gooseberries, from 1680, suggests putting the bottle in cold water which is then brought to the boil. The gooseberries are simmered until they turn white and then stored. The same recipe was still being published, unchanged, 200 years later.

kilner jars

The best bottles to use are kilner jars, which were invented in 1858. Today's are identical; they have screw lids, metal clips and rubber washers, all of which need to be carefully sterilized with boiling water before use. To do this, fill the jars to the brim with boiling water and leave for 10 minutes. Leave to dry in a warm place or a cooling oven. Then you are ready to fill the jars with the fruit or vegetables of your choice.

high altitude tip

Remember if you live at a high altitude that you need to adjust the timings as water takes longer to boil. Allow an extra five minutes per 300 metres for any altitude over 300 metres.

an unusual reason to freeze meat

Freezing is also, in hot climates, a good way of tenderizing beef and lamb. There butchers cannot hang meat unless they have a cold store, so in more primitive countries the meat is cut up and sold almost at once, consequently it can be very tough. If you freeze it, defrost it and repeat the process two or three times, the meat becomes quite tender. Before the health police yell at me, I learnt this trick in the West Indies in the mid-1970s and it has never hurt me yet.

bottling in alcohol

Alcohol is another great preserver and is good for storing soft fruit. Cherries or peaches are particularly good stored in brandy and pears in eau de vie. I am always fascinated as to who came up with the idea of a rumtopf, in which fruits are layered in alcohol and sugar as they come into season. The whole is broached in an alcoholic daze by Yuletide. I have also eaten, in the Lebanon, lemons bottled in brandy and sugar, and quite delicious they were too. You can drink the liqueur afterwards or use it for flavouring puddings.

freezing

This is not really the book for writing about freezing. The practice does, after all, increase food miles, prevent local sourcing, use extra electricity and enable huge food mountains to be preserved almost indefinitely. It also encourages intensive farming and negates seasonality *and* does nothing to enhance the taste of food – in other words, it is definitely not very green. However, it has the advantages of being an easy way to store your gluts, which will encourage home production, and it is also very labour-saving.

To freeze your vegetables, you must first blanch them. Take the largest saucepan you have and fill it with water. Bring to the boil. Meanwhile, fill your sink with very cold water. Fling a batch of vegetables into the boiling water and leave for 1 minute. Using a slotted spoon, scoop the vegetables out and throw them into the cold water. Let the water come back to the boil before blanching the next batch. Remove the vegetables from the cold water, drain and pat dry before freezing. Let the water cool and pour it on your compost heap.

● Always divide the vegetables into batches for blanching. If you blanch too many at once, you will lower the water temperature and they will go soggy.

● Break cauliflower or calabrese into fleurettes and top your beans.

● It is a good idea to freeze vegetables and herbs on baking sheets before transferring them to freezer bags.

● You can freeze fruit to turn into jams later or for cooking, but they don't eat successfully once they have been frozen. Freeze soft fruits on baking sheets before transferring them to freezer bags.

● If you are freezing meat, it must be well wrapped to prevent ice burn. Fish can be frozen in the same way as meat. It freezes very well.

● Don't forget to label everything well or you may have some interesting surprises.

jams, marmalades and chutneys

jams

Jam making is a great way of storing your excess fruit. I once owned a rather pompous 1930s book which stated that, 'If sound fruit and pure granulated or preserving sugar are used, jam making will always be a success.' Through years of unset and burnt jams I have hated the author of that book, then I hit my alcoholic rock bottom over a pan of burnt jam and realised the problem was me. The author had forgotten to add that what you also need are patience and concentration.

Fruit for jam making should always be picked on a dry day and should be unbruised. If the fruit lacks acid, lemon juice or some fruit concentrate should be added. Our cook, Louise, didn't skim her jams whilst they were cooking as she said it caused waste; she just stirred the jam a lot whilst it was coming to the boil and the scum disappeared. I should add that she won prizes for her jams.

apple jam

This is an unusual way to use up apples but I grew up with it and rather like it.

Take good cooking apples, peel, core and thinly slice them then weigh. Stew until tender in a double boiler. Do not overcook. Transfer to a preserving pan and add 450g granulated or preserving sugar and the juice of half a lemon for each 500g of fruit. Add the same of grated lemon rind, a 25g piece of peeled root ginger and three or four cloves. Bring to the boil and simmer for half an hour then apply the cold plate test and pot (see opposite).

currant and raspberry jam

In a world where there are always too many currants and never really enough raspberries, you will welcome this very delicious recipe! It is important to gather the fruit on a dry day, especially the raspberries.

Use 450g currants – red, white or black – to every 100g raspberries, and 450g granulated or preserving sugar to this amount of fruit. De-stalk the fruit. Bring to the boil in your preserving pan with the sugar and simmer gently for 40 minutes. Apply the cold plate test (see opposite) and pot.

mulberry jam

In my childhood garden we had a 400-year old mulberry tree which would have seen the capture of Babbington in the reign of Elizabeth I on that self same spot. To commemorate the coronation of another queen Elizabeth in 1953 I, with a little help from the gardener, planted another mulberry tree, so I have always been very attached to mulberries.

This jam is made partly with fruit juice and partly with fruit. Use 450g granulated or preserving sugar and 570ml juice from crushed mulberries to 450g whole fruit. Put the juice and sugar in a preserving pan and simmer to dissolve the sugar. In this instance, do skim off the scum. Add the whole fruit and simmer rather fiercely for 30 minutes stirring well. Apply the cold plate test (see right) and pot.

plum jam

All jams of fruit of the plum family – plums, greengages, myrtles, damsons, and so on – benefit from the addition of the kernels. However, the EU in its wisdom, frightened by the minuscule amount of cyanide in plum stones, will not allow you to sell jam made like this, so if you are making jam to sell, leave out the kernels. It is alright to include them for your own use.

Weigh the plums, cut them open and remove the stones. Keep about half the stones. Allow 450g granulated or preserving sugar to 450g fruit – less if the fruit is very sweet. Put a layer of plums in a dish and sprinkle with sugar. Continue until both are used up. Leave until the next day. Place the fruit and sugar in your preserving pan and simmer gently for about 15 minutes. Meanwhile crack the reserved stones and blanch the kernels in boiling water. Add the kernels to the jam and cook quickly for another 15–20

when is it ready?

No precise time can be given as to when a jam sets; there are so many different variants of fruit type and weather conditions during the growing season that the plate test is the only safe method. Put a little jam onto a cold plate and if it sets as a jelly, it is done. If not, keep cooking.

minutes, stirring repeatedly as this jam tends to burn. Apply the cold plate test (see above) and pot.

raspberry jam

Pick the fruit on a dry day, ensure it is ripe and use at once. Remove the stalks, add a scant 450g sugar to each 450g fruit plus 2 wineglasses of raspberry or redcurrant juice for each 450g fruit. Bring to the boil and simmer for 35–40 minutes. Apply the cold plate test (see above) and pot.

decanting and storing your jam

When the jam is done, remove from the heat and let it stand for a few minutes before decanting it. The jars you use for storing your jam should be clean and perfectly dry as the slightest moisture will cause the jam to turn mouldy. Our cook, Louise, always made a great ritual of washing them the day before, setting them to dry and covering them with a cloth to keep out bugs and impurities.

Use screw-top jars where possible, pour the jam in but don't fill the jars too full. Once the jam has cooled, lay a round of greaseproof or silicon paper over the top, then close the jars. If you don't have screw-top jars, tie the greaseproof or silicon paper covering down securely. Label the jam with the date and type before storing in a dry, airy place.

marmalade

Marmalade can be made with all citrus fruits, but their skin is tougher than other fruits and has to be softened. Apart from the marmalades below and marmalade made from quinces, all fruit marmalades are technically jams, although I have seen them referred to as marmalades as early as 1710 in a Scots household book.

orange marmalade

Weigh 12 Seville oranges, cut them up small and thin, removing the pips. Reserve the pips. Put the oranges in a non-metallic crock and add 4.5 litres cold water for each 450g fruit. Leave to stand for 24 hours.

from Turkey to Dundee via Mary Queen of Scots

Whatever you may believe about Turkish marmelo, Mary Queen of Scots' migraines or the many other theories that surround this preserve, to me marmalade belongs to Dundee and Mrs Keiler's challenge, and represents the triumph of Scots' housewifery over commerce.

What am I on about? Well, one day in the 1780s, Mr Keiler, merchant of Dundee, received a shipment of bitter Seville oranges instead of the sweet oranges he had ordered. In those days there was no way they could be sent back and he faced ruin. In despair he turned to his wife who used them to produce the first proper marmalade, thereby establishing a great Industry and amassing a fortune, which enabled her descendants to build one of the finest art collections of modern times.

Today, no marmalade is made in Dundee but, according to Sue Lawrence, that town's other great cooking daughter, the cake that bears its name is made with orange peel left over from marmalade production.

Transfer to a preserving pan and boil until the fruit is tender. Wrap the pips in muslin and boil them with the fruit for added pectin. Remove from the heat and leave to stand for a least 12 hours and no more than 24.

Remove the pips. Add 450g sugar (I use half white and half Muscovado) to every 450g fruit. Boil, stirring constantly, until the fruit is clear, the liquid has reduced by half and the syrup jellies, about 1 hour. Apply the cold plate test and pot (see page 209). You can add the juice and grated rind of 2 lemons if you want a sharper marmalade.

oxford marmalade

900g Seville oranges
juice and grated rind of 1 small lemon
30g black treacle
2.7 kg preserving sugar
3.4 litres water
200g crystallised ginger

Proceed as for orange marmalade, but add the ginger just before potting.

three-fruit marmalade

2 grapefruits
juice and grated rind of 4 lemons
2 sweet oranges
2.9 kg granulated or preserving sugar
3.4 litres water

The total amount of fruit should weigh 1.4 kg. Proceed as for orange marmalade.

chutneys

You either love chutneys or you hate them. Personally I am not a great fan but they are a splendid way of using up fruit and vegetables that are a bit battered and you can always give your chutneys away.

You can make chutneys with any fruits and vegetables – runner beans, beetroot and apple, blackberries, cranberries, gooseberries, pears, plums, rhubarb and of course, tomatoes, both red and green. I particularly like quince and lemon with garlic, coriander and cloves. Whatever you make, the principle is always the same.

apple and marrow chutney

675g marrow, peeled, sliced and cubed
675g apples (not Bramleys), peeled, cored and chopped
50g salt
2 medium onions, peeled and chopped
425ml vinegar (any will do)
1/2 tsp salt
1 tsp mustard seed
350g brown sugar
1 tsp black peppercorns
root ginger, small piece

Put the marrow in a bowl, sprinkle with salt and leave for 12 hours. Strain. Put all the ingredients in a preserving pan, bring to the boil and cook until tender and reduced to a thick consistency. Pot in sterilised containers.

jellies, curds
and cheeses

jellies

Making fruit jellies is another good way of
keeping fruit. The jellies are delicious with
hot or cold meat or can be eaten with
bread and butter. The fruit must be
skimmed while it is cooking to give a fine
clear product.

crab apple jelly

Halve the apples, put them in your
preserving pan and add 1.7 litres cold water
to every 450g of fruit. Boil rapidly for
30 minutes and strain through your jelly
bag into a bowl. Measure the amount of
juice you collect and boil it up with 450g
sugar to every 500ml strained juice. Bring
to the boil and cook for 30 minutes,
stirring well. At this stage you can add a
teaspoon of lemon juice if desired. Apply
the cold plate test and pot (see page 209).

You can use this method for all currant
jellies too but reduce the sugar by 100g.

redcurrant jelly

You can either cook as for blackberry jelly
(see opposite) or put your fruit in the
preserving pan with 8 tbsp water to each
500ml of fruit. Cook until the juice runs
freely and strain through your jelly bag.
Measure the strained juice and add 300g
sugar to each 500ml juice. Cook gently
until the sugar melts then bring to the boil.
Simmer for 30 minutes. Apply the cold
plate test and pot (see page 209).

This method can also be used for black and
white currants.

using a jelly bag

You will need a jelly bag, preferably on a stand, though you can hang it from a pole secured between two chairs or from a hook over the bowl in which it will drip. The fruit must be dry but I don't bother to remove any but the largest stalks. Having once had to deal with 35 kg of currants in one session, I've learned to be quick. Don't squeeze your jelly bag or your end result will be cloudy. Just walk away and let it drip, giving it a stir with a wooden spoon occasionally.

blackberry jelly

Put the fruit in a double boiler or in a jar in a pan of boiling water and simmer for 30 minutes, until the juice flows freely. Strain though a jelly bag. Transfer the juice to a preserving pan and boil up with 300g sugar to each 500ml juice. Stir well. Apply the cold plate test and pot (see page 209). This jelly is improved if you add equal quantities of bullace (wild plums).

Use this method for raspberries, strawberries, mulberries etc.

quince jelly

Take ripe sound fruit, slice them and put in a preserving pan with just enough water to float them. Simmer for 2 hours until the fruit is a pulp. Strain twice through a jelly bag, rinsing the bag out between strainings. Boil the strained juice with 450g of sugar per 500ml juice for 45 minutes. Apply the cold plate test and pot (see page 209).

curds

This is a way of preserving food short-term when you have an egg glut. Curds do not have long eating qualities but they will add a few months to your eggs.

lemon curd

4 lemons
340g sugar
100g unsalted butter
8 egg yolks or 4 whole eggs, beaten

If the lemons are waxed wash them, if unwaxed there is no need. Grate or finely peel the lemon rind. Squeeze the lemons. Mix the lemon peel with the sugar and place in a double saucepan with the butter, lemon juice and eggs. Place over a low heat and stir until the sugar is dissolved. Continue cooking over a low heat, stirring until the curd thickens. Pot as for jam (see page 209).

apple curd

1 kg apples, any variety, pulped and sieved
225g unsalted butter
225g sugar
2 medium eggs, beaten
juice and rind of 1 lemon

Make as for lemon curd. You can also make apricot curd in the same way.

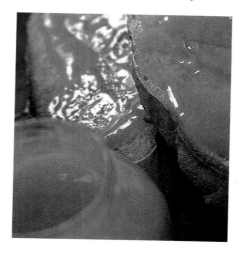

blackberry curd

450g blackberries
100g green apples, pulped and sieved
2 medium eggs, beaten
225g caster sugar
juice and rind of 1 lemon
100g unsalted butter

Cook the blackberries separately, then sieve them. Mix with the apple pulp then continue as for lemon curd.

fruit cheeses

A fruit cheese is a thickly set fruit jelly that is made to be sliced.

basic fruit cheese

1.4 kg fruit
450g sugar to each 450g fruit
olive oil for brushing

Brush sterilized containers with olive oil to enable the cheese to be turned out. Put the fruit in a pan with just enough water to cover. Simmer until soft. Pass through a nylon sieve, weigh and add the sugar accordingly. Put the sieved fruit and sugar in a preserving pan and stir until the sugar has dissolved. Simmer until it reaches the required consistency. Put in the containers, cover and store for at least 3–4 months to allow the flavour to develop.

damson cheese

1.4 kg damsons
450g sugar to each 450g pulp

Bake the whole fruit at Gas Mark 2/150°C/300°F until soft. Remove the stones and crack several for the kernels. Add these kernels to the pulp, then continue as for fruit cheese. Store for at least 6 months. It will continue to improve for up to 2 years.

farmers' markets

Eighteen years ago, as I came out of my alcoholic haze, the world and I became re-acquainted. I was appalled at the state of the food industry. Supermarkets stalked the land like great dinosaurs, keeping farmers and food producers in thrall. To all intents and purposes, farmers' markets had died out both in Britain and in the USA, whereas in mainland Europe, people had the good sense to hang onto and treasure them.

One person alone stood against the supermarkets in Britain, like Horatius at the bridge or David facing up to Goliath. Whenever you drink a toast, remember the name Henrietta Green. She, to my mind, has been insufficiently honoured by the world she fought for in her tremendous battle of the small producer against the Philistines.

the start of the farmers' market movement

Henrietta, a food writer of long standing, started her campaign by writing a compendium of small British food producers called *British Food Finds*, published in 1987. At the time I was running the London bookshop Books for Cooks and we were one of the few places that sold it. When Delia Smith mentioned it on her programme I sold 800 copies in four days, but the printers didn't reprint. BBC Books picked it up and it became the *Food Lovers' Guide to Britain*.

I once had the pleasure of accompanying Henrietta on a day's fact finding. I thought we would have a jolly day out, but not a bit of it. Henrietta and I and

her socially inept rescued Yorkshire terrier, Violet, put in more kilometres a day than any trans-European lorry driver and she cross-examined food producers with the vigour of a top Queen's Counsel. If you passed Henrietta's tests and got into *Food Lovers' Guide to Britain*, you were it. There hasn't been any guide since that I would trust.

Henrietta also started Food Lovers' Fairs all around the country. The only other bastion for the small producer at that time were the Women's Institute markets (see page 216), the W.I. then being a much smaller enterprise than it has now become. When I dubbed the W.I. 'the SAS of British Cookery', I was paying a huge compliment to a splendid institution.

the introduction of certification in Britain

Certification was introduced in 2003 because the success of the farmers' markets had led to a proliferation of markets that weren't following our rigorous practices.

I believe that certification is very necessary. Success brings in the cowboys, bad practices proliferate, the customer

shies away and everything fails.

When visiting a market, look for the FARMA green-and-white logo. If it is not there it doesn't necessarily mean the market is bad but just be more careful and question the producers before buying. After all, if you want to buy eggs brought from several hundred kilometres away you can go to a supermarket.

farmers and retailers unite

In 2003, the National Association of Farmer's Markets (NAFAM) merged with the Farm Retailers' Association and they go happily forward together. I launched the project in Edinburgh, the idea behind it being to protect the integrity of farm shops as well as the exchange of information throughout the network.

beating the supermarkets

I know that we are winning because supermarkets try to woo us to hold markets in their forecourts, and also because of the lip service paid to local produce in supermarkets. Don't shop for food in supermarkets. They have an arrogant disregard for food miles, and I'm

'Eighteen years ago, as I came out of my alcoholic haze, the world and I became re-acquainted. I was appalled at the state of the food industry.'

not talking just about their imported fruit and vegetables. One major British chain of supermarkets slaughters all its beasts at an abattoir in Cornwall, driving the cattle and sheep in lorries hundreds of kilometres, then driving the carcasses back all over the country.

Nor do supermarkets sell British organic food much because of appearance and price. Instead they import from suspect countries where you can use sprays that are banned in the UK and then register as organic 3 days before harvesting. I could go on forever. Trust me. Don't shop there.

other London food markets

When I was a child, my father would often take me to Petticoat Lane on a Sunday, a colourful place where Orthodox Jews with ringlets in their hair and curious clothes sold delicious pickled cucumbers, gefilte fishballs and tasty cold fried fish in matzo meal.

When I was young and wild, I would go off to Covent Garden, not then stuck out on the South Bank, and eat bacon butties and drink at the late-opening pubs and talk to producers around the braziers.

Which brings me to that other great London food market, Borough Market, situated by London Bridge. There has been a wholesale fruit and vegetable market at Borough for centuries but in 1998, again under the auspices of Henrietta Green, Jennifer Paterson and I opened the Gourmet Food Market. The Council was unfriendly, the railway arches leaked and we thought we'd last two years if we were lucky. I remember milking a goat to celebrate the opening. It wouldn't let down its milk, due to all the excitement no doubt.

Today Borough boasts 70 stalls, and growing. It has a footfall of 55,000 a month outside the Christmas period, when there is more. Borough is a true

London market. Here a man in a dish dash will sell lemons next to a stallholder from Devon selling fallow deer. Peter Gott, in his moleskin britches, red socks and brown Derby, discusses his bacon with an apple brandy seller from Hampshire or with Alastair from Brindisia, who is arguing about Cumbrian ham versus Pata Negra. I go whenever I'm in London and feel very proud to have been involved.

women's institute markets

The other great collection of markets is the Women's Institute markets. These have been around for 30 years, allowing members to sell their flowers, vegetables, baked goods, jams, chutneys and pickles. In 1995 the W.I. decided that the markets should break away and become self-financing. Now individuals can sell there subject to the organization's criteria.

You may wish, when your self-sufficiency is producing more than you need, to sell at either a farmers' market or a W.I. market in your area. You can contact either locally for advice.

farmers' markets in the USA

The Farmers' Markets idea started in America, and again, one name really stands out, that of Alice Waters, creator of the restaurant Chez Panisse in California. Alice was unable to source the vegetables she wanted. In the 1970s, what we now call New Wave American Cuisine started in California. It was the most important food revolution since the nineteenth century. New Wave took all the centuries' old national formulas and bust them, creating dishes that broke all the rules.

We forget how exciting it was. Alice, Deborah Maddison at Greens, Wolfgang Puck, Jeremiah Tower and Mark Miller collectively took the ball and ran with it straight past the fullback. New wave led to the growth of fusion food, the pan-Asian movement, slow food and, above all, of farmers' markets. The local farmers who grew for Alice and her friends found they had food surplus to requirements, so, in the 1980s, Alice encouraged them to set up local markets.

meeting farmers' market requirements

Today there are 212 certified farmers' markets in England, 69 north of the border in Scotland and 27 in Wales. The first one in London opened in Islington in 1999 and there are today 11 certified London markets, a fact which, as a Londoner by origin, gives me huge pleasure.

● The Association requires that any stallholder should have grown, reared, caught, brewed, pickled, baked or smoked the produce sold within a required radius of the market. This is usually 50km but in the case of cities or remote regions, it can extend to 80km.

● Where there is no local producer, the markets are allowed to invite a limited number of producers on a fixed number of occasions in order to fill the gap, but produce must never be brought from more than 160km away.

● The stallholder must be the producer or be directly involved in production. The reason for this is that one of the aims of the Association is to bridge the gap between shopper and producer and to enable the public to ask questions about farming and food production.

● Animals must be reared locally for baked, pickled and other such goods.

● A minimum of one major ingredient must be local.

● In the case of fatteners, the beast must have spent at least 50 per cent of its life on the producer's land.

● Game must be sold in the markets from local sources only by those who have shot or caught it under license in the locality.

●● Fish must be sold by the fisherman or by a representative of a number of local boats, and it must have been caught in local inshore waters.

● Documentation must be available for inspection by the public and by the Trading Standards authority.

christmas markets

Another place you might think of trying to sell your produce are Christmas markets. These are much more successful in mainland Europe, especially in Germany and Eastern Europe. Prague has a famous Christmas market but they are growing in the UK. They are a good outlet for specialist goods and can bring in much-needed cash in the period before Christmas for the dark unproductive days of January and February. Whether you go as a supporter or a stallholder, if you want a greener life, markets are where you must do your food shopping.

home brewing

One of the many wonders of nature is the existence of sugar in plants and fruit and the presence of the yeast fungus in the atmosphere. Quite when it was discovered that yeast ferments sugars to create alcohol has been lost in the mists of time, but that discovery has been a most powerful influence on civilization. As well as giving us 'the cup that cheers', it is a valuable source of vitamin B and provides the wherewithal to preserve food. When the fermenting action is negated by exposure to air and vinegar is created, it also provided the earliest form of antiseptic and household cleaning fluid. The art of making wine, beer, cider, mead, vinegar and verjuice was once a common household skill. The old recipes were faithfully recorded and I offer a few here to tempt the home producer into an immensely rewarding, if bibulous, new hobby. Though I have not drunk alcohol for over twenty years, I was once a dedicated home brewer.

beer

The difference between ale and beer is that beer uses hops as a flavouring. Hops came into Britain from the Low Countries during the reign of Henry VIII. Before then, ale was flavoured with a variety of different plants, depending on where you lived and what grew locally. Germander, a small, yellow-flowered woodland plant, was once popular, giving ale a dark colour and a bitter taste. Germander would probably be used in commercial brewing today, if hops had not been introduced. Heather and bracken were used to flavour

ale in the north of England and Scotland. Bracken is still used in Norway and Russia. It might help to get rid of the pernicious stuff if someone starting manufacturing bracken beer here. Monks were great brewers and made particularly potent ales flavoured with cinnamon and other spices. For centuries, the county of Kent was famous for its cherry ale.

In my grandparents' day, there was a brew house at the Home Farm. Here beer was made for the hundred or so farm men, gardeners and household staff. They made a light, thirst-quenching beer for harvest time, a stronger beer for the autumn and a type of stout called October Ale for Christmas and the winter months. As machinery replaced manpower, the estate brew houses became redundant, but the old recipes survive.

Home brewing is easy, enormous fun and the results of one's labours are infinitely better than anything mass-produced.

bitter

The following is the simplest, most traditional recipe for making beer. There are many permutations to achieve a different texture, taste or strength by increasing the quantity of hops and sugar. You can also add black malt granules to make stout.

MAKES 4 LITRES

500g Barbados sugar
400g extract of malt
30g hops, plus an extra handful
4 litres water
7g granulated yeast
8 scant tsp unrefined sugar

Dissolve the sugar and malt in 1 litre of warm water and pour into a sterile 4-litre container. Boil the hops in 1 litre of water for 10 minutes. Strain through a sieve into a sterile jug and then into the container. Re-boil the hops twice more, adding 1 litre of water each time. Add all the hop liquid to the 'wort' in the container. Seal the container with a bung and airlock to which you have added a little water mixed with a drop of bleach. Allow to cool overnight. Next morning, add the yeast to the wort with a handful of hops, and replace the bung. Fermentation will start in a few hours. Leave until fermentation ceases.

Rack, or bottle, the beer using a syphon tube, into sterile half-litre bottles to within 1.5cm of the top. Make sure to keep the tube clear of the sediment in the bottom of the container. Add a level teaspoon of sugar to each bottle and seal. The sugar creates a secondary fermentation in the bottles without which the beer would be flat and lifeless. Stand the bottles somewhere cool.

The beer will quickly clear to a healthy brilliance as the yeast deposit settles to the bottom of the bottles. It will be drinkable in two weeks, but infinitely better the longer you leave it. It is advisable to refrigerate the beer for a day before you drink it. This stops the yeast sediment from rising and makes the beer easier to pour.

'Home brewing is easy, enormous fun and the results of one's labours are infinitely better than anything mass-produced.'

wine

Virtually all the country people who worked on the land when I was a child made wine from a wide range of plants and flowers, to recipes that were centuries old. The different varieties – flower wines, like cowslip and dandelion, or berry wines such as elder and blackberry – brought the scent and taste of spring, summer or autumn, to bleak mid-winter evenings. Other wines – such as parsnip, potato, birch and rhubarb – were more full-bodied.

Country wines are delicious, easy to make and considerably better for you than anything bought from an off-licence. And they are a fraction of the price. The main considerations in wine-making are sterility – boil everything well – and avoiding contaminants like fruit flies.

elderflower champagne

Elder trees grow wherever the nitrogen content of the soil is high. Typically, this might be where there once was an old household midden and the soil has been enriched by the breakdown of organic matter. They also often grow beside churchyards, deserted gardens, rabbit warrens and badger setts. In early summer, the trees are covered in heavily scented white flowers that are rich in vitamin C. These can be used in an infusion, to treat coughs (see page 172). The flowers also make a delicious, slightly effervescent, refreshing wine, not unlike a Frontingac. No yeast is required as the flowers provide enough.

MAKES 4 LITRES

15 elderflower heads
700g unrefined sugar or honey
2 lemons, juice and zest
4 litres water, boiling

Pick the elderflower heads when they are in full bloom, on a warm day when the scent is at its best. Remove any leaves and twigs and shake out any insects that may be feeding on the nectar. Place in a 4-litre crock and scatter the sugar or honey over the flowers. Add the lemon juice and zest to the crock. Pour over the boiling water and stir well. Leave to cool for at least 24 hours, stirring occasionally. Sieve through muslin and decant into sterile screw-top bottles. Leave for a fortnight and drink over the following 3–4 weeks.

elderberry wine

This is a beautiful, rich, port-like drink and well worth the effort. It can be made using any berries – raspberries and blackberries for example.

MAKES 4 LITRES

3 kg elderberries
4 litres water, boiling
1.4 kg unrefined sugar or honey
2 lemons, juice and zest
piece of toast
2 tbsp wine yeast

Pick 3 kg of elderberries – about two bucketfuls. Remove any leaves and twigs, and cut the stems holding each little cluster. Spread the clusters on a baking sheet and warm in an oven at Gas Mark 4/180°C/350°F until they start to split. Mash with a heavy wooden spoon, scrape into a 4-litre crock and cover with boiling water. While they are still warm, scatter on the sugar or add honey. If using honey, warm it slightly so that it is runny. Add the lemon juice and zest. Stir well and leave for 24 hours. Add a piece of toast spread with the wine yeast, cover with a muslin cloth and leave in warm place at 21°C/70°F until fermentation ceases (2–3 weeks).

Once all signs of fermentation have ceased, rack the wine into sterile bottles, making sure to leave the lees (sediment) behind. Leave the wine at least 12 months – the longer you leave it the better it will taste.

dandelion wine

Dandelions were traditionally picked and the wine made on St George's Day, 23 April, to be drunk at Christmas. When you pick the dandelion heads, take the opportunity to gather some dandelion leaves for a salad, too. This recipe can be used to make wine from any flowers – elderflower, cowslip, broom, gorse, rose petals – whatever catches your fancy.

MAKES 4 LITRES

2 kg dandelion heads
4 litres water, boiling
1.4 kg unrefined sugar or honey
2 lemons, juice and zest
piece of toast
2 tbsp wine yeast

Fill two buckets with dandelion heads in full blossom, picked on a warm day in the early afternoon. Remove as much greenery as possible and shake out any insects. Put the flowers into a 4-litre crock and pour over the boiling water. Cover and leave for 2 days, stirring occasionally. Transfer to a saucepan, add sugar or honey and the lemon zest. Bring to the boil and simmer for 1 hour. Return to the crock and allow to cool. Add the lemon juice and wine yeast on toast. Cover with muslin and leave to ferment out in a warm place at 21°C/70°F.

Once all signs of fermentation have ceased, rack into sterile bottles, and store in cool place. It is ready to drink at 6 months but, like most wine, it improves with maturity.

parsnip wine

This was a great favourite with Joe the gardener but his version was dangerously potent. Traditionally, it was made in winter after the first hard frost. Any vegetable wine can be made the same way. Try celeriac, turnip, rhubarb, potato or beetroot. Beetroot makes a lovely heavy port-type wine. The beets need to be boiled and mashed before straining.

MAKES 4 LITRES

2 kg parsnips
4 litres water
2 kg unrefined sugar or honey
2 lemons, juice and zest
500g wheat
500g best raisins
piece of toast
2 tbsp wine yeast

Chop the unpeeled parsnips, add the water and boil until al dente. Strain the liquor into a crock. The parsnips can now be eaten if you wish. Add the sugar or honey and stir until dissolved. Add the lemon juice and zest, together with the wheat, raisins and yeast on toast. Cover with a muslin cloth and allow to ferment out in a warm place at 21°C/70°F.

Once all signs of fermentation have ceased, rack into sterile bottles and store for 12 months.

mead

This is the oldest known fermented drink. It was certainly being drunk in vast quantities in the heyday of Babylon. There it was sometimes mixed with borage to give it an extra kick and to enable the revellers to keep going, when they might otherwise have rolled under the table. Newly-weds were recommended to drink mead every night for a month after the nuptials to ensure a fruitful union, hence 'honeymoon'.

If you want to make sack, a very sweet, almost liqueur wine that was popular among medieval clergy and nobility, simply double the quantity of honey. Metheglin, a type of invalid's tonic, was made by adding nutmeg, coriander, cinnamon and cloves.

MAKES 4 LITRES

1.4 kg heather honey
4 litres water
500g crab apples, mashed
3 lemons, juice and zest
2 big roots ginger, bruised
pieces of comb honey (optional)
piece of toast
2 tbsp wine yeast

Bring the honey, water, crab apples, lemon zest, ginger and any pieces of comb honey you may have to the boil. Simmer for 30 minutes. Pour into a 4-litre crock and when cool, add the lemon juice and yeast spread on toast. Cover and leave to ferment out in a warm place at 21°C/70°F. It can ferment for a long time and often a double or triple fermentation takes place. Once fermentation appears to have stopped, syphon the mead through muslin into a demijohn with a fermentation lock. Nothing is more alarming or messy than bottles of mead exploding all over the place. Leave for a few weeks.

Once fermentation has ceased, rack into sterile bottles and store for 12 months.

vinegars and ciders

verjuice

Verjuice is the naturally fermented, acidic juice of crab apples, cider apples or sour grapes. It had hundreds of culinary and household uses until well into the last century, when lemons became a readily available alternative. The best verjuice is made from crab apples. The word 'crab' means sour and in Scotland, a 'crabbit woman' is to be avoided. Pick ripe crab apples in October and pile them in a heap, somewhere dry and under cover, to sweat. After a few days, discard any that are rotten, remove the stalks and stems, mash and put through a cider or fruit press if you have one. If not, mash until very fine and squeeze through sacking. Strain through muslin into sterile bottles, seal and store. Verjuice may be used to substitute vinegar or lemon juice in any recipe.

vinegar

Any bottle of red or white wine, rice wine, cider, mead or beer will turn to vinegar if it is left for 24 hours with the top off. Exposure to air negates the fermenting action and allows the bacteria, acetobacter, to turn the alcohol to the acid we call vinegar. You can leave your wine, beer or cider to do this naturally, but it is much easier and more effective to create your own acetobacter.

Sterilize a 4.5 litre glass, porcelain or plastic container. Pour in 500ml of the alcohol you wish to turn to vinegar. Add 600ml pasteurized vinegar and 150ml water. Stir vigorously. If you are using commercially bought plonk, this will help remove any gas that may have been added as part of the manufacturing process to protect it against the very bacteria you want to form.

Cover with muslin to allow air in and keep vinegar flies out. Place in a dark place where the temperature is a consistent 27°C/80°F. Leave for a month, checking regularly. During this period, a whitish gelatinous scum will appear. This living bacterium is known as 'the mother'. You may now add 1 litre of the same alcohol you started with together with 600ml water.

Cover with clean muslin and return to a dry dark place for 1–3 months. During that time, the mother will thicken and eventually sink to the bottom. Another will form in her place. Take this off to start the next batch of vinegar. When the mixture tastes strong enough, pour through several layers of muslin and bottle.

To stop a mother forming in your bottled vinegar, store it in a cold place or pasteurize it by bringing it to the boil. Allow to cool, bottle and store.

For much of history, the antiseptic properties of vinegar have been highly valued and it was frequently used as the mixing agent with medicinal herbs. Vinegar can also be sweetened with honey or spices, or heated with chillies. If you want to flavour your vinegar, simply add any seasonal herb or fruit to the vinegar and leave it for a month.

flavoured vinegars

Nothing is more delicious than the flavour of herbs infused in white-wine vinegar.

Herb vinegars are so simple to make and a bottle makes a wonderful Christmas present. The variety and permutations for different flavours from herb garden or hedgerow are endless.

elderflower vinegar

This is delicious with salads and, curiously enough, a small amount adds a certain nimbus to strawberries. You can use this recipe for any flower-petal vinegar.

Fill a sterile 1-litre kilner jar with elderflowers. Cover with 600ml good white-wine vinegar. Seal and store in a cool dark place for 3–4 weeks, the longer, the better. Decant through muslin into a sterile bottle.

tarragon vinegar

This is probably the most traditional herb vinegar. It is ideal for making salsa verde to go with brawn and cold meats.

Pound a double handful of chopped tarragon leaves, stripped off the stalks, in a big stone mortar. Bring 150ml white-wine vinegar to the boil and pour into the mortar. This has the effect of utilizing all the herb oils that have accumulated on the sides of the mortar. Continue crushing the tarragon in the vinegar for a few moments and leave to cool. Pour into a wide-necked sterile container and add a further 450ml wine vinegar. Seal and store in a cool dark place for 3 weeks, giving the container a shake every day or two. Decant through muslin into a sterile bottle and cork.

garlic vinegar

Garlic vinegar is always useful for salad dressing on its own and is one that lends itself to additions of pretty well anything – basil, burnet, dill, chillies, and so on.

Peel and chop 5 large cloves of garlic. Pound and crush in a mortar. Bring 150ml white-wine vinegar to the boil and pour over the garlic. Allow to cool. This is when the garlic flavour is absorbed. Pour into a sterile wide-necked container. Store and seal for 3 weeks, giving a shake every so often. Decant through muslin into a sterile bottle and cork.

fruit vinegars

Raspberry, blueberry, blackcurrant and strawberry are among the fruit vinegars that are delicious with duck and roe deer.

Wash 450ml of the fruit of your choice and place in a large ceramic or glass bowl. Pour over 650ml white-wine vinegar, cover with a cloth and leave for 10 days, stirring periodically as the fruit breaks down. Strain into a heavy-bottomed pan and add

450g unrefined sugar or, better still, honey. Bring to the boil and simmer for 10 minutes, stirring to dissolve. Allow to cool and decant into sterile bottles, and cork. Store in a cool, dark place for 3 weeks.

cider

Cider is autumn's golden liquid. Historically, the French have always produced wonderful, high-quality ciders, particularly in Normandy and Brittany. Up until about 50 years ago, before farming in Britain became so mechanized, every farm had its apple orchard and the centuries-old culture of cider making remained still very much intact, with each region growing its own variety of apples – Foxwhelps, Woodcocks, Rusticoats, White Swans, Kendrik Wildings, Jews' Ears and dozens of others. Many of the old orchards became redundant, were grubbed out and the land used for other purposes, but a surprising number have survived and there is now a renaissance in cider making, particularly in North America.

A small orchard always had a mix of cooking and eating apples and home-made cider was made from a mix of the windfalls of both, to get the right combination of sweetness and acidity, with some crab apples thrown in, to provide extra tannin and tartness.

MAKES 4.5 LITRES

Pick 6 kg assorted ripe apples. Pile them in a heap for 3 days so that they 'sweat', or soften a little. Roughly chop the apples. Putting enough as will fill a shallow box on the ground and chopping them with a clean spade is the most popular method. Shovel the apples into a fruit press and squeeze the juice into a 4.5-litre fermentation bin. The apple pulp can be fed to the pigs if you have any, or added to the compost heap.

Put the fermentation bin into a sink as there will be rapid natural fermentation

which will froth over the sides of the bin. Once this ceases – in roughly 48 hours – decant the apple juice through muslin into another bin, to start the fermentation proper.

Add 1 tbsp dried yeast and 1 kg demerara sugar mixed in 600ml boiling water. Put a tight-fitting lid on the bin and store somewhere warm, such as an airing cupboard, for 3 weeks or however long it takes the sugars to convert to alcohol and the bubbling to stop.

When the bubbling has completely ceased, move the bin to a cool place and syphon the cider into sterile bottles. To ensure a nice fizz, add 1 level tsp unrefined sugar to each bottle. Seal and store in a cool place for 12 months.

perry

This is a wine made from pears and was another very popular drink. The Roman historian, Palladius, refers to a beverage called castomoniale, which was made from fermented pears. In a burst of spirited creativity during the early Middle Ages, the monks at the monastery of Grand Saint Michel in Normandy were responsible for developing pear orchards specifically for perry making. The Cistercian monks brought many varieties with them when they established their abbeys in Britain and more were introduced during successive reigns – particularly Henry VIII's. However, pears for perry making are tart and they were gradually replaced by the sweeter eating varieties. There are, though, enough of the old varieties to be found, particularly in Gloucestershire. They have splendidly evocative names – Mumblehead, Merrylegs and Devil Drink, for instance. The art of perry making was taken to America by early colonists and is now enjoying a revival in popularity.

Perry is made in the same way as cider but replacing the apples with pears.

the green house

alternative energy

With a world energy crisis and ever-escalating fuel bills, it seems crazy not to utilize nature's resources – the sun, wind, water or biomes, in the form of waste woods or bracken – to generate our own power. Even here in the north there is enough daylight through the winter to warm solar-heating panels and there is no shortage of wind, water or bracken.

water power

Water power depends on a constant flow of water and if you are lucky enough to have a stream through your property, however small, it is well worth making use of it. To calculate the strength of water flow, start by measuring the depth of the stream from bank to bank along a given length. Area equals depth multiplied by width. A corked bottle is then timed as it floats along the measured length of stream and the flow is calculated by multiplying 75 per cent of the time the bottle takes to cover the distance, by the area.

Harnessing your water power will almost certainly involve building a simple dam to provide increased velocity and, possibly, a trench or leat to carry water from the dam to the turbine, but the initial outlay is more than compensated for by a continuous supply of free electricity. A further requirement will be a shelter to protect the generator from the elements. Such a shelter can range from a tin shack to the sort of brick, stone or wooden building that develops into a summer house and becomes something of a feature of your property.

Renewable energy, and mini-hydro

electric generators in particular, have become such a science in the last twenty years, that there is no shortage of specialist surveyors to accurately assess the electricity-generating potential of your water supply and to give advice on the most suitable turbine.

wind power

The power of wind has been harnessed since the dawn of time and windmills were a common sight everywhere until electricity became the universal source of energy. Now, of course, clusters of huge wind turbines are sprouting across the countryside, destroying some of the most beautiful landscapes in the world. Although I abhor industrial wind turbines, there is a place for small domestic ones and these are becoming increasingly sophisticated and affordable. A turbine with a 1.5m, three-bladed propeller mounted on the roof of a house or on an exposed area of wind-catching high

some historical notes

Having always lived beside running water, I am fascinated by the historical uses of water as a source of energy as well as water's potential today. For centuries, any farm that grew grain had its mill pond – a lagoon of water that could be used to drive a water wheel for grinding corn. Incredible feats of engineering went into harnessing water in the early days of the Industrial Revolution during the nineteenth century – the nearby town of Hawick is built on a complex labyrinth of tunnels that used to carry water from the river Teviot to drive the machinery in dozens of tweed mills.

ground, and connected to the conversion box by cables will supply about 1kw of electricity, supplementing the property's supply from the National Grid and reducing bills by a third. Rough electricity generated by the turbine is converted directly to mains frequency via the conversion control box. The average householder in the UK can expect to recoup the cost within about five years.

solar power

Sunlight – the solar power that is the basis of all life on earth, even in Scotland, where there is not much of it – can now be utilized to generate electricity and heat water via solar panels. The technology is improving all the time and solar panels are commonly used to generate heat for water in high-usage situations like blocks of flats and hospitals.

For domestic use, solar panels represent an enormous eco-friendly saving in electricity. The beauty of them is that they sit outside, sucking up sunshine. They are sufficiently recognized as simple energy-saving devices for grants to now be available in parts of Europe for their installation. Solar panels have really come into their own in America, Australia and New Zealand where many new lifestyle homes are not on the national grid.

Another method of utilizing the sun's power is through a Trombe wall – a south-facing wall of the house built with a double skin. The inner skin is traditional masonry fitted with ventilators and painted black, to act as a thermal mass to absorb heat. The outer skin is sheet glass that increases the heat in the cavity between the two skins. Warmth is released into the house through the ventilators. A strategically placed conservatory can be a marvellous heat trap for even thin winter sunlight.

fossil fuel alternatives

Alternatives to fossil fuels are being sought all the time and biomasses as fuel for heating are easily accessible to the home producer. Those that were commonly utilized in the past are now being looked to again to generate energy. In the days when hazel, poplar, willow and chestnut were all coppiced for wattle fencing, baskets, paling and charcoal, any waste was scrupulously saved, taken home and burnt. A hedger carrying a bundle of trimmings home on his back was once a familiar sight in the winter. Dried bracken, which gave a fierce heat, was burnt in brick kilns and the ash was used in soap making. Gorse, another fierce burner, was cut and used in bread-baking ovens. Grown timber was rarely used as fuel. It was far too precious and was saved for ship and house building.

Poplar and willow are now being grown again as short rotational crops to be harvested for fuel use, as is miscanthus, a woody perennial grass which can be baled and harvested. Aberdeen University has carried out research on using bracken, dried and compressed into cubes, as an alternative to coal. Gorse could also easily be used in the same way. Both these plants have become damaging, invasive pest species on a global scale so this would be an excellent use for them.

So what should you, the home producer, burn your biomass fuel in? I have several friends who have installed Scanfield boilers imported from Denmark, of which there are now any number of different makes and sizes designed for the domestic market, which will burn virtually anything – bales of straw and bracken, timber offcuts which are of no commercial value, even dried chicken dung and leaves.

a variety of turbines

There are a number of different turbines available to suit different water-flow strengths.

● The Pelton wheel turbine is driven by water forced through a nozzle at high speed into spoon-shaped deflector buckets set round the periphery of the turbine wheel. The revolving wheel turns a generator which converts mechanical energy into electrical energy, either via a shaft or through a system of pulleys, depending on where the generator is sited. The Pelton is designed for fast-flowing water and is 80 per cent efficient, producing 1.8 horse power which equates to 805 watts.

● A propeller turbine is the next best converter. Water passes down an outlet pipe set below the water level at the bottom of your dam and rotates a propeller positioned inside the pipe and connected to the generator. This suits slower-flowing water and is a correspondingly less effective generator, operating at about 75 per cent efficiency.

● The Banki turbine looks like a miniature water wheel and works in much the same way. It is positioned beneath a sluice. Water channelled down a chute strikes curved fins set at angles round the periphery of a wheel. The weight of water revolves the wheel, which in turn charges a generator. This is the simplest form of hydroelectric turbine, operating on the least volume of water pressure, and is the easiest to maintain. However, it is only 65 per cent efficient.

natural paints

If you use natural paints, you can experience much the same thrill of creativity, using almost identical materials, as the first caveman artist did 50,000 years ago. Natural paints are basically made from chalk, water, a binder of some sort and a pigment, while mass-produced paints are based on derivatives of the petrol industry – polyurethane, acrylic, synthetic latex and vinyl. Natural paints have the advantage in that they are porous, allowing the surface underneath to breathe. This was an important consideration in old buildings that had no damp course. What is more, the chalky, matt finish of natural paints is infinitely more attractive than the modern equivalents.

Painting with natural materials is enormously rewarding but anyone embarking on it must appreciate that it is going to be an adventure that is full of experimentation and, unlike what most people have come to expect from modern barrier paints, the fruits of one's labours never last for long.

limewash

The most ancient form of weather-proofing is limewash, used by the ancient Greeks and Romans to protect statuary and commonly used on all buildings until well into the nineteenth century. It is made by crushing and burning limestone or chalk and slaking it with water to produce slaked lime, otherwise known as lime putty. The lime putty is then diluted with water to make a thin paint – basic limewash. Tallow or linseed oil were sometimes added to the water, to improve waterproofing, particularly for painting woodwork. In some areas, horse and cattle hair, gleaned from tanning-yard waste, were mixed in to strengthen the wash.

Colour, in the most basic form, was provided by whatever soil was handy, washed several times and then added (see below). Different colours were obtained by burning earth containing different minerals – for example, soil from areas where iron oxide was present produced the different hues of ochre. Umber and sienna derive from other different clays.

basic earth colouring

For colouring your limewash, use your own soil. It will be fun experimenting with the different colour permutations.

Fill a 2-litre bucket with soil and sieve to remove the stones, etc. Boil the soil three times in 4.5 litres water. Strain off the water and replace it after each boiling. After the third boiling, strain off the soil and mill it as finely as you can with a block of wood (correctly known as a maul) on a board. Either add the milled soil straight to the limewash or, put it in a cast-iron pot over a fire and see what the heat does to the colour.

soft distemper

Soft distemper is a lovely natural paint with a soft matt finish for interior walls. It is made with a fine powdered chalk, known as 'whiting' and rabbit glue as the binder. All the ingredients can be obtained from specialist art material suppliers. Several hours before you need it, mix the pigment with water to make a runny paste. This will allow the colour to 'breathe'.

COVERS THE WALLS AND CEILINGS OF AN AVERAGE ROOM

100g pigment powder
5.5 kg whiting
350g rabbit-glue granules

Put the whiting in a bucket, covered with water, and leave to soak for a couple of hours. Pour off the excess water. Using another bucket, mix the glue granules with just enough water to soak and, after a few minutes, add 3 litres boiling water. Stir until completely dissolved. Allow to cool then add to the whiting paste. Mix thoroughly then add the pigment paste. Continue to mix until thoroughly incorporated.

non-earth colours

The quality and range of pigments that have survived in murals from the Egyptian, Minoan, Phoenician and Roman empires are extraordinary. Although the peoples of the east retained the knowledge of how to make vivid colours from the murex shellfish, and from cinnabar, lapis lazuli, lead and malachite, this knowledge was lost to the west during the Dark Ages and had to be laboriously learnt all over again. Many of the following pigments can still be obtained from specialist suppliers and may be used to colour a variety of different washes and paint bases.

● Until the Industrial Revolution, when paint colouring became a by-product of the chemical industry, white was made from burning lead ore.

● Green came from the verdigris formed on copper by soaking it in verjuice (see page 151).

● Red, the colour most sought after by artists, came from cinnabar, a soft red mineral that is the principal ore of mercury.

● Orange was achieved by heating white lead.

● Yellow came from gamboges, a resin from trees in Asia and later, in the 1700s, Indian Yellow was made from the urine of cows denied water and force-fed on mangoes .

● Blue, so precious to early manuscript illuminators that they only painted the hem of the Virgin's robes with it, was made by grinding up lapis lazuli, mixing it with beeswax and repeatedly washing it.

● Charcoal, lampblack and scraps of ivory, fired in a kiln, created the important base colour, black.

Dyes made from plants, fruit and flowers (see page 161) may also be used with some of the finer non-lime-based washes for beautiful soft interior colouring, although they are not lightfast and tend to fade. However, this is an effect that I find extremely attractive.

gilder's gesso

This provides a hard surface that is used as a base for gilding or, with the addition of pigment, makes a very good paint for softwood furniture.

75g rabbit-glue granules
750ml water
750g whiting

Add the rabbit-glue granules to the water and warm through in the top of a double boiler. Leave to cool overnight. In the morning it will be gelatinous. Add the whiting to the rabbit-glue mixture, followed by the pigment paste.

binders with a difference

● Milk curd is an effective binder. It makes the paint slightly adhesive, which is useful on uneven or decorative surfaces. To make milk curdle, add 1 tbsp lemon juice, verjuice or vinegar, to 1 litre skimmed milk and leave overnight in a warm place. Mix the pigment into the curds before adding to the rest of the liquid.

● Egg yolks and egg whites were used by the early Christian monks as binders for manuscript illumination and for decorating religious artefacts, particularly where gold dust was used. The yolks produced egg tempera and the whites glair.

● Another binder, and one that is very good for vegetable dyes, is starch. This can be used either in the form of beer – handy for the home-brew fanatic – or in the form of sieved water in which potatoes have been boiled up with a little unrefined sugar.

turpentine

Turpentine comes from the sap of pine trees and if you have access to some trees, it is worth tapping the sap. Cut a strip of bark off the trunk at about 1 metre from the ground, leaving a 'V' at the bottom. Tape a 5cm piece of copper pipe, cut in half lengthways to form a gutter, into the trunk at the bottom of the 'V'. Tie a bucket to the trunk so that the sap runs into it along the pipe. When the sap is heated through a glass retort, the vapour that is given off is turpentine spirit.

coloured oil glaze

Some years ago, we stayed in a farmhouse in the hills above Ravello in southern Italy. The pine floorboards of the bedroom had been stained a delicate blue, which highlighted the grain of the wood, producing a fresh, clean effect. When we returned home, we tried to copy the idea in deep red for one of our bedrooms that was too big to carpet. We thought it would give the room a warm feel, which is quite important in this part of Scotland. After sanding the floorboards clean, we used the following coloured oil glaze with great success. A similar effect could be achieved by painting the floor with a natural dye. If you wanted a blue you might consider using indigo from the woad plant – and covering with a basic oil glaze or light varnish to seal it.

COVERS APPROX. 3 SQUARE METRES

150ml boiled pure linseed oil
120ml pure turpentine thinners
2 tbsp whiting
1 tsp red ochre pigment or more depending on depth of colour required

Mix the linseed oil and turpentine thinners together. In a separate container, mix the whiting and the pigment. Mix the two batches together and apply.

wood tar

This is wonderful for weatherproofing garden furniture or any unpainted wood. It is obtained from burning pinewood. Dig a pit on the edge of a raised piece of ground and place a pipe in the bottom so it runs out to a bucket. Fill the pit with dried pine cones and get a good heat going by burning them. Feed the fire with freshly cut pinewood, cut small. Keep the heat up by adding more cones as and when the fire dies down. The black fluid that trickles down the pipe is wood tar. Mix this with turpentine to make the protective coating.

caution!

Lime putty is readily available from natural building and paint product manufacturers and I would recommend obtaining it from them, rather than trying to make it yourself. Remember, too, when handling lime, that it is very toxic and corrosive so you should always wear rubber gloves and goggles.

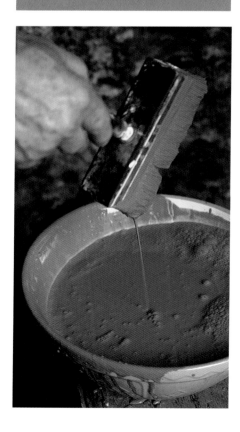

around the house

What does it mean 'a greener life'? Well, let's be brutal. It doesn't mean meditating in a centrally heated room on a macramé mat in front of an Amerindian dreamcatcher and a home-made beeswax candle surrounded by ugly spider plants, then rushing off in a gas-guzzling 4-wheel drive to collect the children from school and feeding them a supermarket ready meal from the microwave.

If you have a faith, living a greener life demands a certain amount of self-sacrifice. You don't save the planet with notions and lip service. Like every adventure it requires a degree of suffering and getting your hands dirty.

services

Heating
Start by turning off the central heating unless the temperature drops below freezing. This simple step, if practised universally, would save more fossil fuel than is imaginable. 'I'll be cold,' you say, 'I'll get ill.' No you won't; you'll put on more clothes if you're cold, and not made of synthetic fibres but of wool which will clasp you in its cosy embrace and which you will have to hand-wash, or at least wash on a cool temperature in your washing machine, so saving fuel again. Soon you will get used to the cold and will find your friends' houses uncomfortably hot. You will also find that you get ill less, as heat breeds germs.

If you have central heating, make sure that your radiators don't need 'bleeding', that each has a thermostatic control, that the thermostat works and that you don't have furniture in front of them blocking the heat. Radiators placed against cold outside walls use more fuel.

An alternative to central heating is a wood-burning stove, which is very cosy and less trouble than an open fire. It gives a warm centre to the room and can also be used for boiling kettles, making toast and leaving soups and stews to slow cook. Remember to burn either wood or coal, not both together as this will gum up your chimney. It also means that, if you wish, you can collect the wood ash for the garden separately from the cinders for your anti-slug paths.

Cooking
Kitchen ranges are economical heat and cooking sources and can also be used to heat the water, though this can lead to rows over who wants to bathe while dinner is being cooked. However you will need another cooker to use during the summer months or the hot range causes the kitchen to become unbearably hot. During the summer, when the range is off, you can heat the water through solar panels on the roof.

Gas is a better heat source than electricity and is also better to cook on. Ceramic hobs and convection ovens use less fuel than other electric hobs and ovens.

Lighting
Use energy-saving light bulbs in all your lights but allow yourself a lamp with an ordinary bulb where you do most reading. There is a tendency among energy-saving manufacturers to be so proud of the energy-saving talent of their products that they forget customer

'You don't save the planet with notions and lip service.'

convenience. Turn your lights off when not using them.

Water

Bathing and showering are something we do far too much of and it results in a huge wastage of fuel and water. You don't need to bathe every day, let alone twice a day. I'm not advocating returning to once a year or even once a month like Queen Elizabeth I, but bathing every other day or every third day will serve just as well if you have a good wash on the other days. A girl I knew tried the thing of never washing her hair. After three months it becomes self-cleansing and non-greasy – a little extreme although very ecological.

Guard against dripping taps and replace washers promptly.

insulation

Insulation is very important to stop heat loss from your home. Heat rises and uninsulated attics result in a huge amount of heat loss, as do uninsulated cavity walls. Use thermafleece to insulate cavity walls and attics, not that horrid artificial glass fibre. Thermafleece is made from the treated fleeces of Swaledale, Herdwick, Welsh Mountain, and Scots Blackface sheep, all hill breeds with extra-large medullas in the wool (see page 156) to protect them against the cold of their living conditions.

Wool is hydroscopic and as such is both absorbent and desorbant. Thus in cold weather it absorbs the moisture from the atmosphere, preventing any condensation in the building cavities. And as wool creates energy when damp, it releases 960 kilojoules of heat for every kilo of wool. Thermafleece raises the temperature of your house by 4°C more than any artificial alternative. In hot weather the wool becomes desorbant and releases moisture, which acts as a cooling agent and decreases inside temperatures by 7°C.

In addition, thermafleece takes 14 per cent less energy to make than artificial glass fibre and, since no protective clothing is needed when handling it, any escaped fibres into the house space are harmless. Natural treatments are used for fire- and insect-proofing, in other words no permethyn, pyrethroids or formaldehydes, and at the end of its very long life, thermafleece is recyclable as it is a natural product.

Double- and triple-glazing are also excellent ways of conserving heat and they also serve as a noise abater. I would use the type you can remove in summer unless you happen to live in a town.

furnishings, finishes and fabrics

Bedding

Use linen or cotton sheets and pillowcases and, if possible, buy organic. Apart from the fact that they are nicer to sleep on they are natural materials and long-lasting. I have slept on linen sheeps at Ballywalter in Northern Ireland which were at least 100 years old and still in beautiful condition. Nothing is nicer than to go to bed in freshly ironed linen sheets. Moreover, if they rip or wear out in the middle, you can sew them sides to middle, in other words, slit them down the middle, turn the outside edge to the middle, sew the edges together and hem the new outside edges. Blankets should be woollen and if you are using a duvet, ensure that it is a real feather one.

Carpets, Rugs, Wall Coverings and Soft Furnishings

These should all be of of natural fibres. Wool or sisal carpeting or, on a wooden floor, wool or cotton rugs are best. The Swedes make warm, attractive rag rugs from recycled clothing. In markets and car boot sales you can often find old rugs that are worn in the middle but still attractive around the worn patch. Rather than repair them, cut them on either side of the hole, bind the edges and sew the two bits together. If you use a wide band of coloured cloth to make the join, it can be a feature.

Hessian is a good choice of wall covering. It is easy to hang, retains warmth and will take paint. Cover your furniture in natural materials too. Avoid artificial fibres just because they are easy keeping.

Hard Flooring

Your floor should be natural and made with wood from sustainable forests. Pine is obviously a good choice as you are removing those horrible coniferous forests in which nothing really can live. A new product of the mountain for flooring is bamboo. Bamboo is harvested once it has reached 3 years and reaches full maturity at 5–6 years. Most bamboo comes from the Hunan forests in China although some is grown in Vietnam. Bamboo regenerates of its own accord when harvested without the need for replanting. The bamboo is sliced and boiled to remove starch, then dried and laminated into solid boards. The lamination uses urea-formaldehyde but using boric acid, tests show emissions are 50 per cent below the rate allowable by Dutch regulations.

Experiments are in progress with organic glues and laminates but have as yet proved too expensive. Bamboo flooring is attractive and has an elastic feel when you walk on it. It can also be used on walls.

Other eco-friendly hard floor options

Palm wood: The wood of coconut palms that have passed their fruiting life can be made into planks that are both attractive and ecological.

Cork tiles: These are warm and attractive and can be laid straight onto the sub-floor. They are also good for stairs and bathrooms.

Hardwood Trees: These must be harvested from a properly managed forest. Planks made of hardwood are beautiful, durable and will last for centuries, as a trip to any great house will show.

Blood: I once had some friends who lived in a mediaeval cottage with a beautiful, easy-to-maintain dark red floor. It washed well, polished beautifully and was warm on the feet. No one knew what it was. Eventually they sent for an expert and it emerged that this beautiful floor was made of layers of blood, allowed to dry and smoothed off before the next layer was added. It had survived intact since the thirteenth century. I expect in our so-called civilized world you would have trouble with the building regulations or even with obtaining the blood, but bear the idea in mind.

Dung: On the same theme, in Africa and the tropics they use dung for flooring and mix it with plaster. It is a great fly-deterrent. As with a blood floor, you would have problems with the building regulations but it might be worth thinking about.

glues and treatments

You want to avoid all of these where possible if they contain formaldehyde but I can only imagine it will be a problem if the fluffy bunny brigade prevents the use of rabbit glue more extensively. Rabbit glue is made from the dehaired skins of rabbits. It is used as a binder (see page 234) or size in oil painting and an adhesive in the application of gold leaf. The word 'glue' originally meant adhesive made from animal protein, achieved by the boiling down of bones and skin. A return to the use of animal glues, and particularly rabbit glue, would get rid of a lot of chemicals. Ecological is in danger of meaning fluffy and vegetarian. It shouldn't be.

Medium density fibreboard (MDF) is now used universally in building. It is made from wood fibres bonded together with chemical adhesives and is notorious for its chemical emissions.

Formaldehyde by another name

Be careful about commercial shampoos; quaternium16 is present even in baby shampoos and is another name for formaldehyde.

recycling

We have already dealt with composting (see page 27) and scraps to pigs (see page 102).

● The fire or woodburning stove will deal with your surplus paper. Wet the paper, roll it tightly into a log shape and allow it to dry. You will be surprised how long and warmly it burns. It was a tree once, after all.

● Glass and plastic containers that you aren't using in the garden or the store room should be taken to a bottle bank, as should old cans. In Sweden, Holland and probably other places as well, there is a machine at supermarkets into which you feed your bottle and receive a credit note against your shopping. We no longer have returnable bottles in England but when I was young, collecting the empties up and returning them in exchange for a small sum of money was a way of supplementing your pocket money. I think this still happens in parts of the USA.

avoiding excess

● Avoid buying goods with excess packaging. You hopefully have given up ready meals anyway, and these are the worst offenders.

● Always take a basket when you are shopping to avoid the excessive use of plastic bags. An experiment in Ireland recently where stores charged for plastic bags reduced the amount used sizeably.

● For what little rubbish is left, use biodegradable plastic refuse sacks.

transport

● Walk or ride a bicycle whenever you can and make your children do the same. In Edinburgh the Council has spent a fortune on cycle lanes and I never see a bike in them from one month to the next. When I was very broke and spending all my money on gin I used to walk everywhere and despite my huge alcohol intake I was really quite healthy because of it.

● Do you take a train or a bus rather than the car? Probably not as they are inefficient, dirty, unsafe and unpunctual, but do at least nag the authorities to provide better services.

● If you are driving, use diesel rather than petrol and LPG in preference to either. My friend Maggie is forever nagging me about being in the wrong gear and wasting fuel. If you drive at 90 kph or below you save fuel quite considerably.

'...if you keep a pot of basil on the windowsill of your sitting room or kitchen, it will keep flies away and give off a great smell when the sun hits it.'

tea and coffee tips

● Never use teabags, partly because they are made with the sweepings of the drying house and because used tea leaves go well around roses or on the compost heap.

● Never drink instant coffee; it is full of chemicals while coffee grounds are good on the compost heap or against slugs around tender plants.

gadgets

Reduce your use of gadgets to the minimum.

● A washing machine with a horizontally mounted drum is more economical than a tub type.

● Avoid tumble dryers wherever possible. A hanging rack in your kitchen for winter or a clothes line outdoors is far better. I dry my sheets on a rack in the spare room where the sun shines warmly through the glass even in a Scots winter.

● Make sure your washing machine is always full and use it on an economy low-energy cycle.

● For very soiled clothes, soak them first either in a basin or on a pre-wash cycle. Boil washes use a lot more energy.

● If you are using an electric kettle, only put in as much water as you need.

● If you have a range, always keep a kettle on the warm plate or the back so that it will boil quicker when you need it.

● Make sure televisions and particularly computers are turned off rather than left on standby. Standby uses 80 per cent of the power that the equipment uses when it is in use.

● Do not position fridges and freezers near any heat source as this can use up to 15 per cent more energy.

houseplants to clean the air

Houseplants are said to be a good way of cleaning the air, but as a hayfever sufferer of 40 years, I don't much like houseplants and I suspect that you need to put them out at night when they are disgorging carbon dioxide. However, I do like herbs on the windowsill and the scented-leaf geraniums on a warm windowsill are very efficacious as room scenters. Another plant which removes odours is vetiver; a piece of dried root placed in a dish is a great deodorizer. Spider plants are also meant to clean the air but I find them too ugly to live with.

Among the plants I like to see growing indoors are dwarf orange or lemon trees. They have a lovely perfume even when not in bloom or in fruit and they do well, provided you remember to keep the leaves clean with a little warm water. When the weather is warm you can give them a holiday outside. What can be nicer than plucking a lemon or lime and slicing it into drinks to amaze your friends? If your orange or lemon trees are in pots, remember to keep them watered and fed, like all houseplants.

Another species that is good for cleaning the air is the ornamental fig. All ficus plants have this ability and a weeping fig can be an attractive feature of the room. Remember to put it outside now and again for a bit of sun and a leaf-washing rainstorm.

I have talked elsewhere about basil but if you keep a pot on the windowsill of your sitting room or kitchen, it will keep flies away and give off a great smell when the sun hits it. The Asian or holy basils don't have the same impact on flies and tend to be more subject to whitefly. If you like houseplants keep as many as you like; personally I tend to limit mine to the useful or sweet smelling.

seasonal diary

Unless they happen to be farmers, people belonging to the
age group that was born in the 1970s and 1980s, when
imported, out-of-season, 'fresh' produce became readily
available, can have no conception of how important the
gradual movement of the seasons was to previous
generations. This is particularly the case in the northern
hemisphere, where seasonal changes are more defined.

I remember that our diet then was distinctly different
between winter and summer. It changed with the
migration of swallows, swifts and house martins. Their
twittering clamour heralded the arrival of spring
vegetables and summer fruits. They left in the autumn
with the beginning of berry picking and when root
vegetables, turnips and swedes began to replace salads,
peas and beans.

When I was a child, the significance of the changing
seasons was still celebrated in festivals whose origins were
pagan – May Day, Lammas Night, Harvest Festival,
Michaelmas, Martinmas, Lady Day and, of course,
Christmas and the great pagan festival of spring fecundity,
which became Easter.

spring

wild food

Spring is a busy time for the home producer. Winter's drab colours are replaced by the first tentative plant growth. Trees are in bud. Wild garlic, nettles and bracken fiddleheads are the first hedgerow foods ready to be picked, wild garlic leaves for salad or a purée, nettles for nettle beer, nettle tea and nettle spinach and bracken fiddleheads for boiling or frying.

gardening

In the month after the spring equinox:

In the heated greenhouse – Sow marrow, courgettes, all other squashes and tomatoes if not already done. Sow aubergines.

Stop and support greenhouse cucumbers and remove male flowers as they emerge. Harvest greenhouse tomatoes when ready.

Cloches and cold frames – Sow dwarf French beans, sweetcorn and celeriac.

Outside – Sow, salsify, scorzona, spinach, beet, cardoons, broccoli, cauliflower and winter cabbage.

Start sowing leaf lettuce and kale (continue into the next month), calabrese and dill (continue over the next 2 months) Florence fennel (continue over the next 3 months) and kohlrabi (continue over the next 4 months).

Plant second early and main-crop potatoes, asparagus crowns, red cabbage and summer cabbage.

Stake peas.
Thin spinach and start thinning summer lettuce (continue over next 4 months).

Clear winter brassicas.

Fertilize potatoes.

Prepare celery trenches.

Harvest early turnips, overwintered spring lettuce, asparagus, spring cabbage and spring onions.

In the second month after the spring equinox:

Outside – Sow sweetcorn, asparagus, peas, chicory, soya beans, all cucurbits and squashes, runner beans, swedes and late-crop beetroots.

Continue sowing leaf lettuce and kale, calabrese and dill, Florence fennel, and kohlrabi.

Plant Florence fennel, sweetcorn, Brussels sprouts, leeks, celery and celeriac.

Earth up early potatoes and Jerusalem artichokes.

Prepare ground for leeks.

Stake broad beans.

Blanch Florence fennel.

Watch for, spray and dust against all types of fly.

Harvest overwintered lettuce, early carrots, turnips, early beetroot and summer spinach.

In the unheated greenhouse – Sow aubergines, sweet potatoes, cucumbers and okra

livestock

Broody hens, ducks and geese will be sitting, rabbit does go to the buck, goats kid, sheep lamb and, if you have gone for spring calving, the cow will calf. These animals will require extra attention in both feeding and veterinary care. Young piglets will need to be brought in for fattening, to kill in the autumn. Bull calves, billy kids and 'wedder' (ram) lambs must be castrated within 48 hours of birth and all livestock offspring have to be ear-tagged and registered as appropriate. Once the cow has calved and the goat has had her kid, they require milking twice a day.

making and creating

The little dairy becomes a hive of activity as butter and cheese are made. Indoors it's time to spring clean.

summer

wild food

As spring moves to summer, wild plants rich in iron, vitamin C and calcium become available. There are dandelions, chickweed, Good King Henry, common orache and watercress, sea kale, sea purslane, marsh samphire and many others. Some of the early summer wines – elderflower, dandelion and summer-fruit wines are made now as well as beer for drinking through the winter. Fish are dried, salted or smoked.

gardening

In the month of the summer solstice:

Outside – Sow winter beet.

Plant all squashes and marrows from the heated greenhouse.

Plant winter cabbages, autumn, winter and summer cauliflowers, broccoli, calabrese and kale.

Pinch out runner beans if bushy plants wanted, and support tall runner beans. Pinch out broad beans when in full flower.

Earth up potatoes.

Stop and support outside tomatoes and cucumbers.

Spray celery.

Remove the flowering shoots of rhubarb. Cut and dry French tarragon.

Hoe, water and mulch.

In the month after the summer solstice:

Outside – Plant red and Chinese cabbage for overwintering. Plant leaf lettuce, kale, spinach, beet, spring and winter cabbages, and main-crop turnips.

Continue sowing kohlrabi.

Tie up endive and begin to blanch. Pinch out runner beans.

Tie up celery plants at 30cm and begin to earth up.

Hoe and water where necessary.

Look out for insect predators and act against them.

Harvest cucumbers and runner beans, shallots, climbing beans, peas, courgettes, marrows, squashes and globe artichokes as appropriate.

In the second month after the summer solstice:

Outside – Sow onions for overwintering and winter spinach.

Earth up kale.

Plant winter cauliflowers.

Bend down onion tops.

Begin to blanch cardoons.

Stop tomato plants at 4–5 trusses.

Hoe and water as necessary.

Harvest early sweetcorn, summer cauliflowers, second earlies (potatoes), calabrese and anything else that's ready.

livestock

Livestock require some veterinary attention: growing lambs, kids and calves need protection from grass-borne internal parasites. All sheep and goats are prone to footrot, particularly as the grass grows longer. Adult sheep have their fleeces plucked or shorn. Bees are busy and the hives require regular attention – removing the honey-filled combs and replacing them with fresh foundation wax.

making and creating

Bath oils and fragrances can be made, and the ingredients for herbal remedies – the leaves of sage, chamomile, fennel, agrimony, borage, hyssop, comfrey, and so on, can be dried for use through the winter. Start preserving excess food as it becomes ready, for example, make jam and bottle fruit.

autumn

wild food

Autumn is the time to prepare for winter and reap the natural harvest of nuts and berries – hazelnuts, chestnuts, walnuts, rose hips, blackberries, elderberries, sloes and damsons. It's all go in the kitchen as fruit, vegetables and wines are bottled and jams are made.

gardening

In the month of the autumn equinox:

Outside – Sow turnips for tops and lettuce in cold frames.

Plant spring cabbage and spring greens. Bend down spring-sown onions.

Cut asparagus foliage,

Remove sere leaves and blown sprouts from Brussels sprouts.

Clear debris of harvested crops.

Store marrows and squashes for winter use.

Harvest and store where appropriate cardoons, main-crop potatoes, Chinese cabbage and autumn cauliflowers.

In the first month after the autumn equinox:
Outside – Sow spring lettuce in cold frames.

Plant rhubarb crowns

Cut down asparagus fern and mound earth over the crowns.

Leave chicory and rhubarb for forcing.

Cover spinach, winter salads and parsley with cloches.

Clean and store all supports.

Examine stored crops and discard any that are decayed. Continue this throughout the winter.

Lift and store carrots, horseradish and beetroot.

Harvest late beans,

Continue to harvest winter cabbage, celeriac and any other vegetables that are ready.

Start picking and storing apples and pears.

Plough and harrow for spring wheat.

In the second month after the autumn equinox:

In unheated greenhouse – Sow winter lettuce.

Outside – Plant broad beans for overwintering.

Protect late cauliflowers.

Harvest any soft vegetables before first frost.

Protect celery and globe artichokes with bracken or straw before first frost.

Bring in tender plants for overwintering or protect against frost.

Lift tubers for storing.

After first frost begin harvesting swedes, parsnips and turnips as ready, and store. Cut wood for fuel.

Indoors – Order seed catalogues.

In the third month after the autumn equinox:

In unheated greenhouse – Sow tomatoes and peppers.

Outside – Lift and trim swede roots. Clean and repair tools.

Harvest forced celery and winter cauliflowers as needed.

Do winter digging for next 3 months as suits after the rains but before the frosts.

livestock

Some of the lambs, kids, ducklings and geese are ready to kill in September. Bees need to be put to bed with enough honey to last them until the spring, and ewes must be got ready to go to the ram. In northern Europe, November is the month for killing pigs and cattle.

making and creating

This is the time for salting, brining and smoking to preserve meat for the winter. Ensure you have everything you need for spinning and weaving in the months ahead. Make chutneys and pickles with the last of the season's tomatoes, cucumbers and so on. Check summer clothes for mending and clean and store the rest. Make candles with wax from beehives. Make soap with dried bracken.

winter

wild food

I love the dark months of winter when the land sleeps and the embryos in stock gradually form the foetuses of spring re-birth. These are traditionally the game months, when pheasants, partridges, deer and wildfowl used to provide the only source of fresh food.

gardening

In the month after the winter solstice:

In heated greenhouse – Sow leeks.

In unheated greenhouse – Sow onions for transplanting.

In cloches and cold frames – Sow early radishes.

Outside – Clear spent crops and weeds. Prune fruit trees.

Indoors – Order seeds and plan layout of vegetable garden.

In the second month after the winter solstice:

In heated greenhouse – Sow tomatoes, cucumbers and okra.

In cloches and cold frames – Sow early turnips, carrots, parsnips and beetroot. Plant bulb onions over next 2 months.

Outside – Plant rhubarb, shallots, garlic and Jerusalem artichokes.

Top-dress overwintered vegetables. Chit seed potatoes.

Apply fertilizer 2 weeks before sowing early crops

In the third month after the winter solstice:

In heated greenhouse – Sow sweet peppers, courgettes and celeriac for transplanting.

Prick out tomatoes, cucumbers, sweet peppers and okra if planted earlier.

In cloches and cold frames – Sow fennel and celery, also tarragon and parsley.

Outside – Plant seakale, horseradish, globe artichokes and early potatoes. Start planting onion sets, continuing into next month.

Hoe between overwintered and perennial crops.

Clean out herb garden and fertilize chives.

Inspect and weed where necessary. Remove 2 out of 3 spring cabbages and eat as spring greens.

Harvest turnip tops as greens, seakale, rhubarb and radishes.

livestock

Stock must be fed once grass growth diminishes, first with hay and then with a supplement feed on a rising scale as pregnancy advances. Bees should be checked to see that they have sufficient honey. You will still have some lambs, kids, ducks, geese and chickens to be killed through the winter. Excess young cockerels must be killed before they become sexually active and start to crow in January, otherwise they will fight.

Where I live, 1 February is customarily the start of winter's thaw, when the Celts celebrated the festival of Imolc with bonfires and sacrifices to the lengthening hours of daylight. Wild garlic and nettles push through their first green leaves and before you know it, spring is back.

making and creating

This is a time for mending, spinning, weaving, felting and dyeing. Replenish your batteries and dress warmly.

useful addresses

Shooting Organisations

Australia
Australian Sporting Shooters Association
http://www.ssaa.org.au/

New Zealand
Shooting NZ
http://www.shootingnz.com/

Europe
The Federation of Fieldsports Association of the European Union (FACE)
http://www.face-europe.org/

Britain
British Association of Shooting and Conservation
http://www.basc.org.uk/

North America
Ducks Unlimited Inc.
http://www.ducks.org/

Quail Unlimited
http://www.qu.org/

Pheasants Forever
http://www.pheasantsforever.org/

Mule Deer Foundation
http://www.muledeer.org/

US Fish and Wildlife Service
http://www.fws.gov/

Fishing

Australia
Game Fishing Australia
http://www.gfaa.asn.au/

New Zealand
http://www.fishinginnewzealand.com/
http://www.fishing.net.nz/

Europe
Fishing Guide Europe
http://www.go-fish.co.uk/

Britain
Fishing Guide Britain
http://www.fishinginbritain.com/
http://www.gone-fishing.info/

North America
http://www.cybertrout.com/
http://www.total-fishing.com/
or type in: fly, game or coarse fishing and the name of the state.

Dexter Cattle

Britain and Europe
The Dexter Cattle Society
http://www.dextercattle.co.uk/

North America
American Dexter Cattle Association
http://www.info@dextercattle.org/

Australia
Dexter Cattle Inc.
http://dexter.une.edu.au/

New Zealand
Dexter Cattle Society in New Zealand
http://www.dexter-cattle.co.nz/

Shetland Sheep

Britain and Europe
Shetland Sheep Society
http://www.users.zetnet.co.uk/ssbg/

Shetland Sheep Society overseas links:
http://www.users.zetnet.co.uk/ssbg/newlink.html

Chickens (Light Sussex)

Britain and Europe
http://www.poultryclub.org/

North America
Sussex Club
http://www.feathersite.com/Poultry/CGP/Sussex/BRKSussex.html

Australia
Light Sussex stockists
http://www.wilkamdai.com/poultry_index.htm

New Zealand
http://www.rarebreeds.co.nz/

Ducks and Geese

Britain
Domestic Waterfowl Club
http://www.domestic-waterfowl.co.uk/

North America
American Livestock Breeders Conservancy
http://www.albc-usa.org/waterfowl.htm

Australia
Rare Breeds Trust of Australia
http://www.rbta.org/

New Zealand
Rare Breeds of Livestock NZ
http://www.rarebreeds.co.nz/ducks.html

Squabs

North America
Pigeon Management
http://www.ansci.umn.edu/poultry/resources/pigeons.htm

Australia and New Zealand
http://www.agric.nsw.gov.au/reader/poultry/squab-raising.htm

Pigs

Britain and Europe
The pigs I have suggested are among the minority breeds. Information is best found on the Rare Breeds websites.

Rare Breeds Survival Trust
http://www.rbst.org.uk/

North America
American Livestock Breed Conservancy
http://www.albc-usa.org/

Australia
Rare Breeds Trust of Australia
http://www.rbta.org/

New Zealand
Rare Breeds Trust NZ
http://www.rarebreeds.co.nz/

Horses and Ponies

Britain
The Pony Club of Great Britain
http://www.pcuk.org/

Europe
18 European countries belong to the Euro Pony Club.
http://www.pcuk.org/output/about/page_1475.html

Australia
Pony Club of Australia
http://www.ponyclub-australia.org/

New Zealand
New Zealand Pony Clubs Association
http://www.nzpca.org/

For candle making equipment:

Candle Makers Supplies
28 Blythe Road
London W14 0HA

Tel: 020 7602 4031/2
http://www.candlemakers.co.uk/

For natural pigments and materials for making limewash, distemper, etc:

L Cornelissen and Son
105 Great Russell Street
London WC1B 3RY

Tel: 020 7636 1045
http://www.cornelissen.co.uk/

For beer making supplies:

The Beer Shop
14 Pitfield Street
London N1 6EY

Tel: 020 7739 3701
http://www.pitfieldbeershop.co.uk/

For seeds:

Douglas Wayne-Heapy (see page 32)
recommends
Tuckers Seeds
Brewery Meadow
Stonepark
Ashburton
Newton Abbot
Devon

Tel: 01364 652233
http://www.edwintucker.com/

Allotments have their own seed-buying schemes. Use a local seedsman or plantsman wherever you are as they will know local conditions.

For selling your produce:

National Association of Farmers' Markets
PO BOX 575
Southampton
SO15 7BZ

Tel: 0845 45 88 420
http://www.farmersmarkets.net/

Department for Environment, Food & Rural Affairs
Nobel House
17 Smith Square
London
SW1P 3JR

Tel: 020 7238 6000
http://www.defra.gov.uk/

The National Federation of Women's Institutes,
104 New Kings Road,
London SW6 4LY

Tel: 020 7371 9300
http://www.womens-institute.org.uk/

For spinning, weaving, etc:

Your local Women's Institute (see above) or Junior League.

The Association of Junior Leagues International Inc.
90 William Street, Suite 200
New York, NY 10038

Tel: (001) 212 951 8300
http://www.ajli.org/

For workshops:
Sarah Bowen (textile artist)
Sarah's Cottage
Loe Bar Road
Porthleven
Cornwall
TR13 9ER

Tel: 01326 564 965

Sewing shops often have information about different courses.

It is always best to enquire locally, use your imagination and make new friends. There is also the internet.

For organic pesticides and biological pest control:

Grovelands Online
166 Hyde End Road
Shinfield
Reading
Berkshire
RG2 9ER

Tel: 0800 074 7195
http://www.grovelands.com/

Growing Success
Wessex House
Units 1-3 Hilltop Business Park
Devizes Road
Salisbury
Wiltshire
SP3 4UF

Tel: 01722 337744
http://www.growingsuccess.org.uk/

Esoteric Hydroponics
8 Martyr Road
Guildford
Surrey
GU1 4LF

Tel: 01483 596484
http://www.1-hydroponics.co.uk/

Pest Control Direct Ltd.
Unit 1, Leap Cross Enterprise Centre
London Road
Hailsham
Sussex
BN27 3PD

Tel: 01323 846845
http://www.pestcontroldirect.co.uk/

For information on organic lifestyles and on sourcing locally grown food:

The Soil Association
http://www.soilassociation.org/

picture credits

All images are credited to Vanessa Courtier, except:

Page 7 Holt/Primrose Peacock
Page 16 F. Davis/ GWI
Page 17 The Garden Picture Library/Alamy
Page 19 **left:** F. Davis/ GWI; **right:** GardenWorld Images
Page 21 **left:** Holt Studios/ Bob Gibbons; **right:** Mark Bolton Photography/Alamy
Page 22 John Hatcher/Alamy
Page 24 Holt Studios/Nigel Cattlin
Page 34 **top left & bottom right:** Holt Studios/ Primrose Peacock; **top right & bottom** left: Holt Studios/ Phil Mitchell
Page 35 Holt Studios/ Michael Mayer
Page 36 **bottom left:** Holt Studios/ Rosie Mayer
Page 38 **left:** N. Downer/ GWI; **right:** Geoff Hayes
Page 39 **left:** Kathy Wright/ Alamy
Page 44 Rob James/ Alamy
Page 45 **right:** Aqua Image/ Alamy
Page 49 **bottom left:** Kathy Wright/ Alamy
Page 53 **top right:** Holt Studios/ Nigel Cattlin
Page 62 **right:** Holt Studios/ Richard Anthony
Page 63 Holt Studios/ Gordon Roberts
Page 66 GardenWorld Images
Page 68 Geoff Hayes
Page 69 Geoff Hayes
Page 70 Geoff Hayes
Page 71 Geoff Hayes
Page 78 Geoff Hayes
Page 79 Geoff Hayes

Page 80 Pete Cassidy
Page 81 **top left:** J.Dracup/GWI; centre: GardenWorld Images; **top right & bottom left:** A.Beaumont/GWI; **bottom right:** A.Ridley/GWI
Page 82 The Garden Picture Library/ Alamy
Page 83 **left:**M. Keal/ GWI; **right:** Gus Filgate
Page 84 **top left & top centre:** Holt Studios/ Nigel Cattln; **top right & bottom centre:** Holt Studios/ Peter Wilson; **middle left & bottom left:** Holt Studios/ Primrose Peacock; **middle centre:** Holt Studios/ Duncan Smith; **middle right:** Holt Studios/ Jean Hall; **bottom right:** Holt Studios/ Bob Gibbons
Page 86 Gus Filgate
Page 87 Gus Filgate
Page 91 Jeremy Pardoe/ Alamy
Page 93 Agripicture Images/ Peter Dean
Page 96 **top left:** Laurens Smak/ Alamy; **top right:** Holt Studios/ Alamy; **centre:** ImageState/ Alamy; **bottom left:** Agripicture Images/ Alamy
Page 98 John Mottershaw/ Alamy
Page 99 Geoff Hayes
Page 100 Gus Filgate
Page 101 Gus Filgate
Page 103 **top left & bottom:** Holt Studios/ Sarah Rowland; **top right:** Holt Studios/ Duncan Smith
Page 106 Gus Filgate
Page 107 Gus Filgate
Page 108 **top right:** Morley/ Alamy; **middle right:** Renee Morris/ Alamy; **bottom:** Holt Studios/ Gordon Roberts
Page 109 **top left:** Geoff Hayes; **bottom right:** Holts Studios/ Nigel Cattlin

Page 112 Gus Filgate
Page 113 Gus Filgate
Page 116 **top:** Maurice Joseph/ Alamy; **middle:** Cassida Images/ Alamy; **bottom:** Holt Studios/ Gordon Roberts
Page 117 Holt Studios/Mark Fuller
Page 120 Peter Fakler/ Alamy
Page 122 Gus Filgate
Page 123 Gus Filgate
Page 125 Gus Filgate
Page 126 Peter Markus
Page 127 **left:** Mary Evans Picture Library; **right:** Bildagentur Franz Waldhaeus/ Alamy
Page 130 **left:** Holt Studios/ Alamy; **middle:** D. Hunt/ Alamy
Page 132 Holt Studios/ Mike Lane
Page 133 Gus Filgate
Page 134 Geoff Hayes
Page 135 Gus Filgate
Page 139 **top left:** imagebroker/ Alamy; **top right:** Nature Picture Library/ Alamy; **middle left:** blickwinkel/ Alamy; **middle right & bottom right:** Holt Studios/ Nigel Cattlin; **bottom left:** The Photolibrary Wales/ Alamy
Page 140 **top left, bottom left & bottom right:** Holt Studios/ Nigel Cattlin; **top right:** Holt Studios/ Phil Mclean; **middle left:** Holt Studios/ Paul Hobson; **middle right:** Holt Studios/ Jurgen Dielenshneider
Page 167 Jeffr Greenberg/ Alamy
Page 179 Gus Filgate
Page 180 Maximillian Stock Ltd/ ABPL
Page 181 Anthony Blake/ ABPL
Page 183 Gus Filgate
Page 205 Food Stills Library/ Alamy
Page 231 Stephen Roberts/ Alamy

bibliography

Lynda Brown, *Gardeners' World Vegetables for Small Gardens* (BBC Books, 1993)

Build Your Own Poultry House and Runs (A2 Sized Plan) (Broad Leys Publishing Ltd., 2005)

George Bird Grinnell, *American Duck Shooting* (Stackpole Books, 1991

Susan Campbell, *Charleston Kedding: A History of Kitchen Gardening* (Frances Lincoln, 2005)

A. Case, *Starting with Pigs* (Broad Leys Publishing Ltd., 2004)

Mary Castell, *Starting with Sheep* (Broad Leys Publishing Ltd., 2004)

Nicholas Gent Culpeper, *Complete Herbal* (Wordsworth Editions, 1995)

Clarissa Dickson Wright and Johnny Scott, *The Game Cookbook* (Kyle Cathie, 2004)

Peter Gordon, *Starting with Bees* (Broad Leys Publishing Ltd., 2004)

Mrs M Grieve, *A Modern Herbal* (Dover Publications Inc., 1971)

Dorothy Hartley, *Food in England* (Little Brown, 1996)

Dorothy Hartley, *The Land of England* (Macdonald General Books,1979)

Elwyn Hartley Edwards, *Horses* (Dorling Kindersley, 2000)

David Hills, *Starting with a Smallholding* (Broad Leys Publishing Lt, 2004)

Julia Lawless and Lynn Edwards, *The Natural Paintbook* (Kyle Cathie, 2002)

Robin Marshall-Ball, *The Sporting Gun* (Swan Hill Press, 2003)

Roger Phillips, *Wild Food* (Pan Books,1983)

Roger Phillips, *Mushrooms and Other Fungi of Great Britain and Europe* (Pan Books, 1981)

Michael Pollock, *RHS Fruit and Vegetable Gardening* (Dorling Kindersley, 2002)

Oliver Rackham, *The History of the Countryside* (Phoenix Giant Paperback,1999)

Claudia Roden, *The Book of Jewish Food* (Penguin, 1999)

John Seymour, *The New Complete Book of Self-Sufficiency* (new ed. Dorling Kindersley 2003)

Katie Thear, *Starting with Chickens* (Broad Leys Publishing Ltd., 2004)

Katie Thear, *Organic Poultry* (Broad Leys Publishing Ltd., 2004)

Katie Thear, *Starting with Ducks* (Broad Leys Publishing Ltd., 2004)

Katie Thear, *Starting with Geese* (Broad Leys Publishing Ltd., 2005)

Katie Thear, *Cheese Making and Dairying* (Broad Leys Publishing Ltd, 2005)

Dennis Walrod, *Grouse Hunter's Guide* (Stackpole Books, 1985)

Colin Willock, *The New ABC of Fishing* (André Deutsch,1992)

Colin Willock, *The New ABC of Shooting* (André Deutsch, 1985)

The following books are out of print but may be available in second-hand bookshops:

'By the author of Enquire Within', *Consult Me* (W. Nicholson and Sons, London 1883)

ed. 'By an American Physician', *Mackenzie's Five Thousand Receipts in all the Useful and Domestic Arts* (James Kay, Pittsburgh and Philadelphia, 1831)

ed. Boyd, Lizzie, *British Cookery, A Complete Guide to the Culinary Practice of the British Isles* (Croom Helm Ltd, 1976)

Elizabeth Craig, *Cookery Illustrated and Household Management* (Odhams Press, 1936)

W. A. Halstead, *A Textile Guide for Retail Distributors* (Ernest Benn & Co)

ed. I.E.P.C., *The Country House* (Horace Cox, London I883)

ed. Richard Ingrams, William Cobbett, *Cobbett's Country Book: An Anthology of William Cobbett's Writings on Country Matters* (Schocken Books, 1974)

Preserving (Good Cook Series) (Time Life, 1981)

H.T. Williams and 'Daisy Eyebright', *Household Hints and Recipes* (People's Publishing Co. Boston, 1884)

Much information was also sourced from Johnny Scott's family archive of Household and Estate Journals and Ledgers

index

Publisher's Acknowledgements

The publisher would like to thank:

Michael Beer for his help with gardening; Sarah Bowen, textile designer, of Sarah's Cottage, Loe Bar Road, Porthleven, Cornwall, TR13 9ER (Tel: 01326 564 965) for the loan of her felt baby's booties; Katy Bevan for her help with the knitting and crochet photography; the Buccleugh Estate for permission to take photographs; Mr G Burnet of Inveresk, Musselburgh for kindly allowing us to photograph his house; Hamish and Gillian Cathie for kindly allowing us to use their garden and kitchen and for introducing us to their helpful neighbours; David Constable of Candle Makers Supplies for his help with the candle making; Nicholas Walt of Cornelissen and Son for the loan of the muller and pigment bottles; Kay Darnbrook of The Dexter Cattle Society for her Dexter cow; T J and S E Forrester of Cream of Cumbria Butter for their help with the butter making; Peter Gott of Silfield Farm for his pigs and cured meats; Greenfibres for the loan of their organic bedlinen; Peter Hood of The Real Paint and Varnish Company Ltd for his natural paint; Mr and Mrs Michael Hughes-Hallet, neighbours of Hamish and Gillian Cathie; Mike Kelly for help with the beer making; Mrs Jenny Nixon for the loan of her horse; Mrs Joan Nixon for her ducks and chickens; Audrey Pattison for allowing us to photograph on her allotment; Janet Phillips for help with the spinning and weaving photography; Andy of The Beer Shop, Pitfield Street, London N1 6EY (Tel: 020 7739 3701) for help with the beer making; Stephen Rendle of Lovat Mill, Commercial Road, Hawick, TD9 7AQ (Tel: 01450 379378) for help with the weaving photography; Doreen Richardson, neighbour of Hamish and Gillian Cathie; Kate Sharp and Jessie Main of Kate Sharp Knitwear (Tel: 01875 833 215) for their Shetland sheep.